Contemporary Issues
in Science & Christian Faith:
An Annotated Bibliography

Third Printing, Revised and Expanded

A Resource Book

Published by the

American Scientific Affiliation

P.O. Box 668

Ipswich, MA 01938

Second printing, revised and enlarged, 1988.
Third printing, revised and enlarged, 1992.

ISBN: 1-881479-01-3

Books and other sources listed here are subject to change without notice.
The ASA takes no responsibility for price changes, availability, or content of
any product listed herein.

Compiled by the ASA Publications Committee, W. Jim Neidhardt, Chair.

Edited by Robin H. MacLeod, Rebecca Petersen, and Patricia Ames.
Typeset by Tami and Stan Brown.

About This Book

This Resource Book has been designed to put you in touch with a number of science/faith resources including:

Annotated Listing of Books on Science and Religion

Audio and Video Tapes of Papers Presented at ASA Meetings

Program and Meeting Suggestions

Speakers on Science and Christian Faith Issues

Christian Professional Societies

We hope this material will be useful to you. Your feedback and suggestions for additions to the next update of this book will be much appreciated!

About the American Scientific Affiliation

The American Scientific Affiliation is a fellowship of men and women of science who share a common fidelity to the Word of God and to the Christian Faith. It has grown from a handful in 1941 to a membership of over 2,300 in 1992. The stated purposes of the ASA are "to investigate any area relating Christian faith and science" and "to make known the results of such investigations for comment and criticism by the Christian community and by the scientific community."

Table of Contents

ANNOTATED BOOK LIST
Alphabetical Listing By Author

The following book list has been revised and enlarged to include many new listings suggested and compiled by Jim Neidhardt, the ASA Publications Committee, and other members of various ASA committees. Book suggestions and annotations were contributed by Jim Neidhardt, Paul Arveson, Richard Bube, Robert Herrmann, David O. Moberg, George L. Murphy, Richard Ruble, Paul C. Vitz, and David Wilcox. Additional help with annotations was provided by Gary Collins, Wayne Friar, Fred Hickernell, George Jennings, Phillip E. Johnson, Howard Van Till, and Richard T. Wright.

Insofar as possible, each listing consists of:

author name/ book title/ publisher/ date of publication/ short annotation.

If the book has been reviewed in *Perspectives on Science & Christian Faith,* the Journal of the American Scientific Affiliation, a reference to the month and year of the issue follows [i.e., (M-90) = March 1990].

The following marks have also been added for your convenience:

✢ = author/editor is ASA Member

✪ = book is new to list this year

🍂   🍂   🍂   🍂   🍂

ACKERMAN, Paul.
IT'S A YOUNG WORLD AFTER ALL. Baker, 1986. Evidences for a recent creation. The author is editor of the *Creation Science and Humanities Quarterly.* (S-87)

ADAIR, Robert K.
THE GREAT DESIGN: PARTICLES, FIELDS, AND CREATION. Oxford U.P., 1989.

✢ADENEY, Miriam.
GOD'S FOREIGN POLICY. Eerdmans, 1984. An anthropologist looks at tough questions and positive case studies in relief and development. (S-85)

✪✢ADENEY, Miriam.
A TIME FOR RISKING: PRIORITIES FOR WOMEN. Multnomah, 1987.

AESCHLIMAN, Michael D.
THE RESTITUTION OF MAN: C.S. LEWIS AND THE CASE AGAINST SCIENTISM. Eerdmans, 1983. As Dr. Johnson fought an impiously excessive rationalism of the 18th century, so Chesterton and Lewis fought the excessive naturalism that has blighted much of the 20th century. Provides historical context for Lewis's writing. (D-86)

ALEKSANDER, Igor, and BURNETT, Piers.
THINKING MACHINES: THE SEARCH FOR ARTIFICIAL INTELLIGENCE. Knopf, 1987. The authors attempt to demystify artificial intelligence for the lay reader, discussing how the technology works, the human brain itself, and how simple machines can be made to seem "intelligent." Computer graphic illustrations enhance the text.

✪ALLEN, Diogenes.
CHRISTIAN BELIEF IN A POSTMODERN WORLD: THE FULL WEALTH OF CONVICTION. Westminster/John Knox, 1989. An examination of how Christianity and Christian belief are being supported by current philosophical and scientific principles. Helpful insights into the nature of faith, the experience of God's presence, and the interface between science and religion. (M-91)

ALLEN, Diogenes.
PHILOSOPHY FOR UNDERSTANDING THEOLOGY. John Knox, 1985. A very readable introduction to basic philosophical concepts that have deeply influenced theological thought.

1

Many of these concepts in turn are significant in any meaningful dialogue between theology and science.

⊕ALLEN, Diogenes.
QUEST: THE SEARCH FOR MEANING THROUGH CHRIST. Walker & Co., 1990. An excellent piece of work which examines the reasons for the 20th century's "lost sense of wonder" and suggests a fresh look at the life, death, and teachings of Christ. Extremely readable.

ALLEN, Diogenes.
THREE OUTSIDERS: BLAISE PASCAL, SØREN KIERKEGAARD, SIMONE WEIL. Cowley Pub., 1983. An excellent discussion of three thinkers who deeply challenge the Church to take more seriously its relationship with Jesus Christ. Pascal and Weil are well-versed in science.

⊕ALLMAN, William F.
APPRENTICES OF WONDER: INSIDE THE NEURAL NETWORK REVOLUTION. Bantam, 1989. A look into the labs of researchers, known as connectionists, who study neural networks, a type of artificial intelligence mimicking the complex activity of the human brain.

⊕AMBROSE, E.J.
THE MIRROR OF CREATION. Scot. Acad. P./Gower Pub. Co., 1990. An attempt to show that modern science, objectively understood, is not in conflict with, but rather supports and underpins our faith.

AMBROSE, E.J.
THE NATURE & ORIGIN OF THE BIOLOGICAL WORLD. Halsted Press, 1982. An excellent overview of biological science and its compatibility with the Judeo-Christian doctrine of creation.

⊕AMERICAN Association for the Advancement of Science.
SCIENCE FOR ALL AMERICANS. Oxford U.P., 1989. A statement by the 2061 Committee of the AAAS of the minimum essentials for an educational system to achieve scientific literacy in the American population by the time Halley's comet returns. Panel reports are also available including *Biological and Health Science,* by Mary Clark, and *Physical and Information Sciences and Engineering,* by George Bugliarello.

ANDERSON, Bernard W., ed.
CREATION IN THE OLD TESTAMENT (Issues in Religion & Theology Ser.: No. 6). Augsburg/Fortress, 1984. A good collection of essays written by noted Old Testament scholars on different aspects of creation.

⊕ANDERSON, Bernard W.
CREATION VERSUS CHAOS: THE REINTERPRETATION OF MYTHICAL SYMBOLISM IN THE BIBLE. Augsburg/Fortress, 1987.

ANDERSON, Ray S.
MINDING GOD'S BUSINESS. Eerdmans, 1986. A Fuller professor tackles the topic of managing Christian organizations to the glory of God. Provides a biblical and theological basis for managing a business in a Christian way.

ANDERSON, Ray S.
THEOLOGY, DEATH AND DYING. Basil Blackwell, 1986. A discussion of the treatment and denial of death by contemporary Western society, the treatment of death in other religious traditions, and the origins of a Christian theology of death. The author examines the legacy of Judaism and seeks to lay the foundations for a Christian anthropology in the unity of body and soul.

ANDERSON, Ray S., and FUERNSEY, Dennis B.
ON BEING FAMILY: A SOCIAL THEOLOGY OF THE FAMILY. Eerdmans, 1986. A helpful book by a pastoral theologian and family sociologist. The book's central theme is that God has placed human persons in a created order for which the covenant of the love of God provides the foundational paradigm for parenting, sexuality and marriage, and the formation of the foundation of family life.

⊕ANDREWS, Edgar H.
CHRIST AND THE COSMOS. Presbyterian & Reformed, 1986.

⊕ANDREWS, Edgar H.
GOD, SCIENCE AND EVOLUTION. Evangelical Press (UK), Presbyterian & Reformed.

ANDREWS, Edgar H.; GITT, W.; and OUWENEEL, W.J., eds.
CONCEPTS IN CREATIONISM. Evangelical Press (UK), Presbyterian & Reformed, 1986. Written primarily by European scientists, the book covers scientific and philosophical aspects of creation/evolution issues.

✪ANKER, Roy M., et al.
YOUTH, POPULAR CULTURE, AND THE ELECTRONIC MEDIA. Eerdmans, 1990. An indepth exploration of the historical-social dynamics contributing to today's mass-mediated youth culture. Principles for evaluating popular art and entertainment, and strategies for transforming the status quo are suggested.

ARGYLE, Michael.
THE PSYCHOLOGY OF HAPPINESS. Routledge, Chapman & Hall, 1987. The author discusses three sources of happiness—relationships, work and leisure—along with the effects of wealth, social class, sex, age, and health, on happiness. (M-89)

✪ASA INDUSTRIAL and Engineering Ethics Commission.
OVERRULED. Order direct: Ed Allen, 8931 Old Pine Rd., Boca Raton, FL 33433. Materials for a workshop dealing with ethical problems in industry, developed in response to the engineering and management decision conflicts connected with the Challenger disaster of 1986.

AUGSBURGER, David W.
PASTORAL COUNSELING ACROSS CULTURES. John Knox, 1986. A major contribution to the field of pastoral counseling that is readable and exhaustive. The author balances sensitively what is universal, cultural, and individual from a biblical perspective. Highly recommended for Christian workers in today's multi-cultural world, especially those working with international students.

AUGSBURGER, Myron, and CURRY, Dean C.
NUCLEAR ARMS: TWO VIEWS ON WORLD PEACE. Word, 1987. Augsburger is a pacifist while Curry argues for a refinement of nuclear weaponry in order to closely limit its target effect and maintain a balance of power. (M-89)

AULÉN, Gustav.
CHRISTUS VICTOR. Macmillan, 1969. The classic argument for the importance of the "Christ the victor" view of the Atonement.

BABLOYANTZ, A.
MOLECULES, DYNAMICS AND LIFE: AN INTRODUCTION TO SELF-ORGANIZATION OF MATTER. Wiley, 1987.

✪BALSWICK, Jack O., and BALSWICK, Judith K.
THE FAMILY: A CHRISTIAN PERSPECTIVE ON THE CONTEMPORARY HOME. Baker, 1989. The best of social science knowledge and research is integrated with theological and biblical values (especially themes of grace, covenant, empowerment, and intimacy) in this study of the family as a developing system. Topics include marriage, parenting, sexuality, communication, the social dynamics of power, stress, divorce, remarriage, and the family environment.

BARBOUR, Ian G.
ISSUES IN SCIENCE AND RELIGION. Harper & Row, 1971. Dean of American scholars in the science/faith arena. An outstanding scholarly look at relation of science and theology in three critical areas of physics and indeterminacy, the origin and basis of life, and evolution and creation. Includes historical survey of theories from the 16th century. (D-67)

BARBOUR, Ian G.
MYTHS, MODELS AND PARADIGMS: A COMPARATIVE STUDY IN SCIENCE AND RELIGION. Harper & Row, 1976. Discusses and compares types of language and other paradigms used in science and religion. Advocates approach of critical realism. (S-75)

✪BARBOUR, Ian G.
RELIGION IN AN AGE OF SCIENCE (The Gifford Lectures Ser.: Vol. 1). Harper & Row, 1990. An integrated and challenging vision of theology, science, technology, and values.

BARLOW, Daniel L.
EDUCATIONAL PSYCHOLOGY: THE TEACHING-LEARNING PROCESS. Moody, 1985. A major overview of developmental, learning and teaching theory written from a Christian perspective. The book encompasses the teacher's actual functioning in the teaching-learning process.

+BARRETT, Eric C., and FISHER, David.
SCIENTISTS WHO BELIEVE: 21 TELL THEIR OWN STORIES. Moody, 1984. Soviet, American and Third World Christians in science share their stories. Contributors include Dr. Robert L. Herrmann and Dr. Robert W. Newman of ASA.

✪BARROW, John D.
THE WORLD WITHIN THE WORLD. Oxford U.P., 1988. An excellent semi-popular treatment of the concept of laws of nature and the extent to which they can be considered objectively true.

3

Includes some comments on theological implications. (D-90)

BARROW, John D., and SILK, Joseph.
THE LEFT HAND OF CREATION: THE ORIGIN AND EVOLUTION OF THE EXPANDING UNIVERSE. Basic Bks., 1986. Good overall coverage of physical cosmology with integration of the insights of particle physics and general relativity.

BARROW, John D., and TIPLER, Frank J.
THE ANTHROPIC COSMOLOGICAL PRINCIPLE. Oxford U.P., 1986. A "classic" contribution to cosmology in the 20th century, it gives a historical overview of the anthropic principle and proceeds to give closely reasoned arguments for the thesis that the universe is structured for human life. Authors are practicing scientists in astrophysics, general relativity and gravitation physics. (D-86, J-88)

BARTH, Karl.
DOGMATICS IN OUTLINE. Harper & Row. A good introduction to Barth's thought *via* his study of the Apostles' Creed.

✪BARTH, Karl (trans. Clarence K. Pott).
WOLFGANG AMADEUS MOZART. Eerdmans, 1986. Originally published in celebration of the 200th anniversary of Mozart's birth. The author, a prominent 20th century theologian and a lifelong devotee of Mozart and his music, suggests that Mozart's music captures the freedom present in creation, a consequence of God's creative-sustaining activity.

BATCHELOR, Peter.
PEOPLE IN RURAL DEVELOPMENT. Attic Press, 1981. Experienced as a member of Sudan United Mission Fellowship, the author contends that Christians have a distinctive contribution to make in rural development. The key to development lies in working with people rather than relying on technology.

BATESON, Gregory.
MIND & NATURE: A NECESSARY UNITY. Bantam, 1988. Bateson is often classified as a pantheist, but in this book he distinguishes his own views from pantheism. The most rigorously scientific of the new crop of popular science books. In a rambling, spirited discussion, he brings insights from cybernetics and brain science. He rejects determinism and pantheism: "If atoms are conscious, we may as well pack up shop and go fishing." His view of evolution sees an intelligence beyond the universe which he suggests could be equated with God.

BAUER, Henry H.
BEYOND VELIKOVSKY: THE HISTORY OF A PUBLIC CONTROVERSY. U. of Illinois P., 1984. Recommended by Owen Gingerich as the most balanced evaluation of the Velikovsky affair. Velikovsky, author of the controversial best seller *Worlds in Collision*, has been widely criticized by the established scientific community.

BAYLY, Joseph.
THE GOSPEL BLIMP AND OTHER STORIES. David C. Cook, 1983. Reprints 24 of Bayly's finest parables and essays. Includes "Does Man Exist," the story of the emancipated computer who argues that man does not exist, except in a pantheistic sense, as "the original ionization from which we all proceed ... the ultimate core memory which enables us to better serve our fellow computers."

✪BEATY, Michael D., ed.
CHRISTIAN THEISM AND THE PROBLEMS OF PHILOSOPHY (Library of Religious Philosophy, Vol. 5). U. of Notre Dame P., 1990. A collection of essays addressing issues of epistemology, metaphysics, and ethics. Written in response to Alvin Plantinga's essay "Advice to Christian Philosophers." Work includes Plantinga's essay and is intended for Christian philosophers as well as instructors and students of philosophy.

BELL, John S.
SPEAKABLE AND UNSPEAKABLE IN QUANTUM MECHANICS: COLLECTED PAPERS IN QUANTUM MECHANICS. Cambridge U.P., 1988.

BELLAH, Robert N., et al.
HABITS OF THE HEART: INDIVIDUALISM AND COMMITMENT IN AMERICAN LIFE. Harper & Row, 1986. An examination of American values with a compelling challenge for personal and societal evaluation.

BERG, Howard C.
RANDOM WALKS IN BIOLOGY. Princeton U.P., 1984.

✛BERNBAUM, John, ed.
ECONOMIC JUSTICE AND THE STATE. Baker, 1986. A debate between Ronald Nash and

Eric Beversluis over whether the liberal or conservative position, with respect to government involvement, conforms most to biblical morés. Includes bibliography, scripture index, and a study guide for use in Christian colleges.

✪BERTOLA, F.; SULENTIC, J.W.; and MADORE, F.R., eds.
NEW IDEAS IN ASTRONOMY. Cambridge U.P., 1988. A conference proceedings *Festschrift* for Halton Arp, with a number of the papers setting out challenges to aspects of the "standard" Big Bang cosmology.

BILEZIKIAN, Gilbert.
BEYOND SEX ROLES: A GUIDE FOR THE STUDY OF FEMALE ROLES IN THE BIBLE. Baker, 1985. Starting with God's creation design, crucial scripture passages on "the Old-Covenant Compromise," the new creation in Christ, and the early Christian church are examined in a step-by-step evaluation of the arguments and alternative views that pertain to women in contemporary society. This is an indispensable resource for anyone concerned about genuinely Christian perspectives on the reciprocal roles of men and women in the family, church, and society.

✪BIRD, Lewis P., and BARLOW, James.
MEDICAL ETHICS: OATHS AND PRAYERS. AN ANTHOLOGY. Christian Medical and Dental Society, 1989. A compilation of codes and declarations in medical care throughout recorded history.

✪BIRD, Wendell R.
THE ORIGIN OF SPECIES REVISITED. 2 vols. Philosophical Library, 1989. An authoritative and comprehensive work comparing theories of evolution, creation, and abrupt appearance, by a lawyer who has been deeply involved in creation/evolution controversies. Contains 2,000 quotations from many leading authorities. Highly recommended.

BIRTEL, Frank T., ed.
RELIGION, SCIENCE, & PUBLIC POLICY. Crossroad NY, 1987. A set of very useful essays, by such authors as: R.A. Peacocke, L. Gilkey, Stephen Toulmin, K.A. Peters, and P. Hefner.

✪BLACKMORE, Vernon, and PAGE, Andrew.
EVOLUTION: THE GREAT DEBATE. Lion Pub., 1989. An objective, balanced account of the history of the theory of evolution and the controversies that have resulted from it. The authors show commitment to the concept of creation though they reject strict interpretations of creation science. (D-90)

✪BLACKWELL, Richard J.
GALILEO, BALLARMINE, AND THE BIBLE. U. of Notre Dame P., 1991. A fresh approach to the Galileo case in which the author argues convincingly that the maintenance of ecclesiastical authority, not the scientific issues themselves, led to the tragic trial and condemnation of Galileo in 1633.

✪BLAEDEL, Niels.
HARMONY AND UNITY: THE LIFE OF NIELS BOHR. Science Tech. Pub., 1988. The only full-length biography of the great Danish scientist written by a Danish author, offering unusual insight into Bohr's immediate cultural background and illuminating his life and work.

BLAKEMORE, Colin, and GREENFIELD, Susan, eds.
MINDWAVES: THOUGHTS ON INTELLIGENCE, IDENTITY AND CONSCIOUSNESS. Basil Blackwell, 1987.

BLISS, Richard B.
ORIGINS: CREATION OR EVOLUTION. Master Bks., 1988. One of the currently popular works demonstrating a two-sided approach to problems of origins with creationism favored. A teacher's guide is also available.

BLOCHER, Henri.
IN THE BEGINNING: THE OPENING CHAPTERS OF GENESIS. InterVarsity Press, 1984. A definitive work of exegesis on the opening chapters of Genesis by a conservative reformed scholar. Author favors the "framework theory" as being the most sound interpretation from the standpoint of biblical exegesis. Highly recommended.

✪BLOCKSMA, Mary.
READING THE NUMBERS: A SURVIVAL GUIDE TO THE MEASUREMENTS, NUMBERS AND SIZES ENCOUNTERED IN EVERYDAY LIFE. Penguin, 1989. A guide to making numbers more understandable and useful.

✪BLOESCH, Donald G.
THE FUTURE OF EVANGELICAL CHRISTIANITY: A CALL FOR UNITY AMID DIVERSITY.

Helmers & Howard, 1989. An examination of contemporary evangelicalism and a vision for its influence within world Christianity as a unifying force. Some issues addressed include: the problem of evangelical identity; the variety of streams and movements in the new conservatism; the scandal of disunity; and the needed directions for a vital, renewed evangelicalism.

BLOESCH, Donald G.
THE STRUGGLE OF PRAYER. Helmers & Howard, 1988. A classic work which surveys common misunderstandings of prayer, then focuses on the practice of biblical prayer as true and effectual for the Christian. The author distinguishes between the evangelical and mystical traditions, calling for a purified mysticism that is "transformed and directed by faith in the crucified and risen Savior."

✪BLOESCH, Donald G.
THEOLOGICAL NOTEBOOK Vol. 1: 1960-1964. Helmers & Howard, 1989. The first publication in a series of spiritual journals by a noted evangelical theologian. The chronological format gives insight into the development of the author's thought on subjects such as: heresy and orthodoxy, the church and the sacraments, marriage and celibacy, sin and sainthood. Includes a comprehensive index.

BLUM, W., et al, eds.
HEISENBERG: GESAMMELTE WERKE (COLLECTED WORKS) (Series B: Scientific Review Papers, Talks, and Books). Springer-Verlag, 1984.

✪BOCKMUEHL, Klaus E.
BOOKS: GOD'S TOOLS IN THE HISTORY OF SALVATION. Helmers & Howard, 1989. Shows by a few characteristic examples the decisive effect books have had in the history of Christianity and urges Christians to work for the creation and dissemination of Christian literature.

BOCKMUEHL, Klaus E.
THE CHALLENGE OF MARXISM. Helmers & Howard, 1988. A candid examination of the Marxist program and the model for the New Man, countered by a biblical evaluation. The author points out key flaws in Marxist thought as well as crucial deficiencies in Christian practice that gave rise in part to Marx's bitter attack on the Church. Marxist criticism is turned into a stirring challenge to Christians to pursue a more purposeful devotion to Christ which includes social reform.

✪BOCKMUEHL, Klaus E.
LISTENING TO THE GOD WHO SPEAKS: REFLECTIONS ON GOD'S GUIDANCE FROM SCRIPTURE AND THE LIVES OF GOD'S PEOPLE. Helmers & Howard, 1990.

✪BOCKMUEHL, Klaus E.
LIVING BY THE GOSPEL: CHRISTIAN ROOTS OF CONFIDENCE AND PURPOSE. Helmers & Howard, 1989. A motivating call to authentic Christian living which points to the gospel of Jesus Christ. Part I examines three gifts of the Gospel: forgiveness, commission, and a personal counselor. Part II examines three tasks of the Gospel: prayer, sustainment and preservation, and proclamation.

✪BOCKMUEHL, Klaus E.
THE UNREAL GOD OF MODERN THEOLOGY; BULTMANN, BARTH, AND THE THEOLOGY OF ATHEISM: A CALL TO RECOVERING THE TRUTH OF GOD'S REALITY. Helmers & Howard, 1989. An analysis of the unreality of God present in twentieth-century theology as a result of a generation of influential theologians, and leading to developments such as: the accommodation of Christian theology to political ideologies, a nominal and increasingly secularized Christianity, a self-preoccupied church. The author calls for a recovery of the truth of God's reality.

BOHM, David.
WHOLENESS AND THE IMPLICATE ORDER. Routledge, Chapman & Hall, 1983. An appeal from quantum mechanics for studying the world as an unbroken unity.

BOHR, Niels.
THE PHILOSOPHICAL WRITINGS OF NIELS BOHR. 3 vols. Ox Bow, 1987. Volume 1: Atomic Theory and the Description of Nature. Volume 2: Essays 1932-1957 on Atomic Physics and Human Knowledge. Volume 3: Essays 1958-1962 on Atomic Physics and Human Knowledge.

BONHOEFFER, Dietrich.
CREATION & THE FALL AND TEMPTATION. Macmillan, 1965. Important theological reflection on the early chapters of Genesis and their connection with the New Testament.

BONHOEFFER, Dietrich.
ETHICS. Macmillan, 1965.

BONHOEFFER, Dietrich.
LETTERS AND PAPERS FROM PRISON. enl. ed. Macmillan, 1972.

⊘BÖRNER, G.
THE EARLY UNIVERSE: FACTS AND FICTION. Springer-Verlag, 1988. This text explores the connections developed recently between particle physics and cosmology, examining the following major topics: the standard Big-Bang model, particle physics and cosmology, and dark matter and galaxy formation.

⊘BOUMA, Hessel, III, et al.
CHRISTIAN FAITH, HEALTH, AND MEDICAL PRACTICE. Eerdmans, 1989. Five Fellows of the Culver City Center for Christian Scholarship examine the issues of medical ethics.

BOVA, Ben.
WELCOME TO MOONBASE. Ballantine, 1987. A hypothetical moonbase of the 21st century is presented in this manual for lunar pioneers by the scientist and science fiction author and editor, Ben Bova. It provides the reader with a complete "history" of lunar exploration, the establishment of moonbases, and an explanation of all moonbase operations. This book, according to the author, is to make us contemplate living and working on the moon in the foreseeable future.

BOWLER, Peter J.
THE ECLIPSE OF DARWINISM. Johns Hopkins U.P., 1983. Excellent history tracing certain themes from the original Darwinian revolution into early modern biology.

BOWLER, Peter J.
EVOLUTION: THE HISTORY OF AN IDEA. rev. ed. U. of Calif. P., 1989.

BRAND, Paul, and YANCEY, Philip.
FEARFULLY AND WONDERFULLY MADE. Zondervan, 1980. A surgeon looks at the human and spiritual body.

BRAND, Paul, and YANCEY, Philip.
IN HIS IMAGE. Zondervan, 1987. A fascinating study of the human body aimed to shed light on the great New Testament metaphor of the Body of Christ.

BRANDIN, David H., and HARRISON, M.A.
THE TECHNOLOGY WAR: A CASE FOR COMPETITIVENESS. Wiley, 1987. The authors feel that whatever political power controls the development and supply of information technology will come to control the world's resources and will be the next global power. The strategies and objectives of this competition are described.

BRANSON, Mark, and PADILLA, Rene.
CONFLICT AND CONTEXT: HERMENEUTICS IN THE AMERICAS. Eerdmans, 1986. Important issues in biblical interpretation are raised including: "How does a church's cultural context affect its interpretation of the Bible?" and "What dangers exist in contextual hermeneutics?"

⊘BRIGGS, John P., and PEAT, F. David.
LOOKING GLASS UNIVERSE: THE EMERGING SCIENCE OF WHOLENESS. Simon & Schuster, 1984. Quantum uncertainty, relativity, holographic images, order out of disorder, as phenomena of wholeness in the universe.

BROAD, William, and WADE, Nicholas.
BETRAYERS OF THE TRUTH. Simon & Schuster, 1983. Scientific fraud and what it indicates about the way science is really done. (J-84)

BROOKS, Jim.
ORIGINS OF LIFE. Lion Pub., 1985. Covers from the first moments of the universe to the beginning of life on earth and includes a wealth of color illustrations. The author has experience as vice-president of the Geological Society in England, and lectures in geochemistry. (J-86)

BROWN, Colin.
MIRACLES AND THE CRITICAL MIND. Eerdmans, 1984. J.I. Packer states, "clearest survey of the debate about miracles."

BROWN, L.B.
THE PSYCHOLOGY OF RELIGIOUS BELIEF. Academic Press, 1987.

BROWN, Lester R., et al.
STATE OF THE WORLD 1988: A WORLDWATCH INSTITUTE REPORT ON PROGRESS TOWARDS A SUSTAINABLE SOCIETY. Norton, 1988. The fifth in Worldwatch's annual series. Current issues analyzed include: the ecology and economics of urbanization, future of nuclear power, thresholds of change for natural systems, recycling solid wastes, and raising agricultural

productivity in the Third World. *State of the World 1989* and *State of the World 1990* are also available.

BROWN, Robert H.
THE WISDOM OF SCIENCE: ITS RELEVANCE TO CULTURE & RELIGION. Cambridge U.P., 1986. A useful introduction to the role that science and technology have played in society over the last 300 years. Evangelicals may not agree with the theological perspective of the author, but they can benefit from his insights.

◻BROWNING, Don S.
RELIGIOUS THOUGHT AND THE MODERN PSYCHOLOGIES. Fortress, 1989. This book is a significant contribution to the dialogue between religion and the social sciences. It has an excellent discussion of the implications of the psychotherapeutic sciences for ethics.

◻BRUNGS, Robert A.
YOU SEE LIGHTS BREAKING UPON US: DOCTRINAL PERSPECTIVES ON BIOLOGICAL ADVANCE. ITEST Faith/Science Press, 1989. Order direct: ITEST Faith/Science Press, 3601 Lindell Blvd., St. Louis, MO 63108. A call for religious and moral vision to keep pace with technological progress, particularly in the biomedical field, from a Roman Catholic perspective.

BURGESS, Jeremy; MURTEN, Michael; and TAYLOR, R.
MICROCOSMOS. Cambridge U.P., 1987. Color and b&w illustrations introduce the major applications of modern microscopic techniques in the biological and materials sciences. Various images as seen through the light microscope, scanning electron microscope and transmission electron microscope show the differences in resolution and views between these types of machines.

BURKE, Derek, ed.
CREATION & EVOLUTION: SEVEN VIEWS. InterVarsity Press (UK), 1985. Seven prominent Christians: A.G. Fraser, E.H. Andrews, R.J. Berry, V. Wright, D.T. Gish, D.C. Burke, and D.G. Jones debate the issues, with a summation by O.R. Barclay. (S-85)

◻BURRELL, David B., and MCGINN, Bernard, eds.
GOD AND CREATION: AN ECUMENICAL SYMPOSIUM. U. of Notre Dame P., 1990. An important contribution to comparative religious thought in general and to serious theological reflection on the doctrine of divine creation in Judaism, Christianity and Islam in particular.

BUTTERFIELD, Herbert.
ORIGINS OF MODERN SCIENCE. rev. ed. Free Press, 1965. Christian historian from Cambridge University. Valuable resource in the history of science.

BUZZARD, Lynn, and COLBY, Kim.
PUBLIC SCHOOL POLICY MANUAL. Christian Legal Society, 1987. Christian Legal Society believes this will become the standard guide for the issues of religion in public schools.

BYRNE, Kevin, ed.
RESPONSIBLE SCIENCE: THE IMPACT OF TECHNOLOGY ON SOCIETY. Harper & Row, 1986. Contributors include Salvador Luria, Daniel Kevles, Winston Brill, Merritt Roe Smith and J. Robert Nelson.

CAMERON, Nigel.
EVOLUTION AND THE AUTHORITY OF THE BIBLE. Attic Press, 1983. Includes a historical survey of the interpretation of the Genesis account of creation.

CAMPOLO, Anthony.
A REASONABLE FAITH: RESPONDING TO SECULARISM. Word, 1985. A Baptist sociologist takes us on a journey through a wide range of modern thinkers in philosophy, theology and the social sciences, and helps us to see how different thinkers (Freud, Marx, Skinner, Einstein, Chardin and Darwin) both challenge and affirm a Christian world view. (J-85)

CAMPOLO, Anthony.
WE HAVE MET THE ENEMY AND THEY ARE PARTLY RIGHT. Word, 1985. Affirms "Genuine faith can be strengthened and purified by hearing their charges, rather than by dismissing them as unfit to consider."

CAMPOLO, Anthony.
WHO SWITCHED THE PRICE TAGS? Word, 1987. This popularized discussion about the need to clarify our values in a mixed-up world gives special emphasis to values in the work place, family, and church. The main thesis is that fun is a very important consequence of true spirituality, for Jesus came to forgive our sins, straighten out our distorted value systems, and teach us how to live joyfully. The joy of living comes from self-giving, in contrast to society's false values. These sermons with a sociological flair are enjoyable for youth as well as adults.

CANTOR, Norman L.
LEGAL FRONTIERS OF DEATH AND DYING. Indiana U.P., 1987.

+CANTORE, Enrico.
ATOMIC ORDER: AN INTRODUCTION TO THE PHILOSOPHY OF MICRO-PHYSICS. MIT Press, 1970. The author views the development of modern quantum physics as part of a continuous fulfillment of the program of imposing order upon observation. The book discusses very difficult conceptual problems in an extremely readable fashion.

✪CAPON, Robert F.
HEALTH, MONEY, AND LOVE ... AND WHY WE DON'T ENJOY THEM. Eerdmans, 1990. A provocative look at happiness and religion in our lives with health, money, and love presented as false religions from which happiness cannot be obtained.

CAPRA, Fritjof.
THE TAO OF PHYSICS. 2nd rev. ed. Shambhala, 1983. An influential book presenting world views of modern physics and Eastern religions and arguing for their similarities.

CARTER, John, and NARRAMORE, Bruce.
THE INTEGRATION OF PSYCHOLOGY AND THEOLOGY: AN INTRODUCTION. Zondervan, 1979. Fine annotated bibliography.

CARVIN, Walter P.
CREATION & SCIENTIFIC EXPLANATION (Frontiers of Knowledge Ser: No.10). Scot. Acad. P./Gower Pub., 1988. A comparison of the Biblical concept of creation with the background of Babylonian cosmology, Aquinas' concept of creation with the cosmology of Aristole, and Leibniz with Descartes. The author argues that there is a correlation between the theory of creation in each philosophy and the scientific world view of its time. (M-90)

✪CASSIRER, Heinz W., trans.
GOD'S NEW COVENANT: A NEW TESTAMENT TRANSLATION. Eerdmans, 1989. A unique and distinctive translation by a Jewish classicist and philosopher. Relevant for those seeking a deeper understanding of spiritual roots and for Jews interested in Christianity.

✪CASTI, John L.
PARADIGMS LOST: IMAGES OF MAN IN THE MIRROR OF SCIENCE. Morrow, 1989. An examination of recent science's impact on our understanding of life's origin, of genes and behavior, artificial intelligence, extraterrestrial life and reality itself.

CAVALIERI, Liebe F.
DOUBLE-EDGED HELIX: GENETIC ENGINEERING IN THE REAL WORLD. (Convergence Ser.: No.1). Praeger, 1984. A critical and cautionary look at American science which is more concerned with the narrow interests of the scientist than with the impending ecological crises threatening humanity.

CHAISSON, Eric.
COSMIC DAWN: THE ORIGINS OF MATTER AND LIFE. Norton, 1989.

CHAISSON, Eric.
THE LIFE ERA: COSMIC SELECTION AND CONSCIOUS EVOLUTION. Atlantic Monthly, 1987. A look at the current and third major era in the development of the constantly changing universe characterized by the existence of intelligence and consciousness. The author contends that this is only the beginning of the "Life Era." (S-89)

✪CHAISSON, Eric.
RELATIVELY SPEAKING: RELATIVITY, BLACK HOLES, AND THE RATE OF THE UNI-VERSE. Norton, 1990. An authoritative synopsis of modern relativity theory.

✪CHAISSON, Eric.
UNIVERSE: AN EVOLUTIONARY APPROACH TO ASTRONOMY. Prentice Hall, 1988. An updated, non-technical look at astronomy, integrated with evolutionary biology, which offers a full picture of modern science's evolutionary view of the cosmos. (M-91)

✪CHAPMAN, Clark R., and MORRISON, David.
COSMIC CATASTROPHIES. Plenum Pub. Corp., 1989. A non-technical examination of the reality and threat of cosmic phenomena and catastrophies. Includes topics such as supernova explosions, colliding worlds, ice ages, and the global greenhouse effect.

CHASE, Gene B., and JONGSMA, Calvin.
BIBLIOGRAPHY OF CHRISTIANITY AND MATHEMATICS, 1910-1983. Dordt College Press, 1983. A very helpful annotated bibliography of approximately 300 entries that deal with the relationships between mathematics and Christianity. Works exhibiting a wide range of Christian

perspectives (Roman Catholic, Evangelical, Reformed) have been included, and mathematics is broadly construed to include some material from physics and biology.

CHENEVIERE, Alain.
VANISHING TRIBES: PRIMITIVE MAN ON EARTH. Doubleday, 1987. A record of twenty primitive tribes of the 300 studied by the author. Photography and text combine to describe the daily life, and traditional legends of each tribe.

◎CHESTNUT, Glen F.
IMAGES OF CHRIST. Harper & Row, 1984. A good modern introduction to Christological issues and ideas.

CLINE, Barbara L.
MEN WHO MADE A NEW PHYSICS: PHYSICISTS AND THE QUANTUM THEORY. U. of Chicago P., 1987. An excellent and very readable introduction to the history of quantum physics and relativity with a good discussion of the conceptual issues and their philosophical significance.

CLOUSE, Bonnidell.
MORAL DEVELOPMENT: PERSPECTIVES IN PSYCHOLOGY AND CHRISTIAN BELIEF. Baker, 1985. Professor of educational and school psychology presents an introduction to moral development through the integration of psychology and Christianity, with application to daily life.

COBB, John B., Jr.
GOD AND THE WORLD. John Knox, 1969. A basic introduction to the ideas of process theology.

COHEN, Bernard I.
REVOLUTION IN SCIENCE. Belknap Press, 1987. An important and massive study that concerns itself with the following questions: How did "revolution," a term from the physical sciences, become transformed into an expression for radical change in political and socio-economic affairs, and then become appropriated once again by the sciences? What are the elements of continuity and discontinuity in a scientific revolution?

COLES, Robert (ed. Peter Davison).
THE MORAL LIFE OF CHILDREN. Houghton Mifflin, 1987. An important book by a Harvard psychiatrist that has received national acclaim. Coles' craft as a storyteller, combined with interesting case studies of his work with children, makes for fascinating reading.

◎COLES, Robert.
THE SPIRITUAL LIFE OF CHILDREN. Houghton Mifflin, 1990. The latest in a series on the moral and spiritual attitudes and insights of children by a noted psychiatrist.

◎+COLLINS, Gary R.
CAN YOU TRUST PSYCHOLOGY? InterVarsity Press, 1988. Considers thirty questions often raised by critics of psychology, including: "Why should a Christian get counseling if God meets all our needs?" and "Can psychology explain away biblical miracles?"

+COLLINS, Gary R.
CHRISTIAN COUNSELING: A COMPREHENSIVE GUIDE. rev. ed. Word, 1988. Provides an overview of counseling and addresses 30 or more of the most common counseling problems including depression, anxiety, homosexuality and grief. Used as a text in colleges and seminaries.

+COLLINS, Gary R.
THE REBUILDING OF PSYCHOLOGY. Tyndale, 1977. An integration of psychology and Christianity, with a number of constructive suggestions. (D-78)

+COLLINS, Gary R., ed.
RESOURCES FOR CHRISTIAN COUNSELING Series. Word, 1986. Titles are: INNOVATIVE APPROACHES TO COUNSELING (Gary Collins),(M-88); COUNSELING CHRISTIAN WORKERS (Louis McBurney); SELF-TALK, IMAGERY AND PRAYER IN COUNSELING (H. Norman Wright); and COUNSELING THOSE WITH EATING DISORDERS (Raymond Vath). These books provide a good introduction to each area with many helpful insights.

+COLLINS, Gary R., ed.
RESOURCES FOR CHRISTIAN COUNSELING Series. Word, 1987. Titles are: COUNSELING THE DEPRESSED (Archibald Hart), (S-88); COUNSELING FOR FAMILY VIOLENCE AND ABUSE (Grant Martin), (M-91); COUNSELING IN TIMES OF CRISIS (Judson Swihart and Gerald Richardson); COUNSELING AND GUILT (Earl Wilson); COUNSELING & THE SEARCH FOR MEANING (Paul Welter), (J-88); COUNSELING FOR UNPLANNED PREGNANCY AND INFERTILITY (Everett Worthington, Jr.),(M-91); COUNSELING FOR PROBLEMS OF SELF-CONTROL (Richard Walters); COUNSELING FOR SUBSTANCE ABUSE AND ADDICTION

(Stephen Van Cleave, Walter Byrd, Kathy Revell), (J-90).

✪+COLLINS, Gary R., ed.
RESOURCES FOR CHRISTIAN COUNSELING Series. Word, 1988. Titles are: COUNSELING AND SELF-ESTEEM (David Carlson); COUNSELING FAMILIES (George Rekers), (M-91); COUNSELING AND HOMOSEXUALITY (Earl Wilson); COUNSELING FOR ANGER (Mark Cosgrove); and COUNSELING AND THE DEMONIC (Rodger Bufford).

✪+COLLINS, Gary R., ed.
RESOURCES FOR CHRISTIAN COUNSELING Series. Word, 1989. Titles are: COUNSELING AND DIVORCE (David Thompson); COUNSELING AND MARRIAGE (Deloss and Ruby Friesen); COUNSELING THE SICK AND TERMINALLY ILL (Gregg Albers); COUNSELING ADULT CHILDREN OF ALCOHOLICS (Sandra Wilson); and COUNSELING AND CHILDREN (Warren Byrd and Paul Warren).

✪+COLLINS, Gary R., ed.
RESOURCES FOR CHRISTIAN COUNSELING Series. Word, 1990. Titles are: COUNSELING BEFORE MARRIAGE (Everett Worthington, Jr.); COUNSELING AND AIDS (Gregg Albers); COUNSELING FAMILIES OF CHILDREN WITH DISABILITIES (Rosemarie Cook); and COUNSELING FOR SEXUAL DISORDERS (Joyce and Clifford Penner).

+COLLINS, Gary R.
YOUR MAGNIFICENT MIND: THE FASCINATING WAY IT WORKS FOR YOU. Baker, 1988. Draws from research in psychology, physiology, and other cognitive and social sciences, then combines this with biblical teachings on the mind. Discusses intelligence, creativity, faith healing, hypnosis, dreams, religious experience, and mind control.

✪COMISKEY, Andrew.
PURSUING SEXUAL WHOLENESS: HOW JESUS HEALS THE HOMOSEXUAL. Creation House, 1989. Well balanced and up-to-date work on topic of homosexuality. Study guide also available.

✪COMMITTEE on the Conduct of Science of the National Academy of Sciences.
ON BEING A SCIENTIST. National Academy Press, 1989. A book for beginning graduate students in the sciences clarifying the methods of scientific research, some problem areas such as fraud, and the social structures of science which function to support good science.(J-91)

✪CRABB, Lawrence.
INSIDE OUT. NavPress, 1988.This book explores the root cause of problems people face. The author advocates ownership of feelings and deep repentance as essential for growth, and disdains the false gospel of relief from suffering which is preached in modern Christianity. Study guide available. (J-90)

CRAIG, W.L.
THE ONLY WISE GOD. Baker, 1987. An excellent introduction to philosophical arguments concerning the compatibility of divine foreknowledge and human freedom. Arguments making use of current physical understanding (e.g., relativity theory) are discussed.

CREASE, Robert F., and MANN, Charles C.
THE SECOND CREATION: MAKERS OF THE REVOLUTION IN 20TH CENTURY PHYSICS. Macmillan, 1987. Describes, for the general reader, the search for the unification theory in physics and the scientists involved.

CUSHING, James T., et al, eds.
SCIENCE AND REALITY: RECENT WORK IN THE PHILOSOPHY OF SCIENCE. U. of Notre Dame P., 1984. A worthwhile set of essays on recent philosophy of science from the standpoint of critical realism. Non-specialists will find the essays readable.

✪D'ABRO, A.
THE EVOLUTION OF SCIENTIFIC THOUGHT FROM NEWTON TO EINSTEIN. Dover Pub., 1950. A clearly presented history from the essential features of Newton's great discoveries to Einstein's contributions to the realm of physics.

D'ESPAGNAT, B.
IN SEARCH OF REALITY. Springer-Verlag, 1983. The author discusses the philosophical implications of quantum physics.

DARWIN, Charles.
THE ORIGIN OF SPECIES AND THE DESCENT OF MAN. Random, 1977.

DAVIES, Paul.
THE COSMIC BLUEPRINT: NEW DISCOVERIES IN NATURE'S CREATIVE ABILITY TO

ORDER THE UNIVERSE. Touchstone, 1989. An excellent book as an overview of the latest developments in the science of cosmology. (M-90)

⊘DAVIES, Paul.
THE FORCES OF NATURE. 2nd ed. Cambridge U.P., 1986. An excellent introduction to electromagnetic field theory, special and general relativity, quantum physics, and the unity of the forces of nature. Intended for both students and those without special knowledge of fundamental physics.

DAVIES, Paul.
GOD & THE NEW PHYSICS. Touchstone, 1984. A lucid, readable popularizer of quantum physics who does not merge current theory with Eastern thought. He concludes in this book that physics offers a surer path to God than religion. He addresses some of the big questions of existence in an honest and fair manner, and clears up much unclear thinking. (D-84)

DAVIES, Paul.
SUPERFORCE. Touchstone, 1985. Very meaningful remarks on the strange correlation between laws that describe physical reality and mathematical law-structures invented by the human mind.

⊘DAVIES, Paul, and BROWN, J.R., eds.
THE GHOST IN THE ATOM: A DISCUSSION OF THE MYSTERIES OF QUANTUM PHYSICS. Cambridge U.P., 1986. An examination of how quantum physics dominates modern physical science yet is built on foundations that appear to defy common sense. This book is based on interviews with leading quantum physicists.

⊘DAVIS, Percival, and KENYON, Dean H.
OF PANDAS AND PEOPLE: THE CENTRAL QUESTION OF BIOLOGICAL ORIGINS. Haughton Pub. Co., 1989. This book stresses intelligent causation as a scientific viewpoint in contrast with natural causation. Covers fields of biology, chemistry, and geology, and is an excellent supplement for a student taking a one-sided biology course which stresses only naturalistic evolution.

DAVIS, Philip J., and PARK, David, eds.
NO WAY: THE NATURE OF THE IMPOSSIBLE. Freeman, 1987. Collected essays on "impossibilities" in a range of "scientific" fields, from experts in mountaineering, artificial intelligence, biology, and politics, among many other topics. *Publishers Weekly* says: "Combining literary elegance with startling insights, these essays lead the reader to exclaim, with Tertullian, 'It is certain because it is impossible.' "

⊘DEBRUS, Joachim, and HIRSHFELD, Allen C., eds.
THE FUNDAMENTAL INTERACTION: GEOMETRIC TRENDS. Plenum Pub. Corp., 1988. An introductory level presentation of recent developments in modern theoretical physics which addresses topics such as methods in modern field theory, anomalies, and supertheories.

DE JONG, Norman, ed.
CHRISTIAN APPROACHES TO LEARNING THEORY, Vol.3. U.P. of America, 1987. A very valuable collection of essays by Christian educators on Christian perspectives with respect to learning theory. There are important theoretical and practical insights therein. The result of the third annual conference on Christian approaches to education held at Trinity Christian College.

⊘DE JONG, Arthur J.
RECLAIMING A MISSION: NEW DIRECTION FOR THE CHURCH-RELATED COLLEGE. Eerdmans, 1990. A call to church-related colleges to replace the value-free scientific model with one that integrates intellectual and moral education on the basis of Christian beliefs.

⊘DEMARAY, Donald E.
LAUGHTER, JOY AND HEALING. Baker, 1987. The therapy of laughter and joy can bring physical, emotional and spiritual healing and restoration. Designed for easy reading and reflection. (D-89)

DENTON, Michael.
EVOLUTION: A THEORY IN CRISIS. Adler & Adler, 1986. Author states that the evidence from his field of molecular biology lends no support to neo-Darwinian theory on the origin of life. Moreover nature appears to be profoundly discontinuous between classes, and evolution is the "great cosmogenic myth of the twentieth century," embraced only because we have no causal explanation for the origin of man.

DESANTO, Charles P., and POLOMA, Margaret M., eds.
SOCIAL PROBLEMS: CHRISTIAN PERSPECTIVES. Hunter Textbooks, 1985. This is intended to be a text for a college level course on social problems. It has 21 articles written mainly by

sociologists who give Christian insights into issues such as environmental crisis, nuclear militarism, variant sexuality, population and hunger, alcohol and drug abuse. (D-86)

DESOWITZ, Robert S.
THE THORN IN THE STARFISH: HOW THE HUMAN IMMUNE SYSTEM WORKS. Norton, 1987. A description of the human immune system and the possibilities of manipulating it. Diet, vitamins, smoking, and immunology are discussed. A special chapter on AIDS and the possibility of developing a vaccine are discussed in light of our knowledge of immunity and immune deficiency.

DIRAC, Paul A.
THE PRINCIPLES OF QUANTUM MECHANICS. 4th ed. Oxford U.P., 1958. A classic text on quantum theory by one of its founders.

✪DIXON, Patrick.
THE WHOLE TRUTH ABOUT AIDS. Nelson, 1989. Topics considered include health care for AIDS patients, death and dying, burnout of AIDS workers, advice to travelers. (J-90)

DUNBAR, Robin I.M.
PRIMATE SOCIAL SYSTEMS. Cornell U.P., 1987.

DYSON, Freeman.
DISTURBING THE UNIVERSE. Ticknor & Fields, 1988. An autobiographical journey through science to ethics and theology.

DYSON, Freeman.
INFINITE IN ALL DIRECTIONS: AN EXPLORATION OF SCIENCE AND BELIEF. Harper & Row, 1988. The 1985 Gifford Lectures of this very distinguished physicist. Contains much stimulating material, particularly with respect to the Anthropic Principle and design of the Universe, purpose in biological discourse, possible theories of the origins of life, and war and peace in a world of nuclear weaponry. The book is, at times, theologically, philosophically and scientifically "loosely" argued.

DYSON, Freeman.
WEAPONS AND HOPE. Harper & Row, 1985. A broad and well-written discussion of issues posed by modern weapons systems.

EHRLICH, Paul R.
THE MACHINERY OF NATURE. Touchstone, 1987. A tour of ecology, from examination of individual aspects of nature to its governing principles of the entire system, giving the reader a sense of the discipline and how ecological scientists operate. The future of man, the author says, depends on his learning to live without seriously damaging the machinery of nature so that it can no longer support civilization.

EINSTEIN, Albert.
RELATIVITY: THE SPECIAL & GENERAL THEORY. Crown, 1961. This is the best single popular introduction to relativity. It is not up-to-date on the latest developments, but lays their foundations.

✪EINSTEIN, Albert.
SIDELIGHTS ON RELATIVITY. Dover Pub., 1983. Two influential unabridged essays: Ether and Relativity (1920) and Geometry and Experience (1921).

EINSTEIN, Albert, and INFELD, Leopold.
THE EVOLUTION OF PHYSICS. Simon and Schuster, 1967. The development of the basic ideas of physics through relativity and quantum theory.

✪EISELEY, Loren.
THE UNEXPECTED UNIVERSE. Harcourt, Brace, Jovanovich, 1972. The famous anthropologist's story of humankind and evolution.

✪EKELAND, Ivar.
MATHEMATICS AND THE UNEXPECTED. U. of Chicago P., 1990. A look at the mathematics of time through the use of pictures.

✪ELDREDGE, Niles.
LIFE PULSE: EPISODES FROM THE STORY OF THE FOSSIL RECORD. Facts on File, 1989. A reader-involved look at key episodes in the earth's evolution.

ELDREDGE, Niles.
TIME FRAMES: THE EVOLUTION OF PUNCTUATED EQUILIBRIUM. Princeton U.P., 1989. Darwinian evolution in light of modern evolutionary thinking.

ELLER, Vernard.
   CHRISTIAN ANARCHY: JESUS' PRIMACY OVER THE POWERS. Eerdmans, 1987. Contrasts the ideologies of partisan politics with the biblical norms of "Christian anarchy."

ELLUL, Jacques (trans. Joyce M. Hanks).
   THE HUMILIATION OF THE WORD. Eerdmans, 1985. This book discusses the dichotomy between the corresponding phenomena of the visual and the verbal, reality and truth, and imagery and the word. Although the author argues that the ultimate reconciliation between truth and reality may be found in God, he cautions that our modern-day predilection for the visual and "experience" of reality has resulted in a devaluing of verbal truth, of the "word" itself.

✪ELLUL, Jacques (trans. Olive Wyon).
   THE PRESENCE OF THE KINGDOM. 2nd ed. Helmers & Howard, 1989. A new edition of Ellul's classic work, first published in 1948, which calls upon Christians to be a radical presense in the world. Themes include: the tension of the Christian position in the world, revolutionary ideologies vs. true revolution; fate vs. human responsibility in the course of history; and the need for a distinctively Christian style of life. This edition includes a bibliography of Ellul's works and a comprehensive index.

ELLUL, Jacques (trans. Geoffrey W. Bromiley).
   THE SUBVERSION OF CHRISTIANITY. Eerdmans, 1986. The prolific French scholar deals with the scandal of Christianity—the radical contradiction between what we read in the Bible and the opposite nature of the society, civilization, and culture to which it and the church gave birth. Many popular misconceptions about the nature and impact of Christianity are overturned as he addresses moralism, sacralism and secularization, antifeminism, mysticism, missionary work, politics, power, wealth, division, accusations and inquisition, and other topics in the context of the scriptures and the history of our faith.

✪ELLUL, Jacques (trans. Geoffrey W. Bromiley).
   WHAT I BELIEVE. Eerdmans, 1989. The true meaning of science is presented as a search for truth by means of dialogue with physical reality.

✪EMERSON, Allen, and FORBES, Cheryl.
   THE INVASION OF THE COMPUTER CULTURE: WHAT YOU NEED TO KNOW ABOUT THE NEW WORLD WE LIVE IN. InterVarsity Press, 1989. A look at the ways in which computers are changing how we view ourselves, how we relate to others, how we interact with machines, how we understand the world around us.

ERDAHL, Lowell.
   PRO-LIFE/PRO-PEACE: LIFE-AFFIRMING ALTERNATIVES TO ABORTION, WAR, MERCY KILLING, AND THE DEATH PENALTY. Augsburg, 1986.

✪ERLER, Rolf J., and MARQUARD, Reiner, eds.
   A KARL BARTH READER. Eerdmans, 1986. An excellent introduction to Barth's thinking and faith through selections from sermons, letters, addresses and published writings.

✪EVANS, C. Stephen.
   SØREN KIERKEGAARD'S CHRISTIAN PSYCHOLOGY: INSIGHT FOR COUNSELING AND PASTORAL CARE. Zondervan, 1990. Using Kierkegaard's premise that mankind was made for relation with God and that this recognition is basic to self-understanding, the author examines the human desire for wholeness and personal growth. Written for psychologists, pastors, counselors, and those seeking to understand themselves and others.

✪FABIAN, A.C., ed.
   ORIGINS: THE DARWIN COLLEGE LECTURES. Cambridge U.P., 1989. A collection of writings by distinguished scientists. Subjects include the beginnings of the solar system, and the evolution of humans, social behavior, society, and language.

+FARNSWORTH, Kirk E.
   WHOLE-HEARTED INTEGRATION: HARMONIZING PSYCHOLOGY & CHRISTIANITY THROUGH WORD & DEED. Baker, 1986. Proposes methodologies for validating religious experience, and for integration of psychological and theological concepts.

FERRIS, Timothy.
   THE RED LIMIT. rev. ed. Morrow, 1983. This modest look at modern cosmology gives insights into the characters of scientists and questions of the meaning of the universe, as well as a survey of the Big Bang theory and observations which support it.

FEYNMAN, Richard P.
   THE CHARACTER OF PHYSICAL LAW. MIT Press, 1967. A series of lectures focussing on the underlying features of physical laws, invariance principles and conservation laws. The

intimate mesh of physics and mathematics is conveyed with little actual use of mathematics.

FEYNMAN, Richard P., and WEINBERG, Steve.
ELEMENTARY PARTICLES AND THE LAWS OF PHYSICS. Cambridge U.P., 1987.

FIDDES, Victor H.
SCIENCE AND THE GOSPEL (Frontiers of Knowledge Ser.: No.7). Scot. Acad. P./Gower Pub., 1987. Given the cultural rejection of Christ in the 20th century with human effort and thought focused on science rather than theology, the author observes that it is a mistake to assume that a scientific understanding of nature requires a repudiation of the Bible and of Christ.

✚FISHER, David E.
THE BIRTH OF THE EARTH: A WANDERLIED THROUGH SPACE, TIME, AND THE HUMAN IMAGINATION. Columbia U.P., 1987.

✪FLOOD, Raymond, and LOCKWOOD, Michael, eds.
THE NATURE OF TIME. Basil Blackwell, 1988. A collection of essays that bring together some of the latest thinking about time, in both philosophy and modern physical science.

FLORMAN, Samuel C.
THE CIVILIZED ENGINEER. St. Martin, 1987. Underlying philosophical foundations of the engineering profession are explored, defined, and discussed. Some questions addressed here include: Where does the profession originate? How ought engineers to be trained and motivated? What are the underlying views, traditions and purposes of engineering?

FOLSE, Henry J.
THE PHILOSOPHY OF NIELS BOHR: THE FRAMEWORK OF COMPLEMENTARITY. Elsevier, 1985. An excellent book which argues that from within the framework of complementarity, one can accept the completeness of the quantum description and yet retain a realistic understanding of the task of scientific theory. Will be of great use to all who wish to properly use complementarity as an epistemological tool to aid theological understanding.

✪FORD, David F., ed.
THE MODERN THEOLOGIANS: AN INTRODUCTION TO CHRISTIAN THEOLOGY IN THE TWENTIETH CENTURY. 2 vols. Basil Blackwell, 1989. Contributions by leading modern theologians from Europe and North America which aim to give a clear picture of individual theologians such as Barth, Tillich and Pannenberg (Vol. I) or theological movements such as evangelical theology, black theology, and feminist theology (Vol. II).

✪FORD, Norman M.
WHEN DID I BEGIN? CONCEPTION OF THE HUMAN INDIVIDUAL IN HISTORY, PHILOSOPHY AND SCIENCE. Cambridge U.P., 1988. A valuable resource on the biological and philosophical beginnings of human individuality.

FORE, William F.
TELEVISION & RELIGION: THE SHAPING OF FAITH & VALUE. Augsburg, 1987.

FORESTER, Tom.
THE HIGH-TECH SOCIETY: THE STORY OF THE INFORMATION TECHNOLOGY REVOLUTION. MIT Press, 1989. An overview of the high-tech revolution and its effects on society so far. Subjects covered include the development of computers, telecommunications, automated factories, and electronic banking, retailing and offices.

FOSTER, Richard J.
MONEY, SEX AND POWER. Harper & Row, 1985. This book is accompanied by a study guide which can be purchased separately. (M-87).

✪FOUNTAIN, Daniel E.
HEALTH, THE BIBLE AND THE CHURCH. Billy Graham Center, 1989. A wholistic view of healing by a physician who has much missionary experience.

FOX, Matthew, and SWIMME, Brian.
MANIFESTO FOR A GLOBAL CIVILIZATION. Bear & Co., 1982. A brief argument for relating science and religion in the context of Fox's "creation-centered spirituality."

FRASER, J.T.
TIME: THE FAMILIAR STRANGER. Microsoft, 1988. Thirty years of research in the study of time is offered to the reader, including a survey of the history of ideas and experiences of time. Both the everyday and scientific understandings of time are discussed.

FRENCH, A.P., and KENNEDY, P.J., eds.
NIELS BOHR: A CENTENARY VOLUME. Harvard U.P., 1987. Many interesting articles with respect to the pioneering physicist whose principle of complementarity is thought by many to

have significance for theology/science interactions.

FRYE, Roland M., ed.
IS GOD A CREATIONIST?: THE RELIGIOUS CASE AGAINST CREATION SCIENCE. Macmillan, 1983. An extremely helpful collection of essays predicated upon Francis Bacon's admonition that we must recognize the integrity of both "the book of God's Word in scripture and the book of God's Works in science." (S-84)

FULLER, Andrew R.
PSYCHOLOGY AND RELIGION: EIGHT POINTS OF VIEW. 2nd ed. U.P. of America, 1986.

FUNKENSTEIN, Amos.
THEOLOGY AND THE SCIENTIFIC IMAGINATION FROM THE MIDDLE AGES TO THE SEVENTEENTH CENTURY. Princeton U.P., 1989. A very important book that argues that the "warfare between science and religion" was exaggerated from the Middle Ages to the 17th century. Many important and original insights, some of which will be a source of considerable controversy.

GAEDE, Stan D.
BELONGING: OUR NEED FOR COMMUNITY IN CHURCH & FAMILY. Zondervan, 1985. A stimulating sociological analysis of the condition of human communities in the modern world which is clearly rooted in Christian values.

GAEDE, Stan D.
WHERE GODS MAY DWELL: UNDERSTANDING THE HUMAN CONDITION. Zondervan, 1985. As a Christian critique of social science, this book raises basic questions about the nature of science.

✪GALLAVOTTI, Giovanni, and ZWEIFEL, Paul F., eds.
NONLINEAR EVOLUTION AND CHAOTIC PHENOMENA. Plenum Pub. Corp., 1988. Twenty-seven papers by leading international experts in this specialized area.

✪GAL-OR, B.
COSMOLOGY, PHYSICS AND PHILOSOPHY. 2nd ed. Springer-Verlag, 1987. A review of general relativity as applied to cosmology, thermodynamics, the current state of theoretical particle physics, and astrophysics, as well as a summary of the history of Western philosophy.

✪GAMOW, George
THE GREAT PHYSICISTS FROM GALILEO TO EINSTEIN. Dover Pub., 1988. A dramatic explanation of how the central laws of physical science evolved plus personal and biographical data about the great physicists.

GAMOW, George.
MR. TOMPKINS IN PAPERBACK. Cambridge U.P., 1967. An introduction to modern physics via brief and amusing stories in which effects are exaggerated so as to be observable at the everyday level.

✪GAMOW, George.
ONE TWO THREE ... INFINITY: FACTS AND SPECULATIONS OF SCIENCE. Dover Pub., 1988. A readable overview of modern science covering topics such as the fourth dimension, relativity, entropy, and atomic structure.

✪GAMOW, George.
THIRTY YEARS THAT SHOOK PHYSICS: THE STORY OF QUANTUM THEORY. Dover Pub., 1985. An entertaining and rigorous introduction to the development of Quantum Theory. Unabridged republication of original (1966) edition.

GANGE, Robert.
ORIGINS AND DESTINY: A SCIENTIST EXAMINES GOD'S HANDIWORK. Word, 1990. Engineer Gange seeks to counter a materialistic world view of the origin of the cosmos, lower-life and man with a biblical perspective buttressed by the evidence of modern science. The author has pointed out many of the serious problems that confront the case for a non-supernatural view of life. Suitable for the general reader.

GARDNER, Martin.
SCIENCE: GOOD, BAD AND BOGUS. Prometheus Bks., 1981. A respected book, criticizes pseudo-science, New Age physics and catastrophe creationism.

GARDNER, Martin.
THE WHYS OF A PHILOSOPHICAL SCRIVENER. Morrow, 1983. Covers scientific and philosophical topics including a reasoned defense of theism. Debunks bogus claims of paranormal experience.

GARFIELD, Jay L., and HENNESSEY, P., eds.
ABORTION, MORAL AND LEGAL PERSPECTIVES. U. of Mass. P., 1985.

✪GARRISON, Charles E.
TWO DIFFERENT WORLDS: CHRISTIAN ABSOLUTES AND THE RELATIVISM OF SOCIAL SCIENCE. U. of Delaware P., 1988. Analysis of the cultural division that splits American society into two warring camps: the Christian "absolutists," who believe their view represents biblical truth for every person in every place at every time; and the "New Class," who believe truth is relative. The author deals with cultural relativity, biblical religion, and negotiations of relationships between the two camps, advocating a third category, "traditional-but-not-absolutist Christians."

✪GAVENTA, Beverly R.
FROM DARKNESS TO LIGHT: ASPECTS OF CONVERSION IN THE NEW TESTAMENT. Fortress, 1986. A biblical examination of conversion language within the context of first-century Christianity and in comparison to current understanding of being "born again."

✪GAYLIN, Willard.
ADAM AND EVE AND PINOCCHIO: ON BEING AND BECOMING HUMAN. Viking, 1990. The author offers a reassessment of what is special about being human through the story of Adam and Eve, which presents the inherent human nature of human beings, and the story of Pinocchio, which highlights humankind's potential for self-creation and self-abasement.

✪GAZZANIGA, Michael S.
MIND MATTERS: HOW MIND AND BRAIN INTERACT TO CREATE OUR CONSCIOUS LIVES. Houghton Mifflin, 1989. The latest research showing the ways the mind interprets the chemical changes in the brain and provides the substance of human consciousness. Written for the general reader. Includes annotated bibliography.

+GEISLER, Norman L.
CREATOR IN THE COURTROOM. Mott Media, 1982. A valuable and thought-provoking discussion of the controversial Arkansas Creation-Evolution trial. (J-83)

+GEISLER, Norman L., and ANDERSON, J. Kerby.
ORIGIN SCIENCE: A PROPOSAL FOR THE CREATION-EVOLUTION CONTROVERSY. Baker, 1987. A proposal for a different set of laws governing origins.(D-87)

GELWICK, Richard.
WAY OF DISCOVERY: AN INTRODUCTION TO THE THOUGHT OF MICHAEL POLANYI. Oxford U.P., 1977. A standard and very readable introduction to the thought of Michael Polanyi.

✪GHYKA, Matila.
THE GEOMETRY OF ART AND LIFE. Dover Pub., 1978. Discussions about geometric interrelationships between art and life ranging from Plato to modern architecture and art.

GEROCH, Robert.
GENERAL RELATIVITY FROM A TO B. U. of Chicago P., 1981. A modern presentation of relativity theory, with a sharp focus on its basic geometric ideas.

GILKEY, Langdon.
CREATIONISM ON TRIAL: EVOLUTION AND GOD AT LITTLE ROCK. Harper & Row, 1985. Highly recommended reading for those seeking to understand the ongoing conflict between the Creationists and mainstream Christianity. (M-87)

GILKEY, Langdon.
MAKER OF HEAVEN AND EARTH: THE CHRISTIAN DOCTRINE OF CREATION IN THE LIGHT OF MODERN KNOWLEDGE. U.P. of America, 1986. The basic concepts of creation which must be maintained in relating Christianity to modern science are presented.

GILL, Jerry H.
FAITH IN DIALOGUE: A CHRISTIAN APOLOGETIC. Word, 1985. Chapter titles include: "Natural Science—Reductionism," "Social Science—Relativism," "The Humanities—Humanism," "The Arts—Subjectivism," "World Religions—Pluralism." A helpful book for evangelicals, even if they differ at points from the author's perspective.

✪GILL, Jerry H.
MEDIATED TRANSCENDENCE: A POSTMODERN REFLECTION. Mercer U.P., 1989. A fresh approach to the religious problem of transcendence based on the author's advocacy of "dimensional" rather than "realmistic" approaches to reality, and of "relational" rather than "substantialist" categories of experience.

GILSON, Etienne (trans. John Lyon).
FROM ARISTOTLE TO DARWIN AND BACK AGAIN: A JOURNEY IN FINAL CAUSALITY, SPECIES, & EVOLUTION. U. of Notre Dame P., 1986. A philosophical discussion of the differences between Aristotle's and Darwin's views of nature with emphasis on the place of final causality in nature.

+GINGERICH, Owen, ed.
SCIENTIFIC GENIUS AND CREATIVITY (Readings from Scientific American Series). Freeman, 1987. Ten biographies of great scientists from the Renaissance to the Atomic Age show how major breakthroughs were made. Articles by Jacob Bronowski and Gunther Stent probe into the nature of scientific creativity and discovery. (J-89)

GISH, Duane T.
EVOLUTION: THE CHALLENGE OF THE FOSSIL RECORD. Master Bks., 1985. Young-earth creationist viewpoint.

GLEICK, James.
CHAOS: MAKING A NEW SCIENCE. Penguin, 1988. An excellent overview of a new scientific discipline that may point to a new and unusual kind of order: this order may be found deep inside an eerie type of chaos which may in fact exist behind a facade of order.

GOEL, N.S., and THOMPSON, Richard L.
COMPUTER SIMULATIONS OF SELF-ORGANIZATION IN BIOLOGICAL SYSTEMS. Macmillan, 1988.

⊕GOLDSTEIN, B.R.
THE ASTRONOMY OF LEVI BEN GERSON, 1288-1344. Springer-Verlag, 1986. Astronomical writings of Levi ben Gerson, a medieval astronomer, are presented in the original Hebrew text, with English translation, and are placed in historical context.

⊕GOODING, David, and JAMES, Frank A.J.L., eds.
FARADAY REDISCOVERED: ESSAYS ON THE LIFE AND WORK OF MICHAEL FARADAY, 1791-1867. American Inst. of Physics, 1989. Eleven original essays by leading Faraday scholars which give new insights into the man, his life and his science.

GOULD, Stephen J.
THE FLAMINGO'S SMILE: REFLECTIONS IN NATURAL HISTORY. Norton, 1987. Problems in viewing evolution as design.

GOULD, Stephen J.
HENS' TEETH AND HORSES' TOES: FURTHER REFLECTIONS IN NATURAL HISTORY. Norton, 1984.

⊕GOULD, Stephen J.
WONDERFUL LIFE: THE BURGESS SHALE AND THE NATURE OF HISTORY. Norton, 1989. A prominent paleontologist presents a strong case for a very early appearance of all the basic animal forms and a good analysis of cultural influences upon scientific interpretation.

GRANBERG-MICHAELSON, Wesley, ed.
TENDING THE GARDEN: ESSAYS ON THE GOSPEL AND THE EARTH. Eerdmans, 1987. Includes essay by Loren Wilkinson presenting a biblical environmental ethic in contrast to the New Age environmental ethics.

GRANBERG-MICHAELSON, Wesley.
A WORLDLY SPIRITUALITY: THE CALL TO TAKE CARE OF THE EARTH. Harper & Row, 1984. Writer formerly worked for Sen. Mark Hatfield. Deals with issues of economics and politics as well as ecological concerns.

GRANT, George.
BRINGING IN THE SHEAVES: TRANSFORMING POVERTY INTO PRODUCTIVITY. Wolgemuth & Hyatt, 1988. For those opposed to government poverty programs this book provides ideology, examples, and suggestions for a Christian alternative. The author has a 1986 book on the problem of the homeless.

GRANT, George.
TECHNOLOGY AND JUSTICE. U. of Toronto P., 1986. A collection of 6 essays by the author describing how modern technology has shaped our lives, even in ways of which we are not aware. (J-88)

⊕GREEN, Garrett.
IMAGINING GOD: THEOLOGY AND THE RELIGIOUS IMAGINATION. Harper & Row, 1989. An original interpretation of the nature of imagination as the "point of contact" between divine

revelation and human experience and as a means of making contemporary sense of God and scripture without violating traditional Christian doctrine.

GREENE, John C.
DARWIN AND THE MODERN WORLD VIEW. Louisiana State U.P., 1973. A critique of social Darwinism.

GREENSTEIN, George.
THE SYMBIOTIC UNIVERSE: AN UNORTHODOX LOOK AT THE ORIGIN OF THE COSMOS AND THE DEVELOPMENT OF LIFE. Greenwillow, 1989. Reflections of an astrophysicist upon the possible significance of the "strong" anthropic principle. Marred by philosophical bias, uncritical rejection of Judeo-Christian theology, and acceptance of a very subjectivist interpretation of quantum physics. (D-89)

GREGORY, Richard L., and ZANGWILL, O.L., eds.
THE OXFORD COMPANION TO THE MIND. Oxford U.P., 1987. 1001 entries, ranging from brief statements to major essays on concepts within the broad compass of philosophy, psychology and physiology of the brain. The religious dimension to such questions is not ignored; there are important essays by British evangelicals Donald MacKay and Malcom A. Jeeves. A useful collection.

✪GREIDANUS, Sidney.
THE MODERN PREACHER AND THE ANCIENT TEXT: INTERPRETING AND PREACHING BIBLICAL LITERATURE. Eerdmans, 1989. A holistic contemporary approach to the interpretation and preaching of biblical texts. Includes many helpful guidelines for responsible contemporary preaching.

GRIBBIN, John.
IN SEARCH OF SCHRODINGER'S CAT: QUANTUM PHYSICS AND REALITY. Bantam, 1984.

GRIBBIN, John.
IN SEARCH OF THE DOUBLE HELIX: QUANTUM PHYSICS AND LIFE. Bantam, 1987. The story of the search for and discovery of the elusive double helix. Gribbin explores the lives of the men and women involved in all applicable fields, and the trail of discovery from x-rays to mutations to quantum mechanics to the human cell itself.

GRIBBIN, John.
THE OMEGA POINT: THE SEARCH FOR THE MISSING MASS AND THE ULTIMATE FATE OF THE UNIVERSE. Bantam, 1988.

GRIFFITHS, Brian.
THE CREATION OF WEALTH: A CHRISTIAN'S CASE FOR CAPITALISM. InterVarsity Press, 1985. A noted international economist argues that capitalism based on biblical principles offers the best hope for using our resources wisely and meeting the needs of the world. (J-86)

✪GROOTHUIS, Douglas R.
REVEALING THE NEW AGE JESUS: CHALLENGES TO ORTHODOX VIEWS OF CHRIST. InterVarsity Press, 1990. An examination of both Orthodox and New Age views of Jesus. The author compares the claims of leading New Age thinkers with the teachings of biblical Christianity and demonstrates how the Bible gives the only substantial and trustworthy view of Jesus.

GROOTHUIS, Douglas R.
UNMASKING THE NEW AGE. InterVarsity Press, 1986. Recognized by many evangelical cult researchers as the best evangelical critique of the New Age Movement. The author draws heavily on the research of the Spiritual Counterfeits Project. Chapters cover the New Age in relation to wholistic health, psychology, science and politics.

✪GROVES, Colin P.
THEORY OF HUMAN AND PRIMATE EVOLUTION. Oxford U.P., 1989. A work on human and primate evolution which features taxonomy, nomenclature, and evolutionary processes by a prominent taxonomist of primates.

✣GRUENLER, Royce G.
THE TRINITY IN THE GOSPEL OF JOHN. Baker, 1986. A very readable and important book that, in the words of the author, tries "to listen to the disclosures of Jesus in John and draw forth the disclosure of God's social nature in the activity of the incarnate Son." The thesis of this book has profound implications for the social sciences; highly recommended.

✣HALL, Douglas J.
IMAGING GOD: DOMINION AS STEWARDSHIP. Eerdmans, 1986. A very important book in which the author argues that the crisis of nature forces us to rethink our whole understanding between humanity and nature. Such understanding, in turn, is rooted in the concept that human

beings are created in the image of God where such "imaging" is not something that human beings "have;" rather, it is a quality that pertains to our relationship with God.

HAMMOND, Phillip E., ed.
THE SACRED IN A SECULAR AGE: TOWARD REVISION IN THE SCIENTIFIC STUDY OF RELIGION. U. of Calif. P., 1985. Significant original studies by 23 leading researchers and theorists center around the anomolies of the thesis that society is moving from some sacred condition to secular conditions in which the sacred is ever more rare. The persistence and resurgence of conservative Protestantism, the emergence of new religious movements, the prominence of religious issues and elements in the politics of numerous nations, globalism, and other factual and theoretical topics are discussed. The bulk of the evidence refutes the secularization thesis, at least in its traditional form.

✪HARAWAY, Donna.
PRIMATE VISIONS: GENDER, RACE AND NATURE IN THE WORLD OF MODERN SCI-ENCE. Routledge, 1989. A scholarly, historical look at the study of apes, monkeys and humans and how these studies of primates influence ideas of gender and race.

HARDING, Sandra, and O'BARR, Jean F., eds.
SEX AND SCIENTIFIC INQUIRY. U. of Chicago P., 1987.

✪HARDISON, O.B., Jr.
DISAPPEARING THROUGH THE SKYLIGHT: CULTURE AND TECHNOLOGY IN THE TWENTIETH CENTURY. Viking Penguin, 1989.

HARDY, Edward R., ed.
CHRISTOLOGY OF THE LATER FATHERS. Westminster, 1977. Important writings on the person and work of Christ primarily from the fourth and fifth centuries. Especially valuable is Athanasius' "On the Incarnation of the Word."

HARRISON, Edward.
COSMOLOGY: THE SCIENCE OF THE UNIVERSE. Cambridge U.P., 1981. This is not mathematically sophisticated, but does give a thorough and scholarly treatment of modern cosmology. Attention is given to the history of cosmology, the broad significance of the subject, and different cosmological approaches, as well as the current observational and theoretical picture.

HARRISON, Edward.
DARKNESS AT NIGHT: A RIDDLE OF THE UNIVERSE. Harvard U.P., 1989.

HARRISON, Edward.
MASKS OF THE UNIVERSE. Macmillan, 1986. A historical overview of cosmology and man's varying "masks" to describe the universe through the ages, including a discussion of current theories and visions of reality.

+HARTZLER, H. Harold.
KING FAMILY HISTORY. Order direct from author: 901 College Ave., Goshen, IN 46536. Harold Hartzler served as the first executive director of ASA, and also as president. He has produced a two-volume, 1000-page work tracing the descendants of the immigrant Samuel King (Koenig) who arrived in North America in 1744.

✪HAUERWAS, Stanley.
NAMING THE SILENCES: GOD, MEDICINE, AND THE PROBLEM OF SUFFERING. Eerdmans, 1990. A reflective and sensitive look at the issue of pain and suffering, primarily with respect to children. The author does not try to explain why God allows suffering but instead explores why the question seems so important to us in the modern world.

HAWKING, Stephen W.
A BRIEF HISTORY OF TIME: FROM THE BIG BANG TO BLACK HOLES. Bantam, 1988. A very important book on current understanding of the evolution of the universe. Even if one disagrees with his theological and/or philosophical perspective, this book is extremely helpful as an overview of current cosmological thinking.

✪HAWTHORNE, Tim.
WINDOWS ON SCIENCE AND FAITH. InterVarsity Press (UK). An examination of topics currently central to both science and theology, such as evolution, miracles and prayer, genetic mutation, the image of God.

HAYES, Zachary.
WHAT ARE THEY SAYING ABOUT CREATION? Paulist Press, 1980. Professor of theology discusses science and theology as they relate to the creation of man. He accepts evolution as God's method of creation. (M-82)

⊙HEDDENDORF, Russell.
HIDDEN THREADS: SOCIAL THOUGHT FOR CHRISTIANS. Probe Bks., 1990. This overview of sociological theories gives special attention to the ways in which they are both relevant to and in conflict with Christian concerns and values. Sociology unearths many "hidden threads," the meanings and interpretations of Christian social principles given by God that are found in scripture but are obscure without the light that comes from sociological analysis.

+HEFLEY, James C.
THE TRUTH IN CRISIS: THE CONTROVERSY IN THE SOUTHERN BAPTIST CONVENTION. Vol 2 & 3. Criterion Pub., 1986. Chronicles the division among Southern Baptists over the question of Bible inerrancy, and reviews the history of the controversy as sparked by various public events back through the Scopes trial.

HEIE, Harold, and WOLFE, David L., eds.
REALITY OF CHRISTIAN LEARNING: STRATEGIES FOR FAITH-DISCIPLINE INTEGRA-TION. Eerdmans, 1987. Contributions from fourteen scholars (two each in political science, sociology, psychology, biology, mathematics, the arts, and philosophy). In each discipline a principal essayist addresses a significant issue from a Christian perspective which the respondent essayist then analyzes.

HEILBRON, J.L.
THE DILEMMAS OF AN UPRIGHT MAN: MAX PLANCK AS SPOKESMAN FOR GERMAN SCIENCE. U. of Calif. P., 1986. A fine biography of a good man attempting to act morally in very difficult situations. Much "food for thought" for Christians.

HEISENBERG, Werner.
PHYSICS AND BEYOND. Harper & Row, 1971. Heisenberg's autobiography, largely in the form of reconstructed conversations with Pauli, Bohr, Einstein and others. It is useful for insights into the motivations of quantum theory and particle physics.

HENDERSON, Charles P., Jr.
GOD & SCIENCE: THE DEATH AND REBIRTH OF THEISM. John Knox , 1986. Reviews the thoughts of Marx, Darwin, Freud, Einstein, Tillich and de Chardin. Also reviews *The Tao of Physics* by Fritjof Capra and *The Dancing Wu Li Masters* by Gary Zukav, two books that marry physics and Eastern religion. The author seems to have some helpful criticism of New Age Physics for its lack of any transcendent reality (personal God) that makes moral distinctions. On the other hand, the author seems to deny any causative control of a transcendent God over his creation, and seems to endorse de Chardin's deification of the evolutionary process.

⊙HENDRY, John
JAMES CLERK MAXWELL AND THE THEORY OF THE ELECTROMAGNETIC FIELD. Adam Hilger Ltd., 1986. A study of Maxwell's theory from its conception to the completion of Maxwell's *Treatise on Electricity and Magnetism.* This book offers a stimulating challenge to the traditional historiography of nineteenth-century physics.

⊙+HENRY, Carl F.H.
GOD, REVELATION AND AUTHORITY: GOD WHO SPEAKS AND SHOWS, Vol. 6. Word, 1983. An excellent section on "Creation."

+HENRY, Carl F.H.
HORIZONS OF SCIENCE: CHRISTIAN SCHOLARS SPEAK OUT. Harper & Row, 1978. Essays on science and faith in contemporary culture.

HENSHAW, Paul S., and KAPLAN, Sylvan J.
INFOPOWER: BIOPHYSICS AND BIOSOCIOLOGY OF MIND. Dorrance, 1987.

HERBERT, Nick.
QUANTUM REALITY: BEYOND THE NEW PHYSICS. Doubleday, 1987.

HERMANN, Kenneth W.
EVERY THOUGHT CAPTIVE TO CHRIST. Order direct: Radix Christian Studies Program, 1100 E. Summit, Suite 8, Kent OH 44240. This bibliography lists and classifies over 800 books which relate Christianity to major academic disciplines, and 60 professional organizations and periodicals committed to the same goal.

⊙+HERRMANN, Robert L.
GENETIC ENGINEERING. Council of Independent Colleges, 1990. A module in the "Technology and the Liberal Arts" curriculum with science and bioethics created in a balanced way.

HERSCHEL, John F.W.
A PRELIMINARY DISCOURSE ON THE STUDY OF NATURAL PHILOSOPHY. U. of Chicago P., 1987.

HETHERINGTON, Norriss S.
ANCIENT ASTRONOMY AND CIVILIZATION. Pachart, 1987.

HEY, A.J., and WALTERS, P.
THE QUANTUM UNIVERSE. Cambridge U.P., 1987.

⊙HODGSON, Peter E.
CHRISTIANITY AND SCIENCE (Christianity and Science Series). Oxford U.P., 1990. Order direct: Oxford University Press; Freepost; Educational Supply Section; Saxon Way West; Corby, Northants NN18 9BR. A masterful synthesis of key concepts form E. Mascal, S. Jaki, and T.F. Torrance. Author is the series editor for the Christianity and Science Series which also includes: Nuclear Power, by P.E. Hodgson; Creation and Evolution, by C.J. Humphreys; Drug Abuse, by J. and M. Grills; and Life and Death, by D.J. Atkinson. Each booklet is extremely well-written with excellent documentation and argumentation.

HODGSON, Peter E.
OUR NUCLEAR FUTURE? Order direct from author: Corpus Christi College, Oxford 0X1 4JF, UK. A well-documented study of the energy crisis, nuclear and alternative energy sources by a British nuclear physicist. Evaluations are balanced and firmly rooted in a Christian perspective.

HOFSTADTER, Douglas R.
GÖDEL, ESCHER, BACH: AN ETERNAL GOLDEN BRAID. Random, 1989. "A metaphorical fugue on minds and machines in the spirit of Lewis Carroll." A well-written (in a style both playful and thoughtful) exploration of pattern, logic, Gödel's theorem, and the nature of intelligence.

HOFSTADTER, Douglas R.
METAMAGICAL THEMAS: QUESTING FOR THE ESSENCE OF MIND AND PATTERN. Bantam, 1986.

HOLMES, Arthur F.
CONTOURS OF A WORLD VIEW. Eerdmans, 1983. This is the first book in a series of ten studies on a Christian world view. Discusses Christian and secular world views. Praised by J.I. Packer. (J-85)

⊙HOLMES, Arthur F.
SHAPING CHARACTER: MORAL EDUCATION IN THE CHRISTIAN COLLEGE. Eerdmans, 1990. A valuable and practical guide for teaching ethics in every Christian college department. This work reflects insights of many experts, writers and faculty members.

HOLTON, Gerald.
THE ADVANCEMENT OF SCIENCE AND ITS BURDENS: THE JEFFERSON LECTURE & OTHER ESSAYS. Cambridge U.P., 1986. Einstein, Heisenberg, the new physics and the public understanding of science.

HOLTON, Gerald.
THEMATIC ORIGINS OF SCIENTIFIC THOUGHT: KEPLER TO EINSTEIN. rev.ed., Harvard U.P., 1988.

⊙HORNER, John R., and GORMAN, James.
DIGGING DINOSAURS: THE SEARCH THAT UNRAVELED THE MYSTERY OF BABY DINOSAURS. Harper & Row, 1988. Science writer James Gorman presents John Horner's investigation of dinosaur nests and fossilized eggs as well as his discovery of the remains of the largest known dinosaur herd. Photos and illustrations included.

HOOVER, A.J.
THE CASE FOR TEACHING CREATION. College Press, 1980. A history professor, from his creation standpoint, supports his reasons why creation should be presented in schools along with evolution. (J-88)

⊙HOUGHTON, John.
DOES GOD PLAY DICE? A LOOK AT THE STORY OF THE UNIVERSE. Zondervan, 1989. An imaginative and vivid account of the story of the universe based on the integration of Christianity and modern science. (D-90)

⊙+HUMMEL, Charles E.
CREATION OR EVOLUTION? InterVarsity Press, 1989. A description of the relationship between science and theology, explaining the difference between scientific theory of evolution and evolutionist philosophy and addressing the question of evolution versus creation in basic science curriculum.

+HUMMEL, Charles E.
THE GALILEO CONNECTION. InterVarsity Press, 1986. An excellent history of the relationship

between science and Christianity, focussing on the impact of Copernicus, Kepler, Galileo and Newton. Contrasts the role and interpretation of the Bible with those of science. Chapters on miracles and scientific laws, and on the creation/evolution debate. (S-86, M-88)

HUMPHREY, Derek, and WICKETT, Ann.
THE RIGHT TO DIE: UNDERSTANDING EUTHANASIA. Harper & Row, 1986.

✪HUNTLEY, H.E.
THE DIVINE PROPORTION: A STUDY IN MATHEMATICAL BEAUTY. Dover Pub., 1970. A look at the relationship between geometry and aesthetics using simple mathematical formulas which require only a very limited knowledge of mathematics. Philosophical, psychological, musical and biological examples are enlisted to show that the divine proportion or "golden ratio" is a feature of geometry and mathematical analysis.

HURDING, Roger F.
THE TREE OF HEALING: PSYCHOLOGICAL & BIBLICAL FOUNDATIONS FOR COUNSEL-ING & PASTORAL CARE. Zondervan, 1987. This well-done book presents the major approaches to counseling and psychotherapy of both secular (e.g., Freud, Skinner, Rogers, Laing, Berne, Perls) as well as Christian (e.g., Lake, Tournier, Oden, Kelsey, Collins, Crable, Adams) authors in terms of their assumptions, aims, and methods, with biblical critique that is well balanced and helpful. The book's special importance is that it covers how Christian psychologists and critics have responded to secular psychology with their own significant contributions.

✛HYERS, Conrad.
THE MEANING OF CREATION: GENESIS & MODERN SCIENCE. John Knox, 1985. An excellent defense of biblical creationism in terms of the meaning the creation texts would have had in their original setting. Carefully examines the meaning of words and phrases in Genesis 1-11 in the light of the religious controversies between Israel's faith and surrounding polytheistic cosmologies. By closely examining the original meaning of creation in Genesis 1-3, the book demonstrates that scientific discourse and creation discourse cannot be placed on the same level. A biblical creationism is defended vis-a-vis those forms of modernism that would try to dismiss creation as prescientific myth and those that would try to defend it as the only true science. (S-85)

ISBISTER, J.N.
FREUD: AN INTRODUCTION TO HIS LIFE AND WORK. Basil Blackwell, 1985. An evangelical British psychologist presents a significant and balanced treatment of the life and work of Freud. This book has received very favorable reviews in both the British secular and Christian press.

✪JAKI, Stanley L.
THE ABSOLUTE BENEATH THE RELATIVE AND OTHER ESSAYS. U.P. of America, 1988. A collection of 14 essays that deal with various aspects of modern physics in their impact on modern culture, inasmuch as that impact is colored by fashionable interpretations of physical science.

JAKI, Stanley L.
ANGELS, APES, & MEN. Sherwood Sugden & Co., 1983. A discussion of the influence which the rationalist and naturalist notions of man respectively had on the scientific enterprise together with the claim that the great breakthroughs of modern science imply a notion of man which represents a middle road between two extremes. (S-84, D-86)

✪JAKI, Stanley L.
BRAIN, MIND AND COMPUTERS, 3rd ed. Regnery Gateway, 1989. A critique of the notion of artificial intelligence within the context of computer theory, neurophysiology, psychology, and logical positivism. Includes a chapter on artificial intelligence.

JAKI, Stanley L.
CHANCE OR REALITY AND OTHER ESSAYS. U.P. of America, 1987. A collection of the author's most important essays on science/theology related topics. Topics discussed include: the role of faith in science, supposed subjectivity in natural science, the interpretation of quantum physics, and proper epistemologies in natural science and theology.

JAKI, Stanley L.
CHESTERTON, A SEER OF SCIENCE. U. of Illinois P. 1986. Jaki takes a provocative look at one of England's most original thinkers, with respect to his views on modern science, the Darwinian world view, and the role of philosophy in shaping our view of the universe.

✪JAKI, Stanley L.
COSMOS IN TRANSITION: STUDIES IN THE HISTORY OF COSMOLOGY. Pachart, 1990. A

collection of ten essays that deal with the transformation of cosmological ideas during the last five hundred years.

◑JAKI, Stanley L.
GOD AND THE COSMOLOGISTS. Regnery Gateway, 1989. Based on the text of eight lectures, delivered at Corpus Christi College, Oxford, under the sponsorship of Farmington Institute, this book deals with the principal contributions modern science has made to the cosmological argument and with the various views of scientific cosmologists who try to exploit their subject in the opposite sense.

JAKI, Stanley L., ed.
LORD GIFFORD & HIS LECTURES: A CENTENARY RETROSPECT. Mercer U.P., 1987. A useful discussion of these important lectures which have become a quasi-institutional framework for natural theology across the broad spectrum of modern philosophical trends. Helpful reading for anyone interested in the historical development of natural theology in the last 100 years.

◑JAKI, Stanley L.
MIRACLES AND PHYSICS. Christendom Press, 1989. An analysis of the notion of scientific law with respect to the possibility of miracles and a criticism of efforts that seek a loophole for miracles in quantum mechanical indeterminacy.

◑JAKI, Stanley L.
THE ONLY CHAOS AND OTHER ESSAYS. U.P. of America, 1990. A collection of 17 essays that deal with the interaction of scientific and literary cultures, with scientism, questions of modern cosmology, the relation of the Bible to modern science.

◑JAKI, Stanley L.
THE ORIGIN OF SCIENCE AND THE SCIENCE OF ITS ORIGIN. Regnery Gateway, 1978. The first monograph on theories proposed since Bacon to the present day on the rise of science in the 17th century.

◑JAKI, Stanley L.
THE PHYSICIST AS ARTIST: THE LANDSCAPES OF PIERRE DUHEM. Scot. Acad. Press, 1988. Possibly the only major physicist of modern times with a creative ability to draw, Duhem reveals in his landscape art the same kind of perception which underlies his theory of physics, a theory positivist in form but metaphysically realist in essence.

◑JAKI, Stanley L.
THE PURPOSE OF IT ALL. Regnery Gateway, 1990. Based on the text of eight lectures dealing with unreliable sources of the sense of purpose, such as progress, evolution, process philosophies and with the true status of the design argument, together with its grounds: man's inner sense of purpose and his freedom to act for a purpose. Given in Oxford, 1989.

JAKI, Stanley L.
THE ROAD OF SCIENCE AND THE WAYS TO GOD. U. of Chicago P., 1980. The text of twenty lectures, of which the last ten are devoted to science in the 20th century. It is argued that the metaphysical realism embodied in the classical proofs of the existence of God is the only epistemology compatible with creative science. (S-81)

◑JAKI, Stanley L.
THE SAVIOR OF SCIENCE. Regnery Gateway, 1988. An examination of the subtle but crucial impact which the Christian belief in the Incarnation had on the development of science, and the role which the same belief can play in securing science for a constructive role in mankind's future.

JAKI, Stanley L.
SCIENCE AND CREATION: FROM ETERNAL CYCLES TO AN OSCILLATING UNIVERSE. U.P. of America, 1990. The first monograph on the invariable stillbirths of the scientific enterprise in all great ancient cultures and on its sole viable birth in Christian medieval Europe with special emphasis on the biblical doctrine of creation.

◑JAKI, Stanley, L.
UNEASY GENIUS: THE LIFE AND WORK OF PIERRE DUHEM. Kluwer Acad. Pub., 1987. The first monograph on the life and thought of Duhem, a pioneering and most seminal philosopher and historian of science, including a portrayal of the mental physiognomy of the Third Republic and the reaction to Duhem as a physicist, philosopher, and historian of science during the last fifty years.

JASTROW, Robert.
GOD AND THE ASTRONOMERS. Warner Bks., 1980. The author shows how the findings of astrophysics point to the existence of a creator.

JAUCH, Josef M.
ARE QUANTA REAL?: A GALILEAN DIALOGUE. Indiana U.P., 1989.

✪JEEVES, Malcolm A., ed.
BEHAVIOURAL SCIENCES. InterVarsity Press (UK). A collection of essays probing the relationship between scientific theories of behavior and Christian beliefs about human nature.

JEEVES, Malcolm A.; BERRY, R.J.; and ATKINSON, David.
FREE TO BE DIFFERENT. Bks. Demand UMI (Reprint of 1985 Eerdmans ed.) A psychologist, a geneticist, and a theologian discuss human freedom in the context of nature, nurture and grace (God's loving and transforming initiative). (J-86)

✪+JENNINGS, George J.
ALL THINGS, ALL MEN, ALL MEANS—TO SAVE SOME. Middle East Missions Research. Order direct: MEMR, P.O. Box 632, Le Mars, IA 51031. World wide survey by a cultural anthropologist geared for cross-cultural mission work.

✪+JENNINGS, George J.
HADITH: A COMPOSITE MIDDLE EASTERN VILLAGE UNDER A MISSIONS CONSULTANT'S GAZE. Middle East Missions Research. Order direct: MEMR, P.O. Box 632, Le Mars, IA 51031. A detailed analysis of village life and thought in the Middle East.

+JENNINGS, George J.
A MISSION CONSULTANT VIEWS MIDDLE EASTERN CULTURE AND PERSONALITY. Middle East Missions Research. Order direct: MEMR, P.O. Box 632, Le Mars, IA 51031. Extended probe into how Middle Easterners think, feel and act, by an anthropologist who has had extensive field work in the Middle East.

✪+JENNINGS, George J.
WITHOUT A PEER: WELCOME INTO THE MIDDLE EAST. Middle East Missions Research. Order direct: MEMR, P.O. Box 632, Le Mars, IA 51031. An ideal general introduction to the Middle East for mission personnel. Chapters include "Conflicting Values," "Saudi Modal Personality," and "Resistance to Westernization."

JENSON, Robert W.
THE TRIUNE IDENTITY: GOD ACCORDING TO THE GOSPEL. Bks. Demand UMI, 1982. The doctrine of the Trinity is set out as the biblical understanding of who God is.

JOHNSON, Douglas W.
COMPUTER ETHICS: A GUIDE FOR THE NEW AGE. Brethren Press, 1984. Deals with legal and ethical issues concerning computers, video games, protection of information, etc.

✪JOHNSON, Phillip E.
DARWIN ON TRIAL. Regnery Gateway/InterVarsity Press, 1991. An examination of the scientific and philosophical merits of Darwinism by a law professor.

✪JOHNSON-LAIRD, P.N.
THE COMPUTER AND THE MIND: AN INTRODUCTION TO COGNITIVE SCIENCE. Harvard U.P., 1989. A description of cognitive science—including its origins and achievements—and a discussion of topics such as the nature of symbols, the theory of computation, human communication and free will.

JOHNSTON, Jon.
CHRISTIAN EXCELLENCE: ALTERNATIVE TO SUCCESS. Baker, 1985. Christian excellence is contrasted with worldly "success" in this solidly biblical tool to stimulate spiritual growth.

✪+JONES, D. Gareth.
MANUFACTURING HUMANS. InterVarsity Press (UK). The implications of the new reproductive technologies in areas crucial from the standpoint of Christian thinking and practice. Issues addressed include the value of human life, the nature of the family, and attitudes toward procreation and infertility.

JONES, Stanton L., ed.
PSYCHOLOGY & THE CHRISTIAN FAITH: AN INTRODUCTORY READER. Baker, 1986. This volume gives twelve examples of integration of psychology and theology in the major areas of psychology. It would be appropriate as a parallel text in a beginning psychology course for Christian students. Contributors include Donald MacKay, Robert Roberts, Clinton McLemore, and David Myers. (J-88)

JOY, Donald M., ed.
MORAL DEVELOPMENT FOUNDATIONS: JUDEO-CHRISTIAN ALTERNATIVES TO PIAGET-KOHLBERG. Abingdon, 1983. A significant collection of essays on moral development

from a Christian perspective.

JUDSON, Horace F.
THE SEARCH FOR SOLUTIONS. abridged ed. Johns Hopkins U.P., 1987.

⊕KAISER, Christopher B.
CREATION AND THE HISTORY OF SCIENCE. Eerdmans, 1990. A comprehensive survey of the relationship between theology of creation and the history of science, in five major historical sections, beginning with the early church and Greco-Roman science and ending with the creationist tradition and the emergence of post-Newtonian mechanics.

KAISER, Christopher B.
THE DOCTRINE OF GOD. Good News, 1982. An excellent, highly readable historical survey of the development of the doctrine of God from the Old Testament through the 20th century. Stresses how the church formulated its trinitarian understanding of God in order to do full justice to the biblical revelation. Kaiser emphasizes an insight understood by the Patristic fathers that the modern world has lost; the concept of persons, divine and human, is profoundly relational as contrasted to the individualistic interpretation commonly held today.

KAKU, Michio, and TRAINER, Jennifer.
BEYOND EINSTEIN:THE COSMIC QUEST FOR THE THEORY OF THE UNIVERSE. Bantam, 1987. An examination of the modern theory of "superstrings" and its effect on the field of physics throughout the world. The authors discuss this theory in relation to Einstein's quest for a unified theory of the universe.

⊕KASUN, Jacqueline.
THE WAR AGAINST POPULATION: THE ECONOMICS AND IDEOLOGY OF POPULATION CONTROL. Ignatius Press, 1988. An argument for the theory that the earth could support 35 billion people in contrast to the idea that the world is over-populated. (M-90)

KAUFMAN, Gordon D.
THEOLOGY FOR A NUCLEAR AGE. Westminster, 1985. A radical and attention-getting, but inadequate, discussion of the challenge to traditional theology posed by the possibility of nuclear destruction.

KELLER, Evelyn F., and FREEMAN, W.H.
A FEELING FOR THE ORGANISM: THE LIFE AND WORK OF BARBARA MCCLINTOCK. Freeman, 1983.

⊕KETTLER, Christian D., and SPEIDELL, Todd H., eds.
INCARNATIONAL MINISTRY: THE PRESENCE OF CHRIST IN CHURCH, SOCIETY, AND FAMILY. Helmers & Howard, 1990. Essays honoring the significant contributions of Dr. Ray S. Anderson which explore three central themes: the church's nature and life as a ministry of Christ, the church in mission and service in society, and the church's ministry *to* families and *as* family to all of humanity.

KEVLES, D.J.
THE PHYSICISTS: THE HISTORY OF A SCIENTIFIC COMMUNITY IN MODERN AMERICA. Harvard U.P., 1987. A monograph reprint of the 1977 publication.

⊕KIMMEL, Allan J.
ETHICS AND VALUES IN APPLIED SOCIAL RESEARCH. Sage Pub., 1988. A survey of the types of problems that arise in applied social research, with both scientific and personal moral viewpoints applied to discussions, examples,and citations. Topics include ethical standards and guidelines for research, methodological issues and dilemmas, confidentiality and the right to privacy, special problems in explicit settings, and the importance of attitudes and value commitments.

KIPPENHAHN, R.
LIGHT FROM THE DEPTHS OF TIME. Springer-Verlag, 1987. A non-technical examination of the complex ideas of cosmology with reference to the dreams of Herr Meyer and his 2-dimensional Flatland as a means of explaining difficult concepts.

KLAAREN, Eugene M.
RELIGIOUS ORIGINS OF MODERN SCIENCE: BELIEF IN CREATION IN SEVENTEENTH-CENTURY THOUGHT. U.P. of America, 1985. A thorough analysis of the role that the concept of God's sovereignty played in the origin and early conflicts of modern science.

KLAY, Robin.
COUNTING THE COST: THE ECONOMICS OF CHRISTIAN STEWARDSHIP. Eerdmans, 1986. Using the tools of economic analysis, the author applies Christian faith and ethics to questions of political economy in such areas as poverty and military spending.

KLOTZ, JOHN W.
STUDIES IN CREATION: A GENERAL INTRODUCTION TO THE CREATION-EVOLUTION DEBATE. Concordia, 1985. Biologist-theologian examines many of the pertinent current topics in creation/evolution discussions.

✪KOENIG, Harold G.; SMILEY, Mona; and GONZALES, Jo Ann P.
RELIGION, HEALTH, AND AGING: A REVIEW AND THEORETICAL INTEGRATION. Greenwood Press, 1988. A definitive summary of research findings on the physical and mental health of aging and elderly people in relationship to religious beliefs, rituals, experience, and affiliation. Includes studies on perceptions of life satisfaction and well-being.(D-89)

KOHONEN, T.
SELF-ORGANIZATION AND ASSOCIATIVE MEMORY. 2nd ed. Springer-Verlag, 1988.

✪KRAFT, Charles.
CHRISTIANITY WITH POWER: EXPERIENCING THE SUPERNATURAL. Vine Bks., 1989. A study of God's power and why there seems to be little evidence of it in the Christian experience. The author offers biblical understanding of signs and wonders and shows how to break out of the confines of a Western worldview which conditions Christians to fit God into a predictable mold.

KRAMER, William.
EVOLUTION AND CREATION: A CATHOLIC UNDERSTANDING. Our Sunday Visitor, 1986. Examines current debate between creationists and evolutionists and explains the teachings of the Catholic church in this matter.

KREEFT, Peter.
THE BEST THINGS IN LIFE. InterVarsity Press, 1984. Socrates visits Desperate State University. In twelve short dialogues he discusses values such as success, power and pleasure and bursts the modern bubbles of agnosticism and subjectivism.

KUHN, Thomas S.
THE STRUCTURE OF SCIENTIFIC REVOLUTIONS. 2d ed. U. of Chicago P., 1970. Widely read critique on the nature of scientific method. Revised edition of the 1962 classic.

LAMMERS, Stephen, and VERHEY, Allen, eds.
ON MORAL MEDICINE: THEOLOGICAL PERSPECTIVES IN MEDICAL ETHICS. Eerdmans, 1987. Paul Tillich, Paul Tournier, Paul Ramsey, C.S. Lewis and many more are examples of the diversity of theological reflection in this book on medical ethics.

LAMBERT, David, and Diagram Group Staff.
THE FIELD GUIDE TO EARLY MAN. Facts on File, 1987. An introduction to evolution from early hominids to modern man. The text is enhanced by illustrations, diagrams, maps and charts. Outstanding scientists in the field are listed, as are museums worldwide that have early-human exhibits.

✪LANGER, Ellen J.
MINDFULNESS. Addison-Wesley, 1989. Fifteen years of research presented as a chronicle of the effect of mindlessness on society, with an explanation of the nature of mindfulness and how the research applies to problems of aging, creativity, work, prejudice and health.

LARSON, Edward J.
TRIAL & ERROR: THE AMERICAN CONTROVERSY OVER CREATION AND EVOLUTION. Oxford U.P., 1989. The author has a law degree and Ph.D. in the history of science which he uses to produce an illuminating picture of the social and legal forces which have shaped the creation/evolution controversy, especially as it pertains to teaching in public schools, over the course of this century. (D-86)

LAWHEAD, Steve.
HOWARD HAD A SPACESHIP. Lion Pub., 1986. Lawhead has written a whole series of adult science fiction. This is a book for children (gr. K-3) with full color illustrations and space photos. It combines a story with information about the wonders of God's creation.

✪LAYZER, D.
COSMOGENESIS: THE GROWTH OF ORDER IN THE UNIVERSE. Oxford U.P., 1990.

LEAN, Garth.
GOD'S POLITICIAN: WILLIAM WILBERFORCE'S STRUGGLE. Helmers & Howard, 1988. Biography of British Parliament member William Wilberforce, and his example of living faith in his tireless pursuit to abolish the slave trade and reform the social morals of Britain in the late 18th and early 19th centuries.

LEAN, Garth.
ON THE TAIL OF A COMET: THE LIFE OF FRANK BUCHMAN. Helmers & Howard, 1988. This first major biography of Frank N.D. Buchman chronicles his inner life as well as his public story—which is played out against the background of nations at war, the rise of black nationalist independence movements in Africa, leaders like Mahatma Gandhi, Konrad Adenauer, and Harry Truman, and the lives of those influenced by his ideas. Buchman founded the Oxford Group and Moral Re-Armament.

LEFEVER, Ernest W., and HUNT, E. Stephen, eds.
THE APOCALYPTIC PREMISE: NUCLEAR ARMS DEBATED. Ethics & Public Policy Ctr., 1982. Order direct: Ethics & Public Policy Center, 1030 15th Street NW, Suite 300, Washington, D.C. 20005. Representative selection of commentaries on arms control, the peace movement, the consequences of a holocaust, the Church and nuclear arms, and official views. Includes statements by European and Russian political leaders. (J-84)

◑LEITH, John H.
THE REFORMED IMPERATIVE: WHAT THE CHURCH HAS TO SAY THAT NO ONE ELSE CAN SAY. Westminster, 1987. A charge to the church to focus on its only unique skill—the ability to interpret and apply the Word of God through sermons, teaching, pastoral care.

◑+LEITH, T. Harry.
BIBLIOGRAPHY For the Preparation of Research Papers in the History & Philosophy & Sociology of Science, Biography of Scientists, Science & Religion, Science & the Humanities, & Education in Science. 7th ed. Self-published, 1984. Order direct: Dept. of Natural Science, York University, Atkinson College, 4700 Keele Street, North York, Ontario, Canada M3J 1P3. A list of books and articles, grouped by subject, for guidance in researching essays in Natural Science courses.

◑LEMING, Michael R.; DEVRIES, Raymond G.; and FURNISH, Brendon F.J., eds.
THE SOCIOLOGICAL PERSPECTIVE: A VALUE-COMMITTED INTRODUCTION. Academic Bks., 1989. An excellent and insightful summary and critique of numerous sociological viewpoints and topics that are as relevant outside academia as they are inside. The value commitment of this text by eleven authors is the Christian faith.

◑LESLIE, John.
UNIVERSES. Routledge, 1989. A discussion of the alleged evidence of fine tuning; mechanisms by which a very varied set of universes might be generated; various forms of Anthropic Principle; and whether belief in God could be preferable to accepting universes in vast numbers. An important book for those interested in the speculations of contemporary cosmologists.

LESTER, Lane, and BOHLIN, Raymond G.
THE NATURAL LIMITS TO BIOLOGICAL CHANGE. Zondervan, 1984. A scientifically sophisticated case for an intrinsic limit to biological change. Excellent overview of modern genetic and ecological theories, including punctuated equilibrium. (J-86)

LEWIN, Roger.
BONES OF CONTENTION: CONTROVERSIES IN THE SEARCH FOR HUMAN ORIGINS. Simon & Schuster, 1988. An examination of famous controversial discoveries in paleoanthropology and their emphasis on man's place in nature. Differences over interpretation due to the subjectivity of the field are covered in discussions of these discoveries, including the Leakey-Johanson case.

LEWIS, C.S.
MERE CHRISTIANITY. Macmillan, 1986. The classic beginning apologetic for Christianity.

LEWONTIN, R.C.
THE GENETIC BASIS OF EVOLUTIONARY CHANGE. Columbia U.P., 1974. Intensive discussion of the evidence for randomness vs. selection. Especially interesting philosophically.

LINDBECK, George A.
THE NATURE OF DOCTRINE: RELIGION & THEOLOGY IN A POSTLIBERAL AGE. Westminster, 1984. An important treatment of the nature of religion and theology in a postliberal age, prompted by ecumenical dialogues.

LINDBERG, David C., and NUMBERS, Ronald, eds.
GOD & NATURE: HISTORICAL ESSAYS ON THE ENCOUNTER BETWEEN CHRISTIANITY AND SCIENCE. U. of Calif. P., 1986. A collection of extremely significant essays which cover the interaction between Christianity and science through all major periods of history from the early church to the 20th century. (J-87, M-88)

⊙LINDE, A.D.
INFLATION AND QUANTUM COSMOLOGY. Academic Press, 1990. An up-to-date view of the inflationary universe scenario, beginning with the standard Big Bang model. The main principles of inflation and chaotic inflation are discussed and the author's view of inflationary cosmology is summarized in a sequence of instructive and humorous cartoons.

LINGENFELTER, Sherwood G., and MAYERS, Marvin K.
MINISTERING CROSS-CULTURALLY: AN INCARNATION MODEL FOR PERSONAL RELA-TIONSHIPS. Baker, 1986. The incarnation of Christ is presented here as a model for missionary work and other Christian service. Rich personal experiences emphasize the necessity of being personally resocialized into a new cultural context in order to share the Christian faith effectively with people from different cultural backgrounds. Six pairs of contrasting traits related to tensions that arise among Christians provide a basis for a questionnaire that can be used to construct a personal profile in order to understand oneself better and thus to improve one's witness. Recommended for prospective short- and long-term missionaries.

⊙LINN, Matthew; FABRICANT, Sheila; and LINN, Dennis.
HEALING THE EIGHT STAGES OF LIFE. Paulist Press, 1989. Erikson's eight stages of life serve as the basis for this book, emphasizing healthy development and the ability of individuals to heal past wounds. Case studies illustrate the nature of healing prayer. (J-89)

LINZEY, Andrew.
CHRISTIANITY & THE RIGHTS OF ANIMALS. Crossroad NY, 1987.

⊙LINZEY, Andrew, and REGAN, Tom, eds.
LOVE THE ANIMALS: MEDITATIONS AND PRAYERS. Crossroad NY, 1989.

LIU, Zongren.
TWO YEARS IN THE MELTING POT. China Bks., 1984. Must reading for Christian professors, students or others who have friendly contact with Chinese from the People's Republic of China. The book reflects the author's personal experience.

LIVINGSTONE, David N.
DARWIN'S FORGOTTEN DEFENDERS: THE ENCOUNTER BETWEEN EVANGELICAL THEOLOGY & EVOLUTIONARY THOUGHT. Eerdmans, 1987. A critically important analysis of how the evangelical church responded to Darwin's theory during the nineteenth century. Especially interesting are the reactions of the major conservative theologians. (S-88)

LODER, James E.
THE TRANSFORMING MOMENT. 2nd ed. Helmers & Howard, 1989. The thoughts of Michael Polanyi, Martin Heidegger, and major theories of psychoanalysis inform a discussion of human transformation; and the thoughts of the Reformers, SØren Kierkegaard, and Karl Barth inform a theological side of the discussion. A seminal book.

LOEB, Paul.
NUCLEAR CULTURE: LIVING & WORKING IN THE WORLD'S LARGEST ATOMIC COM-PLEX. New Society Pub., 1986. The growth of the Hanford Nuclear Reservation and the culture it spawned. Praised by Kurt Vonnegut, Philip Berrigan and John Kenneth Galbraith.

⊙LONGINO, Helen E.
SCIENCE AS SOCIAL KNOWLEDGE: VALUES AND OBJECTIVITY IN SCIENTIFIC INQUIRY. Princeton U.P., 1990. An argument for the premise that social and cultural values influence the obtaining and structuring of knowledge. The author develops the concept of "contextual empiricism" in which the objectivity of scientific inquiry is maintained by understanding it as a social rather than individual process. Feminist attitudes toward science and criticisms of research are addressed.

LOVTRUP, Soren.
DARWINISM: THE REFUTATIONS OF A MYTH. Routledge, Chapman & Hall, 1987.

LUCAS, Ernest and Hazel.
OUR WORLD: HOW? WHAT? WHEN? WHY? Lion Pub., 1986. A look at our earth and the universe with these questions in mind. Excellent for the young and curious. Full color illustrations. Recommended for grades 4 & up.

⊙LUCKY, Robert W.
SILICON DREAMS: INFORMATION, MAN AND MACHINE. St. Martin, 1989. A semi-technical examination of information theory, cryptology, speech synthesis and recognition, coding and other forms of information confronting society.

LYON, David.
THE SILICON SOCIETY. Bks. Demand UMI, 1986. Some Christian guidelines in the complex

fields of automation, new telecommunications and the emerging computer culture.

LYON, David.
SOCIOLOGY AND THE HUMAN IMAGE. InterVarsity Press, 1983. This study in the sociology of knowledge is consistently centered around the theme that Christian commitment can be a guide to doing sociology, with the result that human distinctiveness and values will be taken seriously in social analysis. (J-85)

LYON, David.
THE STEEPLE'S SHADOW: ON THE MYTHS & REALITIES OF SECULARIZATION. Eerdmans, 1987. An important study of the relationship between Western secularization and the vitality of Christian faith.

+MAATMAN, Russell W.
THE BIBLE, NATURAL SCIENCE, AND EVOLUTION. Dordt College Press, 1980. A thorough and well-reasoned discussion of the problem of evolution, with extensive analysis of scientific evidence and of the biblical revelation. Maatman argues against macro-evolution. (D-71)

+MAATMAN, Russell W.
THE UNITY IN CREATION. Dordt College Press, 1978. A physical scientist discusses unity as perceived within different disciplines, in relation to law, order, causality, power, etc., and its importance for Christians. His book sparked a symposium on the subject in the *Journal of the American Scientific Affiliation*, March 1983. (M-80)

✪MACAULAY, David.
THE WAY THINGS WORK: FROM LEVERS TO LASERS, CARS TO COMPUTERS—A VISUAL GUIDE TO THE WORLD OF MACHINES. Houghton Mifflin, 1988. An illustrated look at key inventions and complex principles of today's technology. Useful for even the least mechanically-minded reader.

MACBETH, Norman.
DARWIN RETRIED: AN APPEAL TO REASON. Harvard Common Press, 1971. A lawyer contends modern evolutionists no longer agree with Darwin on many points, yet on a popular level these teachings of Darwin have not been challenged. MacBeth is often quoted by critics of evolution.

✪MACDONALD, George.
PROVING THE UNSEEN. Ballantine, 1989. A recently found collection of MacDonald's sermons on the subjects of faith, grace, freedom and love.

MACDONALD, Gordon.
ORDERING YOUR PRIVATE WORLD. Oliver-Nelson, 1984. An excellent book for looking at priorities.

✪MACKAY, Donald M. (ed. Melvin Tinker).
THE OPEN MIND AND OTHER ESSAYS: A SCIENTIST IN GOD'S WORLD. InterVarsity Press (UK). Lectures and articles by Donald M. MacKay which explore topics such as human engineering, chance and evolution, responsible use of science. (D-89)

MACKAY, Donald M.
SCIENCE AND THE QUEST FOR MEANING. Bks. Demand UMI. (Reprint of 1982 Eerdmans ed.). This book describes the importance of determinism, mechanism, chance, miracle, and the scientific enterprise for the Christian. (S-83)

+MALONY, H. Newton, ed.
WHOLENESS AND HOLINESS: READINGS IN THE PSYCHOLOGY/THEOLOGY OF MENTAL HEALTH. Baker, 1983. A stimulating and balanced anthology containing many of the seminal writings on religious values and counseling published during the past several decades, ranging in perspective from the emphatic biblicism of Jay Adams to the more philosophical orientation of Paul Tillich. (D-85)

✪MANGUM, John M., ed.
THE NEW FAITH-SCIENCE DEBATE: PROBING COSMOLOGY, TECHNOLOGY, AND THEOLOGY. Fortress, 1989. These papers from a Lutheran-sponsored conference on the significance of science and technology for the churches give a broad introduction to the science-technology-theology-ethics quadrilateral. (D-90)

✪MARCH, Robert H.
PHYSICS FOR POETS. Contemporary Bks., 1983. A very readable and accurate introduction to classical contemporary physics for laypeople.

MARGULIS, L., ed.
ORIGINS OF LIFE. 2nd ed. 2 vols. Gordon & Breach, 1970 (vol.1), 1971 (vol. 2).

❂MARSCHALL, Laurence A.
THE SUPERNOVA STORY. Plenum Pub. Corp., 1988. An up-to-date presentation of the centuries-long and international nature of the study of celestial explosions. Highly recommended for undergraduates.

MARSDEN, George, ed.
EVANGELICALISM AND MODERN AMERICA. Eerdmans, 1984. This book has 13 contributors, and includes the "Dilemma of Evangelical Scientists" by Ronald Numbers.

MARSDEN, George M.
FUNDAMENTALISM & AMERICAN CULTURE: THE SHAPING OF TWENTIETH-CENTURY EVANGELICALISM. Oxford U.P., 1980. Shows how we got to where we are in the evolution/creation controversy. Includes both the trends and forces acting within the church and the external pressures.

MARSHALL, Paul A.
THINE IS THE KINGDOM: A BIBLICAL PERSPECTIVE ON THE NATURE OF GOVERNMENT AND POLITICS TODAY. Eerdmans, 1986. One of the best introductory books on politics from a Christian perspective.

❂MARSHALL, Paul A.; GRIFFIOEN, Sander; and MOUW, Richard J., eds.
STAINED GLASS: WORLD VIEWS AND SOCIAL SCIENCE. Institute of Christian Studies, 1989. Social scientists examine worldviews from a Christian Reformed perspective.(M-91)

❂MARSHALL, Paul A., and VANDERVENNEN, Robert E., eds.
SOCIAL SCIENCE IN CHRISTIAN PERSPECTIVE. U.P. of America, 1988. Fourteen essays by Christians working out their faith and striving for radical reform in the practice of the social sciences. Topics include social theory, sociology, economics, politics, and technology. A rich resource on foundational, philosophical, and theoretical issues of the social sciences.

❂MARX, Jean L., ed.
A REVOLUTION IN BIOTECHNOLOGY. Cambridge U.P., 1989. Twenty-six contributors offer a clear summation of biotechnology—the scientific background, achievements, ethical problems and future outlook.

❂MATHENY, Paul D.
DOGMATICS AND ETHICS: THE THEOLOGICAL REALISM AND ETHICS OF KARL BARTH'S *CHURCH DOGMATICS*. Verlag Peter Lang. A study of Barth's revolutionary decision to integrate ethics within church dogmatics and its profound impact on Barth's unique conception of the task of theology.

MAVRODES, George I.
BELIEF IN GOD: A STUDY IN THE EPISTEMOLOGY OF RELIGION. U. P. of America, 1981.

MCGINNIS, Alan Loy.
BRINGING OUT THE BEST IN PEOPLE: HOW TO ENJOY HELPING OTHERS EXCEL. Augsburg, 1985.

MCGOWAN, Chris.
IN THE BEGINNING: A SCIENTIST SHOWS WHY THE CREATIONISTS ARE WRONG. Prometheus Bks., 1984. This book is one of a large flock of recent books designed to attack the evidence used to support a young-earth creationism. This one is fairly well done, and could serve as a sample of the genre.

MCINTIRE, C.T., ed.
GOD, HISTORY AND THE HISTORIANS: MODERN CHRISTIAN VIEWS OF HISTORY. Oxford U.P., 1977. 22 articles on the meaning of history, nature of history and culture, and the Christian historian. Authors include Latourette, Bultmann, Tannenberg, Toynbee, Herbert Butterfield, Karl Barth, C.S. Lewis, T.S. Eliot, and others.

❂MCIVER, Tom.
ANTI-EVOLUTION: AN ANNOTATED BIBLIOGRAPHY. McFarland and Co., 1988. 1,852 anti-evolution publications are listed with information about contents and some of the authors. Some books predate 1900. Author evidences an extracreationist perspective. (D-90)

MCMULLIN, Ernan, ed.
EVOLUTION AND CREATION. U. of Notre Dame P., 1986. An anthology of useful essays arguing for the compatibility of evolution and creation as ways of understanding the universe.

31

⊙MERMIN, N. David.
BOOJUMS ALL THE WAY THROUGH: COMMUNICATING SCIENCE IN A PROSAIC AGE. Cambridge U.P., 1990. A collection of essays dealing with the process of communicating modern physics to both physicists and non-physicists. Author style is characterized by humor as a commitment to to finding simple ways to present complex ideas.

MIDGLEY, Mary.
EVOLUTION AS A RELIGION: STRANGE HOPES & STRANGER FEARS. Routledge, Chapman & Hall, 1986. A philosopher shows how scientific doctrines, especially the notion of evolution, become distorted by strange myths. Also addresses the question as to the proper nature of both science and religion and their relation to one another. A very helpful book.

MILLARD, Alan.
TREASURES FROM BIBLE TIMES. Lion Pub., 1985. Sixty subjects including Ur, Ebla, the Ark, Solomon's temple and the Dead Sea scrolls. First-rate scholarship and graphics (160 color photos).

⊙MILLER, James B., and MCCALL, Kenneth E., eds.
THE CHURCH AND CONTEMPORARY COSMOLOGY. Carnegie Mellon U.P., 1990. Papers and proceedings of a consultation of the Presbyterian Church, U.S.A., the purpose of which was to study the role of cosmology in the Bible and the theological significance of contemporary cosmology for traditional doctrinal positions.

MISNER, Charles; THORNE, Kip; and WHEELER, John A.
GRAVITATION. Freeman, 1973. A detailed text on the classical general theory of relativity.

MITCHAM, Carl and GROTE, Jim, eds.
THEOLOGY AND TECHNOLOGY: ESSAYS IN CHRISTIAN ANALYSIS AND EXEGESIS. U.P. of America, 1984. A collection of 20 original essays and translations, together with a comprehensive, annotated bibliography. Representative essays include "Technology as a Theological Problem in the Christian Tradition" (Carl Mitcham), "A Christian Philosophical Perspective on Technology" (Egbert Schuurman), "Technique and the Opening Chapters of Genesis" (Jacques Ellul), "The Relation of Man to Creation According to the Bible" (Jacques Ellul).

MITCHAM, Carl and MACKEY, Robert, eds.
PHILOSOPHY AND TECHNOLOGY: READINGS IN THE PHILOSOPHICAL PROBLEMS OF TECHNOLOGY. Free Press, 1983. An important collection of already published essays on the relationships between technology and philosophy. These include selections from "The Technological Order" (Jacques Ellul), "The Abolition of Man" (C.S. Lewis), "Man and Machine" (Nicholas Berdyaer), "Christianity and the Machine Age" (Eric Gill), "The Churches in a Changing World" (R.A. Buchanan), "Technology and Man: A Christian View" (W. Norris Clarke), and "The Historical Roots of our Ecologic Crisis" (Lynn White, Jr.).

MITCHELL, Ralph G.
EINSTEIN AND CHRIST: A NEW APPROACH TO THE DEFENSE OF THE CHRISTIAN RELIGION (Frontiers of Knowledge Ser.: No. 5). Scot. Acad. P./Gower Pub., 1987. To the basic existential questions Mitchell offers answers both orthodox, from the Christian point of view, as well as harmonious with modern scientific thinking. Mitchell sees science moving toward a unity with divinely revealed truth. A strange, but interesting, book.

✛MOBERG, David O.
WHOLISTIC CHRISTIANITY: AN APPEAL FOR A DYNAMIC, BALANCED FAITH. Brethren Press, 1985. Puzzling paradoxes, divisions, and conflicts found among Christians are examined in twelve thought-provoking chapters. Some are a result of the cultural context ("squeezed by the world's mold"), and most reflect a focus upon selected portions of the Bible while ignoring others. Styles of personal Christian commitment, tensions between concern for persons and for society, dilemmas faced by religious leaders and institutions, challenges from social change, and steps toward wholeness are among the topics covered.

MOBERLY, Elizabeth R.
PSYCHOGENESIS: THE EARLY DEVELOPMENT OF GENDER IDENTITY. Routledge, Chapman & Hall, 1983.

MOLTMANN, Jürgen.
GOD IN CREATION: A NEW THEOLOGY OF CREATION & THE SPIRIT OF GOD. Harper & Row, 1985. Moltmann argues that Western theology has been mistaken in subordinating the trinitarian character of God to the unity of God. This book is an attempt to spell out the biblical bases for, and the implications of, a fully trinitarian view.

+MONSMA, Stephen, et al.
RESPONSIBLE TECHNOLOGY: A CHRISTIAN PERSPECTIVE. Eerdmans, 1986. A joint effort of Stephen Monsma, Clifford Christians, Eugene Dykema, Arie Leegwater, Egbert Schuurman, and Lambert Van Poolen who worked together for 11 months at Calvin Center for Christian Scholarship. The authors have backgrounds in politics, communications, economics, chemistry and engineering. (S-87)

MONTAGU, Ashley, ed.
SCIENCE AND CREATIONISM. Oxford U.P., 1984. A collection of essays published in commemoration of the 125th anniversary of *The Origin of the Species*, by Charles Darwin. Arguments of Institute for Creation Research are refuted point by point, case for evolution is presented, and Arkansas court case is reviewed. Evangelical point of view represented. A valuable look at contemporary scientific understanding. (M-85)

MONTENAT, Christian; PLATEAUX, Luc; and ROUX, Pascal.
HOW TO READ CREATION & EVOLUTION. Crossroad NY, 1985. Three French Christians in physics, biology and geology interpret evolution as "a demonstration of the creative activity of God." Includes discussion of determinism and human freedom, man's relationship with the Creator, and evil and death.

+MONTGOMERY, John W.
HUMAN RIGHTS & HUMAN DIGNITY: AN APOLOGETIC FOR THE TRANSCENDENT PERSPECTIVE. Zondervan, 1986. An important book in which a theologian-lawyer argues that any foundation for human rights must be found in a transcendent perspective, in the revelational content of the Bible. (S-87)

+MOORE, James R.
THE POST-DARWINIAN CONTROVERSIES. Cambridge U.P., 1981. Extensive book on the response of Christian and non-Christian thinkers to Darwinism in the late 1800's and early 1900's. A valuable resource book and a necessity for knowing how the Church responded to Darwinism. (M-82, J-83)

MOORE, John N.
HOW TO TEACH ORIGINS (WITHOUT ACLU INTERFERENCE). Mott Media, 1983. Represents a "scientific creationism" viewpoint. The author has taught natural science at Michigan State University.

◎MORELAND, J.P.
CHRISTIANITY AND THE NATURE OF SCIENCE: A PHILOSOPHICAL INVESTIGATION. Baker, 1989. A case for the integration of Christian faith and science in which the author demonstrates how the biblical record regarding the origin of life can and should be a legitimate consideration in scientific study. (M-90)

MORRIS, Henry M.
HISTORY OF MODERN CREATIONISM. Master Bks., 1984. A fascinating and prolific account of the growth of modern creationism by one of its founders and leaders. Includes personal accounts of transitions to this position, and of the difficulties incurred by discrimination against the creationist position. Also distinguishes different views among creationists. (S-85)

MORRIS, Henry M.
MEN OF SCIENCE, MEN OF GOD. Master Bks., 1988. Great scientists who believed the Bible. (J-83)

MORRIS, Henry M. et al, eds.
SCIENTIFIC CREATIONISM. Master Bks., 1974. Addresses catastrophic creationism.

MORRIS, Henry M.
WHAT IS CREATION SCIENCE? Master Bks., 1987. Young-earth creationist viewpoint. (J-83)

MORRIS, Henry M., and PARKER, G.E.
THE BIBLICAL BASIS FOR MODERN SCIENCE. Baker, 1984. Young-earth creationist viewpoint.

MORRIS, Walter F., Jr.
LIVING MAYA. Abrams, 1987. This color-illustrated and photographed book (illus. by Jeffrey J. Foxx) depicts the life of the Maya people today—a life preserved since ancient times—including their daily rituals, religious ceremonies, colorful markets, and stunning landscape.

◎MOTZ, Lloyd, and WEAVER, Jefferson H.
THE STORY OF PHYSICS. Plenum Pub. Corp., 1989. The story of the intellectual evolution of physics, from ancient Greek physics through to the rise of modern physics. Concludes with a discussion of the present state of this science, detailing important features of particle physics.

✪MURCHIE, Guy.
MUSIC OF THE SPHERES: THE MATERIAL UNIVERSE—FROM ATOM TO QUASAR, SIMPLY EXPLAINED. rev. ed. 2 vols. Dover Pub. Vol I: The Macrocosm: Planets, Stars, Galaxies, Cosmology. Vol II: The Microcosm: Matter, Atoms, Waves, Radiation, Relativity.

MURDOCH, D.R.
NIELS BOHR'S PHILOSOPHY OF PHYSICS. Cambridge U.P., 1989.

✢MURPHY, George L.
THE TRADEMARK OF GOD (A Christian Course in Creation, Evolution, and Salvation) Morehouse Pub., 1986. The "trademark of God" is creation out of nothing. Material is provided for an adult class which views evolution in the light of the Incarnation. The biblical doctrines of creation and salvation, modern scientific world-views, the problem of evil, ethics and eschatology are among major topics considered. Leader's guide material and bibliographies also included.

✪MURPHY, Nancey.
THEOLOGY IN THE AGE OF SCIENTIFIC REASONING. Cornell U.P., 1990. An argument for the rationality of Christian belief by showing that theological reasoning is similar to scientific reasoning as described by contemporary philosophy of science.

✢MYERS, David G.
PSYCHOLOGY. 2d ed. Worth, 1988. An introductory textbook to psychology written by a professional psychologist who is also an evangelical. While not overtly biblical, it presents a solid overview without being offensive. Also available, a study guide. (S-87, S-89)

✢MYERS, David G.
SOCIAL PSYCHOLOGY. 2d ed. McGraw-Hill, 1988. An excellent overview of the field of social psychology written by a professional psychologist who is also an evangelical. It would make a good selection as a text, or serve as an introduction to the neophyte interested in learning about the field. Also available, a study guide. (S-87)

✢MYERS, David G., and JEEVES, Malcolm A.
PSYCHOLOGY: THROUGH THE EYES OF FAITH. Harper & Row, 1987. A look at major findings and research in current psychology and the links and parallels that exist between psychology and the conclusions of biblical and theological scholarship. Sponsored by the Christian College Coalition. (M-91)

✪NATIONAL Advisory Group of Sigma Xi.
AN EXPLORATION OF THE NATURE AND QUALITY OF UNDERGRADUATE EDUCATION IN SCIENCE, MATHEMATICS AND ENGINEERING. A Report of the National Advisory Group of Sigma Xi. Sigma Xi, The Scientific Research Society, 1989. Order direct: Sigma Xi, The Scientific Research Society, 345 Whitney Ave., New Haven, CT 06511. The report covers the qualities of instruction, curriculum, and of the human and physical environment for adequate undergraduate education.

✪NATIONAL Aeronautics and Space Administration.
THE SEARCH FOR EXTRATERRESTRIAL INTELLIGENCE. Dover Pub., 1980. A study and evaluation of NASA's methods and approaches for detecting alien signals, including scientific rationale, the Soviet program, searches to date.

NEBELSICK, Harold P.
CIRCLES OF GOD: THEOLOGY AND SCIENCE FROM THE GREEKS TO COPERNICUS (Frontiers of Knowledge Ser.: No. 2). Scot. Acad. Press, 1985. The author shows how the interest in knowing God which directed astronomers' eyes heavenward prevented their actually seeing what was there. So firm was the grip of the perfect cosmic circle on the human mind that this concept captured even Copernicus within its compass. (D-87, J-88)

NEBELSICK, Harold P.
THEOLOGY AND SCIENCE IN MUTUAL MODIFICATION. Oxford U.P., 1981. Written from the perspective of the history of ideas, this book elaborates a Christian context in which scientific development may be understood and clears the ground for mature dialogue between science and religion. (J-83)

✪NEHER, Andrew.
THE PSYCHOLOGY OF TRANSCENDENCE. Dover Pub., 1990. A wide-ranging book on the frontiers of psychology covering topics such as: meditation, deprivation, hypnosis, multiple personality, prophecy, astrology, the use of crystals.

NELKIN, Dorothy.
THE CREATION CONTROVERSY: SCIENCE OR SCRIPTURE IN THE SCHOOLS? Norton, 1982. How an "evolutionist" views the school controversy. (J-86)

NEWBIGIN, Lesslie.
FOOLISHNESS TO THE GREEKS: THE GOSPEL AND WESTERN CULTURE. Eerdmans, 1986. Bishop Newbigin, a leader in Christian missions, asks how biblical authority can be a reality in our modern culture, permeated as it is by a scientistic world view. He gives a thoughtful presentation of how the gospel could be implemented to confront modern science (which he calls the core of our culture), politics and economics.

✪NEWBIGIN, Lesslie.
THE GOSPEL IN A PLURALIST SOCIETY. Eerdmans, 1990. An excellent analysis of contemporary (secular, humanist, pluralist) culture and suggestions for how Christians can affirm their faith within this context.

NEWELL, Norman D.
CREATION AND EVOLUTION: MYTH OR REALITY? Praeger, 1984. "Creationism, that narrowly sectarian religious dogma now masquerading as a science, is no match for Dr. Newell's analysis."—Stephen Jay Gould.

✪NOLL, Mark A.
ONE NATION UNDER GOD?: CHRISTIAN FAITH AND POLITICAL ACTION IN AMERICA. Harper & Row, 1988. Author believes politics can serve God and benefit people and he offers principles for implementing Christian faith in the political arena. Historical case studies indicate that Christian politics have been most successful when implemented on the level of conviction, while efforts to mobilize religious forces for narrowly defined moral objectives have been minimal or even counterproductive.

✪NOLL, Mark A.; HATCH, Nathan O.; and MARSDEN, George M.
THE SEARCH FOR CHRISTIAN AMERICA. exp. ed. Helmers & Howard, 1989. An examination of key questions raised by the movement asserting the Christian heritage of the United States. Questions and issues include: How Christian is America's past? How much Christian action is required to make a whole society Christian? Is the "Christian nation" concept harmful or helpful to effective Christian action in society? (M-91)

NOONAN, John T., Jr., ed.
THE MORALITY OF ABORTION: LEGAL AND HISTORICAL PERSPECTIVES. Harvard U.P., 1970.

✪NOVAK, David, and SAMUELSON, Norbert.
CREATION AND THE END OF DAYS. U.P. of America, 1986. An interesting collection of papers on "Judaism and scientific cosmology."

✪NOVIKOS, Igor (trans. Vitaly Kisin).
BLACK HOLES AND THE UNIVERSE. Cambridge U.P., 1990. An explanation of the properties and cosmic importance of black holes by a distinguished astrophysicist.

NUMBERS, Ronald L.
CREATION BY NATURAL LAW: LAPLACE'S NEBULAR HYPOTHESIS IN AMERICAN THOUGHT. U. of Washington P., 1977.

NYMAN, Michael.
EXPERIMENTAL MUSIC: CAGE AND BEYOND. Schirmer, 1981.

ODEN, Thomas C.
THE LIVING GOD. Harper & Row, 1986. A plausible restatement of classical Christian teaching of God (particularly with respect to his creative and revelatory activity). Very readable for lay theologians. Highly recommended.

OLDROYD, David.
THE ARCH OF KNOWLEDGE: AN INTRODUCTORY STUDY OF THE HISTORY OF THE PHILOSOPHY AND METHODOLOGY OF SCIENCE. Routledge, Chapman & Hall, 1986. Detailed, up-to-date, and readable.

✪OSBORNE, Denis.
THE ANDROMEDANS & OTHER PARABLES OF SCIENCE AND FAITH. InterVarsity Press, 1978. A collection of 25 brief essays which address the intriguing issues of complementarity and compatibility, open minds and empty minds, seeing and believing, reason and proof, how and why.

PAGELS, Heinz R.
THE COSMIC CODE: QUANTUM PHYSICS AS THE LAW OF NATURE. Bantam, 1984. An attempt to explain what Pagels calls "quantum weirdness" and its implications.

PAGELS, Heinz R.
PERFECT SYMMETRY: THE SEARCH FOR THE BEGINNING OF TIME. Bantam, 1986.

PAIS, Abraham.
'SUBTLE IS THE LORD...': THE SCIENCE AND THE LIFE OF ALBERT EINSTEIN. Oxford U.P., 1982. A scientific biography of the great physicist.

PANNENBERG, Wolfhart.
ANTHROPOLOGY IN THEOLOGICAL PERSPECTIVE. Westminster, 1985. A massive, seminal work that relates basic findings of the anthropological disciplines (human biology, psychology, cultural anthropology, sociology, and history) to the core theme of theological anthropology—the image of God in human beings.

✪PANNENBERG, Wolfhart.
CHRISTIANITY IN A SECULARIZED WORLD. Crossroad NY, 1989. Major themes are indicated by the following chapter headings: "The Dispute over Secularization and the Origin of its Historical Causes," "The Problematical Consequences of Cultural Secularization," and "The Task of Christian Theology in a Secular Culture." A significant book for Christians concerned with dialogue with the sciences.

PANNENBERG, Wolfhart.
JESUS: GOD AND MAN. 2d ed. Westminster, 1982. A major attempt to understand christology "from below," studying and criticizing the christological tradition in the light of modern understandings of scripture.

✪PANNENBERG, Wolfhart (trans. Philip Clayton).
METAPHYSICS AND THE IDEA OF GOD. Eerdmans, 1990. The convergence of philosophy and theology with respect to their common concern, the idea of God.

PANNENBERG, Wolfhart.
THEOLOGY AND THE PHILOSOPHY OF SCIENCE. Westminster, 1976. A thorough introduction to the philosophy of science and its interrelationship with theology. Written by one of the leading theologians of our time.

✪PARK, David.
THE HOW & THE WHY: AN ESSAY ON THE ORIGINS & DEVELOPMENT OF PHYSICAL THEORY. Princeton U.P., 1990.

✪PARKER, Barry.
CREATION: THE STORY OF THE ORIGIN AND EVOLUTION OF THE UNIVERSE. Plenum Pub. Corp., 1988. A very readable book which serves as an important bridge between present-day scientific work and lay readers.

PASCAL, Blaise (trans. A.J. Krailsheimer).
PENSÉS. Penguin, 1966. Pascal died in 1662. A great scientist of his day, best known among Christians for his wager concerning the existence of God. He was also a leading spokesman for the Jansenists (Augustinian) against the Jesuits of his day.

PATTEE, Howard H., ed.
HIERARCHY THEORY: THE CHALLENGE OF COMPLEX SYSTEMS. George Braziller, 1973.

✪PAUL, Iain.
KNOWLEDGE OF GOD: CALVIN, EINSTEIN, AND POLANYI. Scot. Acad. P./Gower Pub., 1987. An examination of fundamental thought-forms in modern science and reformed theology for the purpose of helping scientists and theologians communicate effectively with each other. Calvin's theology, and Einstein and Polanyi's scientific premises form the basis for discussion.

✪PAZMIÑO, Robert W.
FOUNDATIONAL ISSUES IN CHRISTIAN EDUCATION: AN INTRODUCTION IN EVANGELICAL PERSPECTIVE. Baker Bks., 1988. A call to evangelical educators to "affirm biblical insights" and "incorporate insights from other disciplines" through critical evaluation of foundations significant to evangelical thought and for the purpose of addressing current needs and future challenges in Christian education.

PEACOCKE, Arthur R.
CREATION AND THE WORLD OF SCIENCE. U. of Notre Dame P., 1985. Penetrating thought by a brilliant scholar. Strongly influenced by process theology and Teilhardian thought.

PEACOCKE, Arthur R.
GOD AND THE NEW BIOLOGY. Harper & Row, 1987. An important book that addresses these questions: What part does chance play in evolution? Is biology nothing but physics and chemistry? How does the new biology change our thinking about humanity, God and evolution?

Discussion of reductionism in biology is extremely helpful. (M-88)

PEACOCKE, Arthur R.
INTIMATIONS OF REALITY: CRITICAL REALISM IN SCIENCE & RELIGION. U. of Notre Dame P., 1984. A biochemist and theological writer, the author explains how scientific models and theological metaphors both have contributed to our understanding of reality. He reviews the recent history of the philosophy of science and suggests ways in which science and theology could benefit each other's perceptions of reality.

✪PEAT, F. David.
SUPERSTRINGS AND THE SEARCH FOR THE THEORY OF EVERYTHING. Contemporary Bks., 1988. A dramatic explanation of the development and meaning of the superstring theory which states that everything in the universe—matter, forces, space—consists of minuscule strings of ten dimensions. Accessible to lay readers.

PECK, M. Scott.
PEOPLE OF THE LIE: THE HOPE FOR HEALING HUMAN EVIL. Simon & Schuster, 1985. This bestselling author has identified himself as a Christian. He faults modern psychology for not taking evil seriously, and presents a tentative exploration of the problem of evil from a psychiatric stance.

PECK, M. Scott.
THE ROAD LESS TRAVELED. Simon & Schuster, 1985. Peck's first best-selling book seeks to integrate psychoanalytic and spiritual insights to help in solving the problems of life. Very readable.

✪PEDOE, Dan.
GEOMETRY AND THE VISUAL ARTS. Dover Pub., 1983. The effects of geometry on artistic achievement and its importance to artists, scientists, architects, philosophers and others.

✪PENROSE, Roger.
THE EMPEROR'S NEW MIND: CONCERNING COMPUTERS, MINDS, AND THE LAWS OF PHYSICS. Oxford U.P., 1989. A semi-popular work in which the central concern is the mind-body problem especially as it relates to the question of artificial intelligence. Author covers a good deal of modern mathematics and physics.

PERKINS, D.
INTRODUCTION TO HIGH ENERGY PHYSICS. 3d ed. Addison-Wesley, 1987. A technical introduction to the field.

PERKINS, Richard.
LOOKING BOTH WAYS: EXPLORING THE INTERFACE BETWEEN CHRISTIANITY & SOCIOLOGY. Baker, 1987. The necessity of keeping the perspective of both Christianity and sociology in active dialogue with each other is emphasized in this interesting discussion of topics relevant to all scholars such as ideology, the nature of science, values and science relativity, positivism, reflexivity, and praxis or applied science. An excellent resource as an introduction to "Christian sociology" and as a constructively critical analysis of the significant issues with which it deals. (J-88)

✪PETERS, Ted, ed.
COSMOS AS CREATION: THEOLOGY AND SCIENCE IN CONSONANCE. Abingdon, 1989. A collection of essays by scholars interested in the science-theology interface, gathered around the theme "theology and science in consonance."

✪PETERSON, Dale.
THE DELUGE AND THE ARK: A JOURNEY INTO PRIMATE WORLDS. Houghton Mifflin, 1989. A look at 12 primate species which illustrate the effects of the "deluge," human-related threats to their survival; and the "ark," wildlife sanctuaries and other protected habitats. Foreword by Jane Goodall.

PETERSON, Michael L. (ed. Stephen C. Evans).
PHILOSOPHY OF EDUCATION: ISSUES & OPTIONS. InterVarsity Press, 1986. A look at traditional and contemporary philosophy of education. Author aims to encourage excellence in schools and develop a Christian philosophy of education.

PEUKERT, Helmut (trans. James Bohman).
SCIENCE, ACTION AND FUNDAMENTAL THEOLOGY: TOWARD A THEOLOGY OF COMMUNICATIVE ACTION. MIT Press, 1986. A complex and technical work developing a theological theory of communicative action which relates ordinary language and social interactions to underlying normative principles. Relates theology to philosophy of science, and to society and politics. (J-86)

PHILIPCHALK, Ronald P.
PSYCHOLOGY AND CHRISTIANITY: AN INTRODUCTION TO THE CONTROVERSIAL IS-SUES IN PSYCHOLOGY. rev. ed. U.P. of America, 1988. This book examines such phenomena as ESP and brainwashing. Each topic is related to the Bible. (M-89)

✪PIERCE, John R., and NOLL, A. Michael.
SIGNALS—THE SCIENCE OF TELECOMMUNICATIONS. Scientific American Library, 1990. Extremely well written with many suggestive references to God.

PITMAN, Michael.
ADAM & EVOLUTION: A SCIENTIFIC CRITIQUE OF NEO-DARWINISM. Baker, 1987. Author contends there is little or no evidence for macro-evolution by natural selection. Holds old-earth view. (S-87)

✪PLACHER, William C.
UNAPOLOGETIC THEOLOGY: A CHRISTIAN VOICE IN A PLURALISTIC CONVERSATION. Westminster, 1988. An examination of religion and the search for truth in a pluralistic society. Issues considered are science and its relation to belief, dialogue among various religions, and the theological method.

PODOLNY, R.
SOMETHING CALLED NOTHING: THE PHYSICAL VACUUM: WHAT IS IT? Imported Publications, 1986.

POLANYI, Michael (ed. Marjorie Grene).
KNOWING AND BEING. U. of Chicago P., 1973. This collection of essays by Polanyi is a very readable introduction to the basic concepts and overall breadth of his thought. Recommended for someone who has not read Polanyi before.

POLANYI, Michael.
PERSONAL KNOWLEDGE: TOWARDS A POST-CRITICAL PHILOSOPHY. U. of Chicago P., 1974. Leading philosopher of science and seminal thinker emphasizes the personal character of all human knowledge as an epistemological dictum. This work has significant resonances with Christian theology and philosophy. Difficult reading.

POLKINGHORNE, John.
ONE WORLD: THE INTERACTION OF SCIENCE & THEOLOGY. Princeton U.P., 1987. Noted mathematical physicist and Anglican priest argues that theologians and scientists are exploring only one world and can fruitfully influence each other. A historical exploration as to how science and theology came to be seen as opposing, rather than complementary, fields is shown in the author's typically flowing and anecdotal style. (J-89)

POLKINGHORNE, John.
THE QUANTUM WORLD. Princeton U.P., 1985. An introduction to quantum theory which presents the basic concepts clearly, while restricting most mathematics to appendices. Problems of interpretation are stressed, with a generally "realistic" view being taken.

✪POLKINGHORNE, John.
ROCHESTER ROUNDABOUT: THE STORY OF HIGH ENERGY PHYSICS. Freeman, 1990. The story behind the science and business of high energy physics based primarily on a sequence of International Rochester Conferences. The author describes the participating physicists and the discoveries that were announced and discussed at these prestigious gatherings.

✪POLKINGHORNE, John.
SCIENCE AND CREATION: THE SEARCH FOR UNDERSTANDING. Shambhala, 1989. Addresses fundamental questions about how scientific and theological worldviews relate to each other.

✪POLKINGHORNE, John.
SCIENCE AND PROVIDENCE: GOD'S INTERACTION WITH THE WORLD. Shambhala, 1989. An examination of Christian understanding of evil, miracles, prayer and providence in a scientific world.

POLKINGHORNE, John.
THE WAY THE WORLD IS: THE CHRISTIAN PERSPECTIVE OF A SCIENTIST. Bks. Demand UMI (Reprint of 1984 Eerdmans ed.). Written by a professor of mathematical physics at Cambridge who resigned to become an Anglican priest. Response to skeptical reactions of fellow scientists. A masterful statement and apologetic for the rationality and inner coherence of the Christian world view. (D-85)

POLLARD, Jeffrey W., ed.
EVOLUTIONARY THEORY: PATHS INTO THE FUTURE. Wiley, 1984. Secondary causal level:

discusses problems with "conventional evolutionary hypotheses" and proposes some solutions. Particularly noteworthy is Chapter 4 by Brian C. Goodwin, "Changing from an Evolutionary to a Generative Paradigm in Biology."

POLLARD, W.G.
TRANSCENDENCE AND PROVIDENCE: REFLECTIONS OF A PHYSICIST AND PRIEST (Frontiers of Knowledge Ser.: No.6). Scot. Acad. P./Gower Pub., 1987. This selection of essays demonstrates how the author reconciles two views of reality: the world of evolution and that of Judeo-Christian tradition. The author served as a Professor of Physics at the University of Tennessee until entering the priesthood in 1952. These papers reflect the work written in the last thirty years since his ordination. (J-89)

✪POLOMA, Margaret M.
THE ASSEMBLIES OF GOD AT THE CROSSROADS: CHARISMA AND INSTITUTIONAL DILEMMAS. U. of Tennessee P., 1989. A thorough study based on participant observation, interviews with ministers, surveys of the members of 16 assemblies, questionnaires from pastors, and more. The core issue interpreted is the tension between a worldview in which religious experiences are central and the pragmatic bureaucratic needs and pressures that result from congregational growth.

✪POSTMAN, Neil.
CONSCIENTIOUS OBJECTIONS: STIRRING UP TROUBLE ABOUT LANGUAGE, TECH-NOLOGY, AND EDUCATION. Knopf, 1988. True stories of resistance and challenge are used to explore myths and conceits of our culture.

POYTHRESS, Vernon S.
SYMPHONIC THEOLOGY: THE VALIDITY OF MULTIPLE PERSPECTIVES IN THEOLOGY. Zondervan, 1987. A distinguished theologian-mathematician argues for the legitimacy of "multiple perspectives" with respect to theological thought; the differing viewpoints reinforcing, improving, or correcting what is understood from each separately. As physical reality is too large and complex to be grasped in its totality by any one way of looking at things, God's truth is too great to be understood by looking at it from a single perspective.

PREISS, Byron, ed.
THE UNIVERSE. Bantam, 1987. A collaborative work by leading cosmologists, popular science fiction authors, space artists, and space photographers about current and future knowledge of the universe. Each scientific essay is accompanied by a fictional piece by a major science fiction writer, along with photographs and illustrations.

✪PRESBYTERIAN Eco-Justice Task Force.
KEEPING AND HEALING THE CREATION. Committee on Social Witness Policy, Presbyterian Church (USA), 1989. A resource paper on environmental concerns and the church, coming from the Presbyterian Eco-Justice Task Force.

✛PRICE, David; WIESTER, John L.; and HEARN, Walter R.
TEACHING SCIENCE IN A CLIMATE OF CONTROVERSY: A VIEW FROM THE AMERICAN SCIENTIFIC AFFILIATION. American Scientific Affiliation, 1989. Order direct: ASA, P.O. Box 668, Ipswich, MA 01938. (Quantity discounts available.) Members of Committee for Integrity in Science Education have masterminded a booklet addressing the issues science teachers must face when teaching creation/evolution and about origins. First printing was sent to 22,000 high school biology teachers (members of the National Science Teachers Assoc.); second printing with revisions, 1987; third printing with revisions, 1989. Over 100,000 copies now in print.

✪PRIGOGENE, Ilya, and STENGERS, Isabelle.
ORDER OUT OF CHAOS—MAN'S NEW DIALOGUE WITH NATURE. Bantam, 1984. A demanding but lucid layperson's introduction to a new scientific formulation which shows how order can arise out of apparent disorder.

✪PROPST, L. Rebecca.
PSYCHOTHERAPY IN A RELIGIOUS FRAMEWORK. Human Sciences Press, 1988. An examination of the interplay between psychology and religious faith in clinical practice. Psychological and theological principles are applied to the problems religious people face. Emphasis is on cognitive psychotherapy in a religious context. (S-89)

PUDDEFOOT, John.
LOGIC & AFFIRMATION: PERSPECTIVES IN MATHEMATICS & THEOLOGY (Frontiers of Knowledge Ser.: No.9). Scot. Acad. P./Gower Pub., 1987. A challenge to the assumption that knowledge and understanding arise primarily from examining axioms in mathematics and from dogmas in theology. The author relocates the center of theological understanding in visions of

God accessible to the community of faith. Highly recommended. (S-90)

+RAMM, Bernard.
THE CHRISTIAN VIEW OF SCIENCE AND SCRIPTURE. Eerdmans, 1954. The classic work on creation in Genesis, proposing progressive creation as an interpretation of Genesis 1.

RATZSCH, Del (ed. Stephen C. Evans).
PHILOSOPHY OF SCIENCE: THE NATURAL SCIENCES IN CHRISTIAN PERSPECTIVE. InterVarsity Press, 1986. A fine overview of the philosophy of science, both traditional and contemporary, and discussion of its significance for Christianity. Includes chapters on what science can and cannot tell us.

RAVETZ, J.R.
SCIENTIFIC KNOWLEDGE & ITS SOCIAL PROBLEMS. Oxford U.P., 1971.

⊘REDEKOP, Calvin, and BENDER, Urie A.
WHO AM I? WHAT AM I?: SEARCHING FOR MEANING IN YOUR WORK. Zondervan, 1988. Biblically based Christian values and social science resources are the basis for the analyses of career choices and changes, mid-life crises, unemployment, tensions in the family and workplace, male-female relationships, and other pragmatic issues related to work. Evaluation of the physical, mental, psychic, social, and spiritual elements of work and how they interact is one of the major foci of attention.

REDONDI, Pietro (trans. Raymond Rosenthal).
GALILEO: HERETIC. Princeton U.P., 1989. A translation from Italian of Redondi's work regarding Galileo's trial for heresy under Pope Urban VIII. A controversial book, Redondi's thesis is based on his discovery of a previously unknown manuscript that he claims is proof of Galileo's innocence of heresy stemming from the "Copernican heresy" of the heliocentric theory, and places Galileo's heresy in the realms of Catholic theology (stemming from "atomic" theory as a disproof of the 17th-century theory of the doctrine of transubstantiation). Interesting, but "loose" in historial proof. (J-88)

⊘REICHENBACH, Hans (trans. Ralph B. Winn).
FROM COPERNICUS TO EINSTEIN. Dover Pub., 1980. A precise description of the development of the special and general theories of relativity beginning with Copernican astronomy.

REICHLEY, A. James.
RELIGION IN AMERICAN PUBLIC LIFE. Brookings Institute, 1985. A secular viewpoint on the role of religion in the formation of public policy throughout American history.

REISSER, Paul C.; REISSER, Teri; and WELDON, John.
NEW AGE MEDICINE: A CHRISTIAN PERSPECTIVE ON HOLISTIC HEALTH. rev. and exp. ed. InterVarsity Press, 1987. A well-written investigation into holistic health techniques in light of the New Age movement. Topics include the holistic phenomenon, ancient Chinese medicine, psychic diagnosis and healing, and a biblical foundation for health and wholeness. Formerly titled *The Holistic Healers*. Intended for a general Christian audience. (M-90)

⊘RICHARDS, Robert J.
DARWIN AND THE EMERGENCE OF EVOLUTIONARY THEORIES OF MIND AND BEHAVIOR. U. of Chicago P., 1987. The history and development of evolutionary theories of human behavior. Recommended for historians of science. (D-89)

RICHARDS, Stewart.
PHILOSOPHY AND SOCIOLOGY OF SCIENCE: AN INTRODUCTION. 2nd ed. Basil Blackwell, 1987.

RIFKIN, Jeremy.
ALGENY: A NEW WORD—A NEW WORLD. Penguin, 1984. An unexpurgated warning against the dangers of biogenetic engineering. (M-87)

RIORDAN, Michael.
THE HUNTING OF THE QUARK. Simon & Schuster, 1987. An account of the discovery of the quark, by a physicist involved in the experimentation, which has led to a transformation of our view of the subatomic world.

ROBINSON, Daniel N.
AN INTELLECTUAL HISTORY OF PSYCHOLOGY. U. of Wisconsin P., 1986. Rather than tracing the important figures in a history of psychology, the author traces the important ideas. In the process, many disciplines are discussed including politics, art, literature and religion.

ROHRLICH, Fritz.
FROM PARADOX TO REALITY: BASIC CONCEPTS OF THE PHYSICAL WORLD. Cambridge

U.P., 1987. A clear introduction to the basic ideas of the two pillars of 20th-century physics: relativity theory and quantum physics. The discussion stresses conceptual issues from a realist perspective; balanced and sane. Highly recommended.

✪ROLSTON, Holmes, III.
SCIENCE AND RELIGION: A CRITICAL SURVEY. Temple U.P., 1986. An interdisciplinary analysis of the methods and central themes of contemporary scientific and religious thought.

✪ROSS, Hugh.
THE FINGERPRINT OF GOD. Promise Pub., 1989. An examination of the Big Bang cosmology and the anthropic principle, and an attempt to use them to show the truth of Genesis and the existence of the Creator.

ROSZAK, Theodore.
THE CULT OF INFORMATION: THE FOLKLORE OF COMPUTERS AND THE TRUE ART OF THINKING. Pantheon, 1987.

ROTHENBERG, Stuart, and NEWPORT, Frank.
THE EVANGELICAL VOTER: RELIGION AND POLITICS IN AMERICA. Free Congress Research, 1984. This report and analysis of a 1983 public opinion survey of adult evangelical Christians reveals their political diversity along side of their significant religious differences from other Americans.

✪ROTHMAN, Tony, et al.
FRONTIERS OF MODERN PHYSICS: NEW PERSPECTIVES ON COSMOLOGY, RELATIVITY, BLACK HOLES AND EXTRATERRESTRIAL INTELLIGENCE. Dover Pub., 1984. Excellent up-to-date discussions for laymen.

✪ROTHMAN, Tony.
SCIENCE À LA MODE: PHYSICAL FASHIONS AND FICTIONS. Princeton U.P., 1989. A collection of witty and wise nontechnical essays explaining why the bandwagon effect is so strong in science and suggesting how to recognize and respond to it.

ROZENTAL, I.L.
BIG BANG BIG BOUNCE: HOW PARTICLES AND FIELDS DRIVE COSMIC EVOLUTION. Springer-Verlag, 1988.

RUCKER, Rudy.
INFINITY AND THE MIND: THE SCIENCE & PHILOSOPHY OF THE INFINITE. Birkhauser, 1982. Rudy Rucker is Hegel's grandson, and an advanced mathematician. His book is a lively excursion through the mathematical, philosophical and theological concepts of infinity, exploring Gödel's incompleteness theorem, set theory, and the idea of robot consciousness of mysticism along the way.

RUPPRECHT, David and Ruth.
RADICAL HOSPITALITY. Presbyterian & Reformed, 1983. A discussion of how to use your home for hospitality to students and needy people.

✪RUSE, Michael.
PHILOSOPHY OF BIOLOGY TODAY. State Univ. of New York Press, 1988. A brief account of recent developments in the philosophy of biology covering topics such as evolutionary theory, population genetics, molecular biology, teleology, and human biology. Includes an excellent bibliography of representative works.

RUSPOLI, Mario.
THE CAVE OF LASCAUX: THE FINAL PHOTOGRAPHS. Abrams, 1987. Photographs of the now-sealed cave in the Dordogne region of France, dated to the prehistoric period, record spectacular animal paintings by the tribe of that region. The text tells what is known of that region: variations in climate, pollen, vegetation, fauna, the way of life of the tribe, their religion, hunting and fishing, and their art. The process of recording this cave-art on film and their meaning is discussed.

RUSSELL, Colin.
CROSS-CURRENTS: INTERACTIONS BETWEEN SCIENCE AND FAITH. Bks. Demand UMI. An assessment of the massive mutual debt of science and faith to each other over the last four centuries. Includes discussion of the Greek and biblical origins of modern science, the growth of technology, the evolution controversy, rise of modern physics and the environmental crisis. (D-86, M-88)

RUSSELL, Colin.
SCIENCE & SOCIAL CHANGE IN BRITAIN: 1700-1900. St. Martin, 1984.

✪RUSSELL, Robert J.; STOEGER, William R.; and COYNE, George V., eds.
PHYSICS, PHILOSOPHY, AND THEOLOGY: A COSMIC QUEST FOR UNDERSTANDING. U. of Notre Dame P., 1989. Eighteen papers which address historical and contemporary relations in science and religion, topics related to realism and myth, and contemporary physics and cosmology and their impact on theology. Includes message by Pope John II calling for dialogue between theologians, philosophers, and scientists. (D-90)

RYAN, Dennis P., ed.
EINSTEIN AND THE HUMANTITIES (Contributions in Philosophy No. 32)., Greenwood Press, 1987.

SANDERS, James A.
CANON AND COMMUNITY: A GUIDE TO CANONICAL CRITICISM. Fortress, 1984. An introduction to a promising approach to biblical study: "canonical criticism."

SCHAEFFER, Francis A.
THE CHURCH AT THE END OF THE 20TH CENTURY: THE CHURCH BEFORE THE WATCHING WORLD. 2nd ed. Good News, 1985.

SCHAEFFER, Francis A.
ESCAPE FROM REASON. InterVarsity Press, 1968. A critique of modern philosophy in light of Christianity.

SCHAEFFER, Francis A.
THE GOD WHO IS THERE. InterVarsity Press, 1968. A detailed critique of modern antitheistic philosophy.

✪SCHINDLER, Craig F.; and LAPID, Gary G.
THE GREAT TURNING: PERSONAL PEACE, GLOBAL VICTORY. Bear & Co., 1989. A discussion of a visionary technique for negotiation, useful not only in arms control negotiations but also in the resolution of international issues.

SCHOVILLE, Keith N.
BIBLICAL ARCHAEOLOGY IN FOCUS. Baker, 1978. A comprehensive summary by an evangelical Old Testament scholar.

✪SCHROEDER, Gerald L.
GENESIS AND THE BIG BANG: THE DISCOVERY OF HARMONY BETWEEN MODERN SCIENCE AND THE BIBLE. Bantam, 1990. A provocative argument for harmony between science and the Bible by a physicist and theologian. Events described as following the Big Bang and events described in Genesis are shown to be identical realities both of which reveal a universe evolving from chaos into order.

SCHULTZ, Duane P., and SCHULTZ, Sydney E.
A HISTORY OF MODERN PSYCHOLOGY 4th ed. Harcourt, Brace, Jovanovich, 1987. This volume traces the history of experimental psychology while not overlooking its ancestors. It gives some attention to the influence Christianity had in the lives of many scientists. (J-87)

SCHUURMAN, Egbert.
TECHNOLOGY AND THE FUTURE: A PHILOSOPHICAL CHALLENGE. Radix, 1980. Order direct: Shiloh Books, 910 Wood St., Pittsburgh, PA 15221. A Dutch legislator, considered a leading philosopher of technology in the reformed tradition, discusses the impact of technology in the future.

SCHWINGER, Julian.
EINSTEIN'S LEGACY: THE UNITY OF SPACE AND TIME. Freeman, 1987. Scientific and human elements of Einstein's quest to reconcile Newton and Maxwell's theories into his own unified theory, and special and general theories of relativity, are recounted here by Nobelist Schwinger. Past and present experiments to confirm or challenge Einstein's theories of matter, energy, space and time are also described.

SCOTT, Drusilla.
EVERYMAN REVIVED: THE COMMON SENSE OF MICHAEL POLANYI. The Book Guild Limited (UK), 1986. Order direct: Helmers & Howard, P.O. Box 7407, Colorado Springs, CO 80933. A lucid presentation of Polanyi's ideas and values. Polanyi, a reknowned scientist, turned to philosophy in an effort to free thinkers from the rigid limitations of a strictly scientific view of human affairs.

✪SEERVELD, Calvin.
ON BEING HUMAN: IMAGING GOD IN THE MODERN WORLD. Welch Pub. Co. (Canada). A devotional exploration of "the miracle of being human, in the image of God" through the use of scripture, songs, prayers, artwork.

●SEIELSTAD, George A.
AT THE HEART OF THE WEB: THE INEVITABLE GENESIS OF INTELLIGENT LIFE. Harcourt, Brace, Jovanovich, 1989. An intelligent journey through modern science by a secular scientist.

SELL, Alan P.F.
DEFENDING & DECLARING THE FAITH: SOME SCOTTISH EXAMPLES, 1860-1920. Helmers & Howard, 1987. Examination of the development of eight Scottish theologians who wrote during the period of 1860 to 1920 when Christianity was struggling with the questions posed by the modern world, including evolution, biblical criticism, materialism, naturalism, and idealism.

SHANNON, Thomas A., ed.
BIOETHICS. 3rd ed. Paulist Press, 1987. An excellent collection of articles by noted ethicists.

SHAPIRO, Robert.
ORIGINS: A SKEPTIC'S GUIDE TO THE CREATION OF LIFE ON EARTH. Bantam, 1987. A chemistry teacher at NYU, examines the many extant theories pertaining to the origin of life in the guise of a skeptic, separating the scientific (rigorously determined) ones from those which really are not, and then proceeding to point out the flaws in the scientific theories. Includes examination of primordial soup, Oparin-Haldane reducing theory, "lifecloud" theory, and creationists' claims. (S-87, D-87)

●SHELDRAKE, Rupert.
A NEW SCIENCE OF LIFE: THE HYPOTHESIS OF FORMATIVE CAUSATION. rev.ed. Tarcher, 1988. An introduction of the mechanistic view of processes into the realm of organismic holistic thinking with morphogenetic fields as the mediator of form based upon the prior history of structures and systems.

SHELLY, Judith A., and John, Sandra D., eds.
SPIRITUAL DIMENSIONS OF MENTAL HEALTH. InterVarsity Press, 1983. Introductory compilation of articles by 13 contributors dealing with spiritual care and needs in relation to mental health. Produced by Nurses Christian Fellowship Mental Health Task Force. (J-85)

SHOPE, Robert K.
THE ANALYSIS OF KNOWING: A DECADE OF RESEARCH. Princeton U.P., 1983. Points out the difficulties inherent in knowing, and compares different types of knowing and the different values placed on them in different societies. Rates the scientific (and mathematical) epistemic method most highly. (J-85)

SHUSTER, Marguerite.
POWER, PATHOLOGY, PARADOX: THE DYNAMICS OF GOOD & EVIL. Zondervan, 1987. Similar in genre to Peck's People of the Lie, though fuller and more conservative theologically, while less complete in its case studies. Stylistically sophisticated, this book treats the relationships between the mind, spirit, body, will, and psychopathology. See ASA member Mary Stewart Van Leeuwen's review in Christianity Today (Apr 8, 1988) for an excellent essay on this book.

●SIDER, Ronald J.
COMPLETELY PRO-LIFE. InterVarsity Press, 1987. Abortion, the family, nuclear weapons, the poor: a plea for consistency. (J-88)

SIDER, Ronald J., ed.
EVANGELICALS & DEVELOPMENT: TOWARD A THEOLOGY OF SOCIAL CHANGE. Westminster, 1982. Contains article by Tom Sine.

SIDER, Ronald J.
RICH CHRISTIANS IN AN AGE OF HUNGER: A BIBLE STUDY 2nd ed., rev. and expanded. InterVarsity Press, 1984. An update of the situation around the world and a response to many of the author's critics by a reconsideration and reformulation of his arguments. (J-78)

●SIEGEL, Bernard S.
LOVE, MEDICINE AND MIRACLES. Harper & Row, 1986. A Yale University surgeon talks about experiences of healing with some exceptional patients.

SILK, Joseph.
THE BIG BANG: THE CREATION AND EVOLUTION OF THE UNIVERSE. 2nd rev. ed., Freeman, 1988. A popular survey of modern cosmology, with a mathematical appendix.

SINCLAIR, Maurice.
GREEN FINGER OF GOD. Paternoster (UK)/Attic Press, 1986. A biblical theology of development by an agriculturalist who was involved in a development project in Argentina.

SINE, Tom.
MUSTARD SEED CONSPIRACY. Word, 1981. Futurist challenges Christians to respond in a

caring way to change. This book won the 1983 gold medallion award in the Christianity and Society category from the Evangelical Christian Publishers Association.

✛SIRE, James W.
THE UNIVERSE NEXT DOOR: A BASIC WORLD VIEW CATALOG. 2nd ed. InterVarsity Press, 1988. Excellent summaries of the major presuppositions and positions of a number of basic world views including: Christian theism, deism, naturalism, secular humanism, existentialism, and the New Age. (D-89)

✪SKEHAN, James, W.
MODERN SCIENCE AND THE BOOK OF GENESIS. National Science Teachers, 1986. A short and well-balanced treatment of the relationship of science to the creation accounts of the early chapters of Genesis.

✛SKILLEN, James W.
CHRISTIANS ORGANIZING FOR POLITICAL SERVICE: A STUDY GUIDE BASED ON THE WORK OF THE ASSOCIATION FOR PUBLIC JUSTICE. Assn. for Public Justice, 1982. A fine introduction to the topic. (J-82)

SMARTO, Donald.
JUSTICE AND MERCY. Tyndale, 1987. The transforming power of Jesus Christ for criminals and for the correctional system of American society is the main theme of this constructive descriptive and evaluative study. The crises of the prison system, the problems of reforming it, alternative methods and means for dealing with offenders, the need for a Christian conscience in dealing with them, the history and present status of prison ministries, and the role of the local church are among the topics covered.

SMEDES, Lewis B.
CHOICES: MAKING RIGHT DECISIONS IN A COMPLEX WORLD. Harper & Row, 1986.

SMEDES, Lewis B.
MERE MORALITY: WHAT GOD EXPECTS FROM ORDINARY PEOPLE. Eerdmans, 1987.

✪SMITH, Gary S., ed.
GOD AND POLITICS: FOUR VIEWS ON THE REFORMATION OF CIVIL GOVERNMENT. Presbyterian & Reformed, 1989. An examination of four major positions on the biblical role of civil government held by Christians in the Reformed community. Theonomy, principled pluralism, Christian America, and national confession are each described and critiqued by representatives of the other three positions. A useful resource on issues associated with church-state relations and other political topics.

✪SMITH, J. Maynard.
DID DARWIN GET IT RIGHT? ESSAYS ON GAMES, SEX AND EVOLUTION. Chapman & Hall, 1989. Short essays addressing key questions of modern biology such as: How did life begin? Does the brain work like a computer? How did social behavior evolve?

SMITH, J. Maynard.
EVOLUTION NOW. Freeman, 1982. Annotated articles from the leaders of the current evolutionary debates.

SMITH, Wolfgang.
COSMOS & TRANSCENDENCE: BREAKING THROUGH THE BARRIERS OF SCIENTIFIC BELIEF. Sherwood Sugden & Co., 1984

SMULLYAN, Raymond.
FOREVER UNDECIDED: A PUZZLE GUIDE TO GÖDEL. Knopf. Through a fairy-tale-like allegory of logic, the author attempts to explain Gödel's two great theorems on incompleteness and undecidability and some of their mathematical and philosophical implications.

SMUTS, Barbara, et al., eds.
PRIMATE SOCIETIES. U. of Chicago P., 1987.

SNOW, C.P.
THE TWO CULTURES: AND A SECOND LOOK. 2nd ed. Cambridge U.P., 1965. A classic presentation of the dangers of a split between scientific and non-scientific cultures, by a member in good standing of both.

SNYDER, S.H.
DRUGS AND THE BRAIN: A SCIENTIFIC AMERICAN BOOK. Freeman, 1987. Knowledge of how different drugs affect the brain is explored by a psychopharmacological research scientist. The development of therapeutic drugs for treating mental disturbances and our understanding of the brain are among topics discussed.

✪SO, Miriam L.
THE BIBLE AND BIOLOGY. 5 vols. Heavenly People Depot, 1988. Order direct: Heavenly Peo;le Depot, P.O. Box 95421, Hong Kong. Collections of easy-to-read articles written in Chinese which focus on the plant and animal kingdoms, genetics, and psychology, and which show the wisdom and the power of the Creator. Some articles require no background, while others are a bit technical. Material is not scientifically or theologically controversial and would be acceptable to the Chinese Christian community. Author comments on human practices, preferring, for example, natural (God-made) to artificial (man-made) things. Volumes lack adequate references and unifying themes.

✪SOKOLOWSKI, Robert.
THE GOD OF FAITH AND REASON. U. of Notre Dame P., 1985. A short, clear presentation of how to gain an intellectual apprehension of deity through philosophical reflection. Unifying discussion of faith and reason is excellent.

✪SOSKICE, Janet M.
METAPHOR AND RELIGIOUS LANGUAGE. Oxford U.P., 1987. An excellent introduction to the concept of metaphors emphasizing the creative and realistic role that models and metaphors play in both theistic theology and natural science.

SPANNER, Douglas C.
BIBLICAL CREATION & THE THEORY OF EVOLUTION. Paternoster (UK)/Attic Press. The author addresses fellow-scientists and clergy about the God-giveness of both scripture and science, and how they can be reconciled. While the book is readable by laypeople, the appendices are devoted to a number of specialized topics for both scientists and theologians. (S-89)

SPERRY, Roger.
SCIENCE AND MORAL PRIORITY: MERGING MIND, BRAIN, AND HUMAN VALUES. Praeger, 1984. A study by a leader in brain research integrating the discoveries in science with ethical values.

SPIELBERG, Nathan, and ANDERSON, Bryon D.
SEVEN IDEAS THAT SHOOK THE UNIVERSE. Wiley, 1987.

✪SQUIRES, Euan J.
THE MYSTERY OF THE QUANTUM WORLD. Adam Hilger Ltd (UK), 1986. An examination of quantum physics and how it challenges our understanding of reality.

✪SQUIRES, Euan J.
TO ACKNOWLEDGE THE WONDER: THE STORY OF FUNDAMENTAL PHYSICS. Adam Hilger Ltd. (UK), 1985. A description of the story of fundamental physics, including recent developments and the latest theories of the nature of space, time, and matter.

✪STAFFORD, Tim.
THE SEXUAL CHRISTIAN. Scripture Press, 1989. A focus on Christian sexuality. Topics include marriage, singleness, homosexuality.

STAFLEU, Marinus D.
THEORIES AT WORK: ON THE STRUCTURE AND FUNCTIONING OF THEORIES IN SCIENCE, IN PARTICULAR DURING THE COPERNICAN REVOLUTION (Christian Studies Today). U. P. of America, 1987.

STANESBY, Derek.
SCIENCE, REASON & RELIGION. Routledge, Chapman & Hall, 1989. A distinguished theologian and physicist presents strong arguments that rationality is essential to both science and theology, indeed to all human thought. A very helpful and significant book.

✪STANNARD, Russell.
GROUNDS FOR REASONABLE BELIEF (Frontiers of Knowledge Ser.: No. 12). Scot. Acad. P./Gower Pub., 1989. Noted physicist compares grounds for believing in God with grounds for other more universally held beliefs. Theology, psychology, socio-biology and philosophy are included in this discussion.

✪STANNARD, Russell.
SCIENCE AND THE RENEWAL OF BELIEF. SCM Press. A British physicist who is a conservative Christian examines biblical revelation in light of modern science, proposing serious attention to new trends in Christian theology and providing interesting historical perspective on the Science/Christian Faith relationship.

✪STEPHENSON, B.
KEPLER'S PHYSICAL ASTRONOMY. Springer-Verlag, 1987. A critical examination of Kepler's

Astronomia nova, a record of his ten year study on pre-Newtonian astronomy.

✪STEPHENSON, G., and KILMISTER, C.W.
SPECIAL RELATIVITY FOR PHYSICISTS. Dover Pub., 1987. A concise account for nonspecialists which examines topics such as Lorentz transformation, optical and dynamical applications, applications to modern physics.

STOKES, William L.
THE GENESIS ANSWER: A SCIENTIST'S TESTAMENT FOR DIVINE CREATION. Prentice-Hall, 1984. An interesting attempt to harmonize the Genesis account with the "facts" of modern science. Assumes the days of Genesis have a celestial and not terrestrial meaning.

✪STROMBECK, Donald R.
THE REASON FOR SCIENCE. Stonegate Pub., 1987. A documentation of scientists' real achievements and what is genuinely new in science.

✪SUGIMOTO, Kenji (trans. Barbara Harshav)
ALBERT EINSTEIN: A PHOTOGRAPHIC BIOGRAPHY. Schocken, 1989. More than 400 photographs, documents and drawings accompany a text chronicling the life of Einstein.

SWARTLEY, Willard M.
SLAVERY, SABBATH, WAR AND WOMEN: CASE STUDIES IN BIBLICAL INTERPRETATION. Herald Press, 1983. A highly detailed examination of the arguments and the principles of interpretation behind the arguments of opposing viewpoints on these four issues. (M-86)

✪SWERDLOW, N.M., and NEUGEBAUER, O.
MATHEMATICAL ASTRONOMY IN COPERNICUS' *DE REVOLUTIONIBUS.* 2 vols. Springer-Verlag, 1984. A monumental analysis of Copernicus.

TEILHARD DE CHARDIN, Pierre.
CHRISTIANITY AND EVOLUTION. Harcourt, Brace, Jovanovich, 1974. A collection of Teilhard de Chardin's essays on important aspects of the relationship between evolutionary thought and Christian concepts.

TEILHARD DE CHARDIN, Pierre.
THE PHENOMENON OF MAN. Harper & Row, 1959. A classic work of Teilhard de Chardin.

✪TEMPLETON, John M., and HERRMANN, Robert L.
THE GOD WHO WOULD BE KNOWN: REVELATIONS OF THE DIVINE IN CONTEMPORARY SCIENCE. Harper & Row, 1989. The new science and its enlargement of our view of God. (D-90)

✛THAXTON, Charles B.; BRADLEY, Walter L.; and OLSEN, Roger L.
MYSTERY OF LIFE'S ORIGIN: REASSESSING CURRENT THEORIES. Philosophical Library, 1984. A valuable summary of the evidence against chemical evolution of life out of non-living matter and a clearly written analysis of the alternatives to the accepted scientific theory of the origin of life. (J-85)

THOMPSON, A.
BIOLOGY, ZOOLOGY & GENETICS: EVOLUTION MODEL VS. CREATION MODEL. U.P. of America, 1983. An evolutionist presents creationist views as compared to evolutionary concepts. Intended as a textbook so that students will know both sides. Comprehensive and introductory.

THOMPSON, John, ed.
THEOLOGY BEYOND CHRISTENDOM: ESSAYS ON THE CENTENARY OF THE BIRTH OF KARL BARTH. (Princeton Theological Monograph Ser.: No. 6). Pickwick Pub., 1986. A set of very important essays relating Karl Barth's theology to current problems including: "Karl Barth's Understanding of Science" (Harold Nebelsick), "Barth & a New Direction for Natural Theology" (R.S. Anderson), "Barth & the Western Intellectual Tradition" (C. Gunton), and "The Abiding Significance of Karl Barth" (G.W. Bromiley).

THOMSON, Alexander.
TRADITION AND AUTHORITY IN SCIENCE AND THEOLOGY (Frontiers of Knowledge Ser.: No.4). Scot. Acad. P./Gower Pub., 1987. Making considerable use of Polanyi's distinction between subsidiary and focal awareness, implicit and explicit thought, the author explores the nature of understanding, authority, and interpretation in the Church. Similarities are noted between science and religion in that both are committed to the authority of truth within their respective frameworks of knowledge and institutions. (M-89)

✛THURMAN, L. Duane.
HOW TO THINK ABOUT EVOLUTION, AND OTHER BIBLE-SCIENCE CONTROVERSIES.

2nd ed. InterVarsity Press, 1978. Suggested methods for students to use in evaluating scientific ideas and theories. (D-79)

TILLICH, Paul.
DYNAMICS OF FAITH. Harper & Row, 1957. A basic discussion of what faith *is* and *is not*.

✪TOOMER, G.J.
PTOLEMY'S ALMAGEST. Springer-Verlag, 1984. A translation of a classic scientific work by one of the most influential early astronomers.

+TORRANCE, Thomas F., ed.
BELIEF IN SCIENCE AND IN CHRISTIAN LIFE: THE RELEVANCE OF MICHAEL POLANYI'S THOUGHT FOR CHRISTIAN FAITH AND LIFE. Scot. Acad. P./Gower Pub., 1980. Christian thinkers discuss the epistemology of Michael Polanyi. Torrance's "Notes on Terms and Concepts" (in Polanyi's works) are a valuable aid for readers of Polanyi's works. (D-81)

+TORRANCE, Thomas F.
THE CHRISTIAN FRAME OF MIND: REASON, ORDER, AND OPENNESS IN THEOLOGY AND NATURAL SCIENCE. Helmers & Howard, 1989. Distinctive contributions of the Christian mind to human life and thought, especially as it applies to the world of modern science today. Chapter headings: The Greek Christian Mind; The Concept of Order in Theology and Science; Man, Mediator of Order; The University within a Christian Culture.

+TORRANCE, Thomas F.
CHRISTIAN THEOLOGY AND SCIENTIFIC CULTURE. Oxford U.P., 1981. A very significant work that in the words of its author "is concerned rather with the deep mutual relation and respect of Christian and scientific thought for each other...but also warns against the dangers of a reactionary retreat from the rigours of scientific thought into fuzzy mythological interpretations of the incarnation, and calls for a deeper appreciation of the Nicene creed upon which all Christendom rests."

+TORRANCE, Thomas F.
GROUND AND GRAMMAR OF THEOLOGY. U.P. of Virginia, 1980. An important contribution in this transitional period when science and theology are coming to recognize each other as partners in their common exploration of the meaning and structure of the universe. (M-83)

✪+TORRANCE, Thomas, F.
KARL BARTH: BIBLICAL AND EVANGELICAL THEOLOGIAN. T & T Clark, 1990. Order direct: Books International, P.O. Box 6096, McLean, VA 22106. A major study of a theologian dedicated to the renewal of Christian theology in light of God's unique self-revelation in Jesus Christ. Barth is shown as a "theological Einstein" who is able to dispel obsolete forms of thought.

+TORRANCE, Thomas F.
THE MEDIATION OF CHRIST. Bks. Demand UMI (Reprint of 1984 Eerdmans ed.). A wholistic perspective on the pivotal role that Christ plays as the mediator between God and man; revelation, reconciliation, sin and atonement, and vicarious suffering all being involved. At appropriate points, insights drawn from good scientific method and science are used to shed light on theological method and concepts. (S-86)

+TORRANCE, Thomas F.
REALITY AND EVANGELICAL THEOLOGY. Westminster, 1982. The author is one of few evangelical theologians who really understands the creative and open-ended nature of all good science. He has seriously grappled with the work of Polanyi, Einstein, Bohr, and Prigogine in integrating the perspectives of Christian theology and natural science meaningfully. This book explores how questions basic to both theology and natural science can inform biblical and theolgical interpretation; it offers a vital statement on the nature of Christian revelation.

+TORRANCE, Thomas F.
REALITY AND SCIENTIFIC THEOLOGY (Frontiers of Knowledge Ser.: No.1). Scot. Acad. Press, 1985. An argument for a rigorous scientific theology under the double constraint of God and the reality of the world of space and time. The author contends that there is a mutual relation between intense intellectual communion with God and a dynamic understanding of the world disclosed through the natural sciences.

+TORRANCE, Thomas F.
SPACE, TIME AND INCARNATION. Oxford U.P., 1969. A provocative study of the meaning of the Incarnation in its relationship with our space-time reality.

+TORRANCE, Thomas F.
THEOLOGICAL SCIENCE. Oxford U.P., 1969. (J-82)

✣TORRANCE, Thomas, F.
TRANSFORMATION AND CONVERGENCE IN THE FRAME OF KNOWLEDGE: EXPLORA-TION IN THE INTERRELATIONS OF SCIENTIFIC & THEOLOGICAL ENTERPRISE. Bks. Demand UMI (Reprint of 1984 Eerdmans ed.). A major collection of important articles of Torrance (many not readily available in the USA), all dealing with explorations in the interrela-tions of scientific and theological enterprize. Some essays are difficult reading but all show integrative thinking with respect to Christian theology and natural science at its best. (S-86)

✪TOURNIER, Paul
A LISTENING EAR: REFLECTIONS ON CHRISTIAN CARING. Augsburg, 1986. A personal account of the events which shaped the author's life. (J-90)

TREFIL, James S.
FROM ATOMS TO QUARKS: THE STRANGE WORLD OF PARTICLE PHYSICS. Scribner, 1982. A popular survey of the way in which our knowledge of the basic structure of matter has developed.

TREFIL, James S.
MEDITATIONS AT SUNSET: A SCIENTIST LOOKS AT THE SKY. Scribner, 1987.

✪TREFIL, James S.
READING THE MIND OF GOD: IN SEARCH OF THE PRINCIPLE OF UNIVERSALITY. Scribner, 1989.

TREFIL, James S.
A SCIENTIST AT THE SEASHORE. Macmillan, 1987. A physicist explains many of the questions involved in a trip to the seashore in an accessible manner for the lay reader: Why is the ocean salty? Why do bubbles form on the water surface? How do waves form?

✪UHLIG, Herbert H.
LIFE, SCIENCE AND RELIGIOUS CONCERNS: THEIR INTERRELATIONS AND LIFE'S MEANING. Academy Bks., 1988. With the premise that the nature and meaning of life is the most important unresolved issue of the present scientific era, the author shows that the truths attributed to science can be reconciled to the established truths of religion, and that living matter differs profoundly from non-living matter.

UNSOLD, A., and BASCHEK, R.B.
THE NEW COSMOS. 3rd ed. Springer-Verlag, 1985. An introduction to astrophysics.

VAN DEN AARDWEG, Gerard J.
ON THE ORIGINS AND TREATMENT OF HOMOSEXUALITY: A PSYCHOANALYTIC REIN-TERPRETATION. Praeger, 1985.

✪VAN HUYSSTEEN, Wentzel.
THEOLOGY AND THE JUSTIFICATION OF FAITH: CONSTRUCTING THEORIES IN SYS-TEMATIC THEOLOGY. Eerdmans, 1989. Award-winning book by theologian presents a strong case for the validity of the claims of theological truth.

✪VAN LEEUWEN, Mary Stewart.
GENDER AND GRACE: LOVE, WORK AND PARENTING IN A CHANGING WORLD. Inter-Varsity Press, 1990. A provocative analysis of the influences of nature, nurture, and faith in shaping the lives and roles of men and women.

✣VAN LEEUWEN, Mary Stewart (ed. Carl F. Henry).
THE PERSON IN PSYCHOLOGY: A CONTEMPORARY CHRISTIAN APPRAISAL. Eerdmans, 1985. An ingenious effort to penetrate critical problems inherent in contemporary psychology from a Christian standpoint. The author creatively demonstrates challenging means of molding a new psychology of great promise for the Christian community. (S-87)

✣VAN TILL, Howard J.
THE FOURTH DAY: WHAT THE BIBLE AND THE HEAVENS ARE TELLING US ABOUT THE CREATION. Eerdmans, 1986. The author argues that both science and theology, undertaken in rigorous fashion, are valid tools for understanding creation and evolution in the universe. He discusses biblical creation and the various processes discerned by science in the formation of the universe in relation to each other. (S-86)

✪✣VAN TILL, Howard J. et al.
PORTRAITS OF CREATION: BIBLICAL AND SCIENTIFIC PERSPECTIVES ON THE WORLD'S FORMATION. Eerdmans, 1990. Recognizing that many persons today view the relationship of natural science and Christian belief as falling short of the mutual respect and harmony that ought to prevail, this interdisciplinary work examines both the historical roots and the present manifestations of the perceived tension, and critiques several of the misperceptions

that encourage an adversarial approach. (J-91)

✪✛VAN TILL, Howard J.; YOUNG, Davis A.; and MENNINGA, Clarence.
SCIENCE HELD HOSTAGE: WHAT'S WRONG WITH CREATION SCIENCE AND EVOLU-
TIONISM. InterVarsity Press, 1988. A critique of creation science and evolutionism, showing
how advocates of both have abused scientific evidence while ignoring alternative explanations.
(J-89)

VARGHESE, Roy A.,ed.
THE INTELLECTUALS SPEAK OUT ABOUT GOD. Regnery Gateway, 1984. Includes writings
of five scientists including Sir John Eccles, Robert Jastrow and Stanley Jaki. Bernard Lonergan
and four other philosophers contribute to this work in addition to Peter Kreeft, Josh McDowell
and Sheldon Vanauken.

VERMEIJ, Geerat J.
EVOLUTION AND ESCALATION: AN ECOLOGICAL HISTORY OF LIFE. Princeton U.P., 1987.

✪VERSCHUUR, Gerrit L.
INTERSTELLAR MATTERS. Springer-Verlag, 1989. A true scientific detective story about the
discovery and acceptance of interstellar matter, from the early work of Edward Barnard to the
recent detection of complex organic molecules amid the galaxies.

VERSCHUUR, Gerrit L.
THE INVISIBLE UNIVERSE REVEALED. Springer-Verlag, 1986. A non-technical up-to-date
report on modern radio astronomy by a capable radio astronomer and writer.

VICKERS, Brian, ed.
ENGLISH SCIENCE: BACON TO NEWTON (Cambridge English Prose Texts). Cambridge
U.P., 1987.

✛VITZ, Paul C.
CENSORSHIP: EVIDENCE OF BIAS IN OUR CHILDREN'S TEXTBOOKS. Servant Pub., 1986.
Results of a two-year study of textbooks used in public school education as to bias and
censorship. Findings of the author reveal the systematic censorship of religion, family values,
and certain political and economic positions from children's textbooks.

✛VITZ, Paul C.
PSYCHOLOGY AS RELIGION: THE CULT OF SELF-WORSHIP. Eerdmans, 1977. The thesis
of the title is well documented and some viable Christian alternatives are proposed. Praised by
Karl Menninger, Paul Tournier and Andrew Greely. (S-81)

✛VITZ, Paul C.
SIGMUND FREUD'S CHRISTIAN UNCONSCIOUS. Guilford Press, 1988. Illustrated biography
focusing on the influence of Freud on Christian culture. The author reconstructs how, through
the Christian mileu of Freud's childhood, Christianity came to form a bedrock of his psyche and
his theory of psychoanalysis. As a major work of Freudian revision, this book raises many
controversial questions usually ignored by Freud biographers. (J-90)

✛VITZ, Paul C., and GLIMCHER, Arnold B.
MODERN ART AND MODERN SCIENCE: A PARALLEL ANALYSIS OF VISION. Praeger,
1983. Thesis is that modern art and modern science have influenced one another and that this
in turn has influenced Christian thought. The book has an interesting discussion of randomness
in art.

VOEGELIN, Eric.
SCIENCE, POLITICS AND GNOSTICISM. Regnery Gateway. Modern intellectual and political
movements are shown to be the culmination of present-day gnosticism; e.g., Marxism, progres-
sivism.

VON RAD, Gerhard (trans. James D. Martin)
WISDOM IN ISRAEL. rev. ed. Abingdon, 1973. A treatment of the important wisdom literature
of the Bible by a major Old Testament scholar.

✪VYUYAN, John.
IN PITY AND IN ANGER: A STUDY OF THE USE OF ANIMALS IN SCIENCE. Micah Pub.,
1988. An account of the emergence of the antivivisection movement in Europe in the nineteenth
century. Author opposes all animal experimentation. (S-89)

WADE, Nicholas.
A WORLD BEYOND HEALING: THE PROLOGUE AND AFTERMATH OF NUCLEAR WAR.
Norton, 1987. A precise account of nuclear war is presented, including how it might start,
weaponry, and effects on people, cities and the environment. Chances of economic and ecologic

recovery are discussed in ways that try to avoid both understatement and exaggeration using present scientific knowledge.

WALDROP, M. Mitchell.
MAN-MADE MINDS: THE PROMISE OF ARTIFICIAL INTELLIGENCE. Walker, 1987. Discusses the developments and progress in artificial intelligence since it became a separate discipline about thirty years ago. Upheavals since the commercial applications boom in 1980, the future of artificial intelligence and intelligent machines, and artificial intelligence's affect on society are explored.

WALLACH, Michael A., and WALLACH, Lise.
PSYCHOLOGY'S SANCTION FOR SELFISHNESS: THE ERROR OF EGOISM IN THEORY & THERAPY. Freeman, 1983.

WALTER, J.A.
NEED: THE NEW RELIGION. InterVarsity Press, 1986. A witty, broad-ranging and provocative discussion. Published in England under the title Love Is All You Need. (M-87)

WANG, Hao.
REFLECTIONS ON KURT GÖDEL. MIT Press, 1987.

✪WARNER, R. Stephen.
NEW WINE IN OLD WINESKINS: EVANGELICALS AND LIBERALS IN A SMALL-TOWN CHURCH. U. of Calif. P., 1988. A thorough analysis of a quarter century of relationships between the evangelical and liberal members of The Presbyterian Church of Mendocino, California. Includes attention to church growth and decline, internal conflict, linkage with the national Protestant scene, and many other topics. An excellent resource for the study of American religion in general.

WEINBERG, Steven.
THE FIRST THREE MINUTES: A MODERN VIEW OF THE ORIGIN OF THE UNIVERSE. Basic Bks., 1988. A clear presentation of what science can tell us about the first three minutes of the universe. (Written before particle theories associated with Weinberg's name were applied to cosmology.) Includes a mathematical appendix. (D-89)

✪WEINER, J.S.
THE PILTDOWN FORGERY. Dover Pub., 1981. Classic analysis of century's greatest scientific fraud by member of scientific team that broke the case.

WEIR, David.
THE BHOPAL SYNDROME: PESTICIDES, ENVIRONMENT AND HEALTH. Sierra Club Bks., 1987. A writer for the Center for Investigative Reporting looks at the global proportions of pesticide manufacture, use, and the problems associated with it. Reports on the conditions of pesticide plants around the world are accompanied by possible solutions and reforms suggested by the author.

✪WEISSKOPF, Victor F.
THE PRIVILEGE OF BEING A PHYSICIST. Freeman, 1988. Sixteen essays about the life and work of a theoretical physicist who has devoted himself to the pursuit of intellectual and ethical integrity in science. Includes many anecdotes from the author's life, beginning in the 1920s with scientists such as Bohr and Heisenberg.

WENNBERG, Robert N.
LIFE IN THE BALANCE: EXPLORING THE ABORTION CONTROVERSY. Eerdmans, 1985.

✪WHEELER, John A.
A JOURNEY INTO GRAVITY AND SPACETIME. Scientific American Library, 1990. Extremely well written book with many suggestive references to God.

WHITCOMB, John C., Jr., and MORRIS, Henry M.
THE GENESIS FLOOD. Baker. The "classic" defense of a young earth which started the present creation/evolution controversy.

WHITE, John.
PUTTING THE SOUL BACK IN PSYCHOLOGY. InterVarsity Press, 1987. Critical of contemporary psychology, the author believes the church should seek to provide emotional, physical, and spiritual health to the needy.

WHITEHEAD, Alfred N.
SCIENCE AND THE MODERN WORLD. Free Press, 1967. A discussion of the development of physical science through relativity and quantum theory, with an attempt at a process philosophy synthesis. Serious reading, though not scientifically difficult.

⊘WHITROW, G.J., ed.
EINSTEIN: THE MAN AND HIS ACHIEVEMENT. Dover Pub., 1973. An excellent analysis of Einstein's life, from his childhood to his search for the "united field theory."

⊘WHITTAKER, Edmund T.
A HISTORY OF THE THEORIES OF AETHER AND ELECTRICITY. Dover Pub. An unabridged republication of a rare, hard-to-find classic. Two volumes bound as one. Vol. I: The Classical Theories; Vol. II: The Modern Theories, 1900-1926.

WICKEN, Jeffrey S.
EVOLUTION, THERMODYNAMICS AND INFORMATION: EXTENDING THE DARWINIAN PROGRAM. Oxford U.P., 1987.

⊘WILLIAMS, Redford.
THE TRUSTING HEART: GREAT NEWS ABOUT TYPE A BEHAVIOR. Times Bks., 1989. New research on Type A behavior that offers specific strategies for self-help in the areas of behavior modification, religion, and medicine.

WINFREE, Arthur T.
WHEN TIME BREAKS DOWN: THE THREE-DIMENSIONAL DYNAMICS OF ELECTRO-CHEMICAL WAVES & CARDIAC ARRHYTHMIAS. Princeton U.P., 1987. A very readable introduction to the field of chaos. The author, a physiologist, investigates the breakdown of biological timekeeping and rhythms, and the timelessness involved in the resulting chaos.

+WONDERLY, Daniel E.
GOD'S TIME-RECORDS IN ANCIENT SEDIMENTS: EVIDENCES OF LONG TIME SPANS IN EARTH'S HISTORY. Crystal Press, 1977. Order direct: Interdisciplinary Biblical Research Institute, P.O. Box 423, Hatfield, PA 19440. Designed to help Christians understand the origin and nature of the thick sedimentary rock layers of the earth. Cites and explains examples of the natural, slow formation of limestone, and biologically-formed structures in rock formations, in contrast to "flood geology" theory. First chapters of Genesis are accepted as basically literal, but long geologic periods are defended. Issues of evolutionary theory not discussed.

+WONDERLY, Daniel E.
NEGLECT OF GEOLOGIC DATA: SEDIMENTARY STRATA COMPARED WITH YOUNG-EARTH CREATIONIST WRITINGS. Interdisciplinary Biblical Research Institute, 1987. Order direct: IBRI, P.O. Box 423, Hatfield, PA 19440. Not only points out errors of young-earth studies in sedimentary strata, but gives solid evidence for long periods of time. More scientifically oriented than his previous book *God's Time-Records in Earth's History.*

⊘WORTHINGTON, Everett L., Jr.
MARRIAGE COUNSELING: A CHRISTIAN APPROACH TO COUNSELING COUPLES. Inter-Varsity Press, 1989. An integrated, biblically based theory of marriage and marriage therapy with analysis at three levels: the individual, the couple, and the family. Specific techniques are offered for enhancing cooperative change, intimacy, communication, conflict resolution and forgiveness with the marriage.

⊘+WRIGHT, Richard T.
BIOLOGY THROUGH THE EYES OF FAITH. Harper & Row, 1989. The purpose of this book is to help those interested in the life sciences to develop a biblical world view by exploring the issues raised when biology is examined in a context of Christian faith and thought. Major issues covered are: how God interacts with his created order; reconciling creation, evolution, and early Genesis; the biomedical and genetic revolutions; and environmental stewardship. (J-91)

⊘WUTHNOW, Robert.
MEANING AND MORAL ORDER: EXPLORATIONS IN CULTURAL ANALYSIS. U. of Calif. P. 1987. An examination of four prominent levels of cultural analysis in the social sciences—subjective, structural, dramaturgic, and institutional. The author concludes that the concepts of meaning and moral order that have legacies in nineteenth century classical theories still require careful consideration, for the issues related to them are central to society and to the world's religions.

+YAMAUCHI, Edwin M.
HARPER'S WORLD OF THE NEW TESTAMENT. Harper & Row, 1981. Informs readers of the cultural setting and background for the New Testament, focusing on Jewish religious and historical background, Greek and Near Eastern intellectual culture, and on the Roman Empire. Numerous illustrations. (M-85)

+YOUNG, Davis A.,
CHRISTIANITY & THE AGE OF THE EARTH. Zondervan, 1982. A geology professor states

that present scientific arguments for a young earth are not valid. Highly recommended. (J-83)

❂YOURGRAU, Wolfgang, and MANDELSTAM, Stanley.
VARIATIONAL PRINCIPLES IN DYNAMICS AND QUANTUM THEORY. Dover Pub., 1979. Historical and theoretical survey of variational principles and their relationship to dynamics and quantum theory.

YOXEN, Edward.
THE GENE BUSINESS: WHO SHOULD CONTROL BIOTECHNOLOGY? Oxford U.P., 1986. Reviews the history of biochemical research and its concomitant ethical concerns. Examines the politics and social ramifications involved, and the question of control of research. Prospects for the future are touched upon. (D-85)

YU, Carver.
BEING AND RELATION: AN EASTERN CRITIQUE OF WESTERN DUALISM (Frontiers of Knowledge Ser.: No. 8). Scot. Acad. P./Gower Pub., 1987. Philosopher and theologian examines dualism as a fundamental concept in Western philosophy from the perspective of the Eastern tradition. Using modern philosophers MacMurray, Husserl, and Heidegger as pointers, Yu describes the current spiritual predicament of the West as it plays a decisive role affecting socio-cultural transformations of Asia and Africa.

❂ZEE, A. (ed. Elisa Petrini).
AN OLD MAN'S TOY: GRAVITY AT WORK AND PLAY IN EINSTEIN'S UNIVERSE. Macmillan, 1990. A witty examination of the conception of the universe that followed from Einstein's insight into gravity and how it is still confounding modern physics.

❂ZEH, Heinz D.
THE PHYSICAL BASIS OF THE DIRECTION OF TIME. Springer-Verlag, 1989. An investigation into the different ways in which this asymmetry of nature shows up in the various fields of physics, such as radiation and thermodynamics.

ZIMAN, J.
AN INTRODUCTION TO SCIENCE STUDIES: THE PHILOSOPHICAL AND SOCIAL ASPECTS OF SCIENCE & TECHNOLOGY. Cambridge U.P., 1987.

Watch for These New Books...

FENNEMA, Jan, and PAUL, Iain, eds.
SCIENCE AND RELIGION: ONE WORLD—CHANGING PERSPECTIVES ON REALITY. Kluwer Acad. Pub., date not set. Papers presented at the second European Conference on Science and Religion, March, 1988, by contributors such as T.F. Torrance *(Fundamental Issues in Theology and Science)*, A. Gierer *(Physics, Life and Mind)*, W.B. Drees *(Theology and Cosmology Beyond the Big Bang Theory)*, and J. Hüber *(Science and Religion Coming Across)*.

MACKAY, Donald M.
BEHIND THE EYE. Edited by Valerie MacKay. Basil Blackwell, Ltd. Based on MacKay's Gifford Lectures. A discussion of the brain, its nature and relation to the functioning individual — and the implications of such understanding for our view of human nature, the meaning of freedom and moral responsibility, the knowledge of God, and Christian belief in particular.

JOHN TEMPLETON Foundation.
WHO'S WHO IN THEOLOGY AND SCIENCE: 1991 EDITION. Winthrop Pub. Co., due fall, 1991. A comprehensive international guide for those actively engaged in the ongoing dialogue between science and theology. Major books and essays are listed for each individual, and a cross-referencing system facilitates identifying individuals actively involved in specific areas in the field. For more information call Winthrop Publishing Company at (800)562-8283.

NEBELSICK, Harold P.
THE RENAISSANCE, THE REFORMATION AND THE RISE OF SCIENCE. Scot. Acad. Press. A masterful reflection on the historical development of science in a mutual modification with Judeo-Christian theology, written from the interpretative framework of a leading Barth scholar.

PRIEBE, Duane A.
THE GENESIS OF THE UNIVERSE: THE CULTURAL MATRIX OF CHRISTIAN VISIONS OF CREATION. Augsburg, 1991. An exploration of ideas about the world's origin in other religions, the variety of biblical pictures of creation, different interpretations of Genesis in Christian history, and scientific cosmology. Offers suggestions about how to think about creation in this context.

OUT OF PRINT BOOKS

The following books are worthy of your consideration, but are now unfortunately listed as "out of print." We hope that you will take the time to search for them in your local library or used bookstore.

(Note: these books have been verified as out of print as of the 1989-90 edition of *Books in Print*. This means that the publisher is no longer printing new copies of the book in question. Some books may be back in print since this edition was printed. Unfortunately, publishers bring books in and out of print so quickly that it is almost impossible to keep track of them all. If you suspect a book on this list may be in print, or has gone out of print only within the last year, check in your local bookstore for copies still on the shelf.)

These books are also included in the Categorical Listing of Books (marked with an asterisk) starting on page 63.

ALEXANDER, Denis.
BEYOND SCIENCE. Holman, 1972. Shows bankruptcy of scientism and humanism and then presents the Christian option. (D-73)

ALLEN, David F. and Victoria.
ETHICAL ISSUES IN MENTAL RETARDATION: TRAGIC CHOICES/LIVING HOPE. Abingdon, 1979. A sensitive discussion of concerns for the mentally retarded by a Christian psychologist with broad training in medical ethics and his journalist wife.

OALLEN, David F.; BIRD, Lewis P.; and HERRMANN, Robert L.
WHOLE PERSON MEDICINE: AN INTERNATIONAL SYMPOSIUM. InterVarsity Press, 1980. Twelve essays on education for whole person medicine.

ANDERSON, J. Kerby.
GENETIC ENGINEERING: THE ETHICAL ISSUES. Zondervan, 1982. Deals with artificial reproduction and genetic manipulation. Subjects are evaluated from scientific, legal, ethical and theological stances.

ANDERSON, J. Kerby, and GUFFIN, Harold G.
FOSSILS IN FOCUS. Zondervan, 1977. Very interesting analysis of the gaps and patterns of the fossil record supporting a progressive creationist perspective.

ANDERSON, Norman.
ISSUES OF LIFE & DEATH: ABORTION, EUTHANASIA, GENETIC ENGINEERING, BIRTH CONTROL. InterVarsity Press, 1976. A survey of a number of controversial issues, taking a balanced and moderate stance. Based on five lectures, the London Lectures in Contemporary Christianity, given in 1975. (M-78)

+BARCLAY, Oliver R.
THE INTELLECT AND BEYOND: DEVELOPING A CHRISTIAN MIND rev. ed. Zondervan, 1985. Excellent in presenting a description of the Christian mind and how it relates to everyday matters such as work and culture. (M-87)

BENZ, Ernst.
EVOLUTION AND CHRISTIAN HOPE. Doubleday, 1966. A critical yet positive study of Christian understanding of evolution.

+BERGMAN, Jerry.
THE CRITERION: RELIGIOUS DISCRIMINATION IN AMERICA. Onesimus Press, 1984. Documents over 40 cases of religious discrimination in Europe and America.

BIRCH, C., and COBB, John.
THE LIBERATION OF LIFE. Cambridge U.P., 1981. An integration of evolution and process theology. John Cobb is a leading advocate of process theology, which is perhaps the leading challenge to evangelical theology today.

BROWNE, S.G.; DAVEY, F.; and THOMSON, W.A.R., eds.
HERALDS OF HEALTH: THE SAGA OF CHRISTIAN MEDICAL INITIATIVES. Christian Medical Fellowship (UK), 1985. A remarkable record of devoted service to the Third World by men and women whose Christian faith contributed to the progress of public health and benefitted medical science. (D-87)

+BUBE, Richard H.
SCIENCE AND THE WHOLE PERSON: A PERSONAL INTEGRATION OF SCIENTIFIC AND BIBLICAL PERSPECTIVES. American Scientific Affiliation, 1985. An attempt to integrate a total scientific and biblical perspective across the whole range of issues and concerns that characterize active life in both Christian and scientific communities. This book seeks to present a single perspective adequate to the task of dealing with a whole range of particular issues.

+BUBE, Richard H.
THE ENCOUNTER BETWEEN CHRISTIANITY & SCIENCE. Eerdmans, 1968.

+BUBE, Richard H.
THE HUMAN QUEST: A NEW LOOK AT SCIENCE & CHRISTIAN FAITH. Word, 1971.

+BURKE, Thomas, ed.
MAN AND MIND. Hillsdale College Press, 1987. Six authors contribute to this book of readings and present ideas on Christian faith as related to personality theory. (M-88)

CALLAHAN, D.
ABORTION: LAW, CHOICE AND MORALITY. Macmillan, 1970.

+CANTORE, Enrico.
SCIENTIFIC MAN: THE HUMANIST SIGNIFICANCE OF SCIENCE. Institute of Scientific Humanism Pub., 1977. [May still be able to order direct: World Institute for Scientific Humanism, 113 West 60th St., NY, NY 10023, (212) 841-5519.] The author, a Jesuit philosopher of science, affirms the conviction that true science always points beyond itself to a transcendent dimension of human experience which is ultimately religious. Science is thus seen to affirm true human dignity defined in a realist context as openness to the richness of all human experience including the religious dimension.

CLIFT, W.B.
JUNG AND CHRISTIANITY. Crossroad NY, 1986.

CLOUSE, Robert G., ed.
WEALTH & POVERTY: FOUR CHRISTIAN VIEWS OF ECONOMICS. InterVarsity Press, 1984. Gary North for free-market capitalism, William Diehl for the guided-market system, Art Gish for decentralist economics, and John Gladwin for centralist economics. (J-85)

COHEN, B.D.
HARD CHOICES: MIXED BLESSINGS OF MODERN TECHNOLOGY. Putnam, 1986. A general examination of the major ethical, legal and financial dilemmas arising from the applications of modern medical technology. Case histories of patients from a wide range of backgrounds and conditions are offered for consideration.

+COLLINS, Gary R., ed.
OUR SOCIETY IN TURMOIL. Creation House, 1970. A collection of essays (including Russell Heddendorf on crime and civil disobedience) discuss major social problems of the day and encourage Christians to become involved. (M-72)

DARVILL, Timothy.
PREHISTORIC BRITAIN. Yale U.P., 1987. Archaelogical evidence and photographs combine to examine the development of human societies in Britain from the prehistoric period to the Roman conquest.

DAVIES, Paul.
THE ACCIDENTAL UNIVERSE. Cambridge U.P., 1982. A semi-popular treatment of physical cosmology, culminating in the anthropic principle.

DAVIES, Paul.
OTHER WORLDS. Touchstone, 1982. The anthropic principle that "the parameters of earth are precisely suited to human life" is addressed.

DE JONG, Norman, ed.
CHRISTIAN APPROACHES TO LEARNING THEORY. Vol. 1 & 2. U.P. of America, 1985 (Vol.1), 1986 (Vol. 2). A very valuable collection of essays by Christian educators on Christian perspectives with respect to learning theory. There are important theoretical and practical insights therein. The result of the first two annual conferences on Christian approaches to

of Churches.
NEERING: SOCIAL AND ETHICAL CONSEQUENCES. Prepared by the Panel
ncerns of the NCC, 1984. Comprehensive.

BIBLICAL PERSPECTIVE FOR BIOETHICS. Fortress, 1984. A comprehens-
erstanding of human life in all its dimensions—biological, psychological and
ritten, with deep biblical insight.

and ROHRICHT, Jo Anne.
INE: ETHICAL PERSPECTIVES ON TODAY'S MEDICAL ISSUES. rev. ed.
. An excellent primer on medical ethics.

, and ECKLEMENN, Herman.
& THE ORIGIN OF THE EARTH. A proposed "age-day" reconciliation by two
onomers.

OF THE UNIVERSE. Oxford U.P., 1965. A thorough study of cosmology
ly modern period."

ES CLAP THEIR HANDS: FAITH, PERCEPTION AND THE NEW PHYSICS.
3. An introspective and subjective summary of a sensitive person's reaction to
her, tied tenuously to some thoughts under debate in the philosophy of physics.

OWARD, Thomas.
: THE TRUE HUMANISM. Word, 1985. Who offers the highest hope for modern

lfhart.
'S CREED IN THE LIGHT OF TODAY'S QUESTIONS. Westminster, 1976.

lfhart.
ALITY. Westminster, 1977. Central theme is the connection between God and
ng of reality. The author discusses first how the biblical understanding of reality
by Israel's experience of God, and then deals with problems in understanding
d raised by the natural sciences. The chapter "Man—The Image of God" deals
tiny and human history.

THEOLOGY IN EINSTEIN'S PERSPECTIVE (Frontiers of Knowledge Ser.: No.
Press, 1986. Drawing on writings by Einstein and Athanasius, the author
e ways in which modern science and Christian theology share in common belief
unded in reality, in its independence, intelligibility, and rationality. Authentic
both encourages individuals to act on the hope that personal life based on
edge is more real than anything a closed conceptual system has to offer. (M-88)

OLOGY AND EINSTEIN. Oxford U.P., 1982. Part of Torrance's Science and
A good discussion of the continual interplay of faith and reason in Einstein's

John.
Y. Freeman, 1979. An excellent popular introduction to particle physics.

PROVIDENCE. Scribner, 1958.

ATURE & SCRIPTURE IN CONFLICT? Zondervan, 1982. A biology professor
sive creationist position takes a careful look at several positions. Extensive
-84)

CAL CHRISTOLOGY: ECUMENIC & HISTORIC. Nelson, 1985. A very readable
basic issues in Christology and the enduring validity of orthodox and historic
e author integrates a careful exegesis of Scripture with his expertise in philoso-
ence and psychology. Extremely helpful book.

(trans. John Bowden).
F THEOLOGY: A BRIEF ACCOUNT OF THE RELATIONSHIP BETWEEN

58

education held at Trinity Christian College.
+DUNN, Jean.
ASTRONOMY FOR THE YOUNGER SET. Vantage Press, 1984. Intended for grades 1-5, with simple explanations of complex phenomena, nice line drawings and a helpful glossary.
+DYE, David.
FAITH AND THE PHYSICAL WORLD. Eerdmans, 1966. Thorough exposition of scientific method related to an evangelical interpretation of Christianity by a theistic evolutionist.(J-68)
ELLISON, Craig, ed.
MODIFYING MAN: IMPLICATIONS AND ETHICS. U.P. of America, 1978. Distinguished contributors include Sen. Mark Hatfield, Robert Herrmann and Donald MacKay. These papers come out of a 1975 conference in Wheaton. MacKay's lecture, "Biblical Perspectives on Human Engineering," is regarded as one of the finest lectures in existence on this topic. The book represents a major contribution by outstanding experts in the fields of genetics, brain modification, and behavior modification, with responses from an evangelical perspective.
+FISCHER, Robert B.
GOD DID IT, BUT HOW? Zondervan, 1983. Former president of ASA has written a minor masterpiece. Good book to give to new Christians or people interested in science-faith questions. Excellent definition of terms and concepts often confused. (S-82, S-84)
+FRAIR, Wayne, and DAVIS, Percival.
A CASE FOR CREATION. 3rd ed. Moody, 1983. (May still be able to order direct: Creation Research Society Books, P.O. Box 14016, Terre Haute, IN 47803). Frair is a young-earth creationist with a Ph.D. in biology. His epilogue, "Creationism's Unfinished Business," is a rallying call for further research in specific areas conducted in a civil but uncompromising spirit. (D-86)
FREUDENBERGER, C. Dean.
FOOD FOR TOMORROW? Augsburg, 1984. A Christian agronomist calls for renewal of the biblical covenant to meet the world crisis in agriculture. Includes policy suggestions in response to land and water abuse in America. Also discusses worldwide problems and solutions.
GILLESPIE, Neal C.
CHARLES DARWIN AND THE PROBLEM OF CREATION. U. of Chicago P., 1982. An unbiased account of the religious roots of Darwin's thought, and how the creation debate shaped him.
GISH, Duane T.
EVOLUTION: THE FOSSILS SAY NO! Creation-Life Pub., 1972. The best known analysis of the fossils by the best known spokesman for special creation/young earth concept.
GODFREY, Laurie R., ed.
WHAT DARWIN BEGAN. Allyn & Bacon, 1985. A series of articles by experts in the field outlining present controversies.
GOUDZWAARD, Bob.
IDOLS OF OUR TIME. InterVarsity Press, 1984. Author is former member of the Dutch parliament and Professor of Economics at the Free University in Amsterdam. Excellent work in exposing the skeletons of our popular ideologies. (S-86)
GRANVILLE, H.
LOGOS: MATHEMATICS AND CHRISTIAN THEOLOGY. Bucknell U. P., 1976. Book has section on classic math and traditional theology, and one on modern math and contemporary theology.
GRAY, Asa.
DARWINIANA. Harvard U.P., 1963. Integrative articles by a conservative Christian botanist who was Darwin's major American defender.
+GRUENLER, Royce G.
THE INEXHAUSTIBLE GOD. Baker, 1983. Former advocate of process theology has made a highly praised critique of it from a biblical perspective.
GRUNLAN, Stephen, and REINER, Milton, eds.
CHRISTIAN PERSPECTIVES ON SOCIOLOGY. Zondervan, 1982. An introductory reader with twenty essays written by social science professors at Christian colleges on a variety of topics centering around sociology and the Christian point of view. (M-84)
GUINNESS, Os.
THE GRAVEDIGGER FILE: PAPERS ON THE SUBVERSION OF THE MODERN CHURCH. InterVarsity Press, 1983. This fictionalized account in the style of C.S. Lewis' Screwtape Letters

55

is a thorough sociological and soundly Christian critique of contemporary Christianity.

GUTHRIE, Shirley C., Jr.
DIVERSITY IN FAITH, UNITY IN CHRIST. Westminster, 1986. In a helpful way, Guthrie presents an interpretation of the Christian faith that captures the strengths of pietism, orthodoxy, and liberalism and corrects their weaknesses. Evangelicals of all persuasions can be greatly helped by this book; its comments on science-related issues (i.e., care for the environment) are insightful.

HAYWARD, Alan.
CREATION & EVOLUTION: THE FACTS & FALLACIES. SPCK (UK), Fortress (US), 1985. (May still be able to order direct: SPCK Books, Holy Trinity Church, Marylbone, London, England NW1 4DU).This book provides a critique of both theistic-evolution and recent-creation theories, especially those of "flood geology." Evidence for an "old earth" is presented. In addition to the scientific arguments, Hayward reviews various Christian views of Genesis and presents his own interpretation. (D-86)

HAYWARD, Alan.
GOD IS: A SCIENTIST SHOWS WHY IT MAKES SENSE TO BELIEVE IN GOD. Thomas Nelson, 1978. An apologetic for the existence of God arguing from the complex designs revealed by science. Also reviews various Christian views of creation. (J-83)

✝HENRY, Carl F.H.
QUEST FOR REALITY: CHRISTIANITY & THE COUNTER CULTURE. InterVarsity Press, 1973.

✝HERRMANN, Robert L., ed.
MAKING WHOLE PERSONS: ETHICAL ISSUES IN BIOLOGY & MEDICINE. ASA Reprint Volume. American Scientific Affiliation, 1980. A collection of articles from the ASA Journal organized around human engineering and human medicine. Articles by Gareth Jones, reports from the National Conference "Human Engineering and the Future of Man" and reprints of articles on genetic and brain manipulation and behavior modification. The medicine section contains articles by Carl Henry, James Jekel and Stan Lindquist.

HOFFMANN, Banesh.
THE STRANGE STORY OF THE QUANTUM. 2nd ed. Dover, 1959. An amusingly written, sometimes novelistic, treatment of quantum theory by a former collaborator of Einstein. The treatment emphasizes the development of the different approaches to quantum theory.

HOLMES, Arthur F.
ALL TRUTH IS GOD'S TRUTH. InterVarsity Press, 1983. A fine introduction to the placement of human learning in the context of God's truth. The author rejects a dichotomy between the sacred and the secular.

HOOYKAAS, R.
RELIGION & THE RISE OF MODERN SCIENCE. Eerdmans. Author is perhaps the first Protestant (reformed) thinker to document the thesis that modern science is in good part a product of Judeo-Christian influence on Western thought. Highly recommended.

HOUSTON, James M.
I BELIEVE IN THE CREATOR. Eerdmans, 1979. A wide-ranging and powerful reflection on God as our creator by a geography teacher who migrated from Oxford to Regent College. Highly praised. (J-81)

JAKI, Stanley L.
COSMOS AND CREATOR. Regnery Gateway, 1980. An analysis of the bearing of modern cosmological theories on the Christian dogma of the creation of the universe, followed by the history of that dogma, its philosophical presuppositions, and its relation to evolutionary theories of man. (J-83)

JAKI, Stanley L.
THE RELEVANCE OF PHYSICS. U. of Chicago P., 1967. A brilliant overview of the significance and limitations of physics as a form of human inquiry. The section headings indicate the book's broad scope: The Chief World Models of Physics, The Central Themes of Physical Research, Physics and Other Disciplines, Physics: Master or Servant?

JASTROW, Robert.
TWO FACES OF REALITY. Norton, 1987.

JEEVES, Malcolm A.
THE SCIENTIFIC ENTERPRISE & CHRISTIAN FAITH. InterVarsity Press, 1969. A good overall survey of the relationship, including a good historical perspective.

JOHNSON, Cedric B.
THE PSYCHOLOGY OF BIBLICAL INTEI
book that deals openly and honestly with t

✝JONES, D. Gareth.
BRAVE NEW PEOPLE: ETHICAL ISSUE
1985. A discussion from a Christian persp
pre-natal diagnosis, artificial insemination
cloning. Highly recommended. (J-86)

✝JONES, D. Gareth.
OUR FRAGILE BRAINS: A CHRISTIAN P
Press, 1981. A discussion for nonprofessio
and how this understanding relates to a C

JUNGEL, Eberhard.
GOD AS THE MYSTERY OF THE WORLI
theology of the crucified one in the dispute

✝KIRKPATRICK, William K.
PSYCHOLOGICAL SEDUCTION: THE I
Nelson, 1983.

✝KOTESKEY, Ronald L.
PSYCHOLOGY FROM A CHRISTIAN PEI
sor discusses structuralism, functionalism,
ism from a Christian perspective, and prop

✝LEITH, T. Harry.
THE CONTRASTS AND SIMILARITIES
CULT AND RELIGION. 4th ed. Self publis
resources. Includes 12 pages of books and
and critiques of gradualistic evolution.

✝LINDQUIST, Stanley E.
REACH OUT: BECOME AN ENCOURAG

LINDSAY, Robert B., and MARGENAU, Henry
FOUNDATIONS OF PHYSICS. Dover, 1
physics, including general relativity and qu

MACKAY, Donald M.
BRAINS, MACHINES & PERSONS. Eerdr
biophysicist. (J-81, J-82)

MACKAY, Donald M., ed.
CHRISTIANITY IN A MECHANISTIC UNI

MACKAY, Donald M.
THE CLOCKWORK IMAGE. InterVarsity
ism, mechanism, chance, miracle, and the

MACKAY, Donald M.
HUMAN SCIENCE & HUMAN DIGNITY. In
cannot destroy personal significance. (J-8(

MESSENGER, Ernest C.
EVOLUTION AND THEOLOGY. Macmilla
evolution questions. Study of the Church F

✝MOBERG, David O.
THE CHURCH AS A SOCIAL INSTITUTIC
2nd ed. Baker, 1984. This sociological ana
or institutional religion, especially Christia
types of religious organizations, how they
contributions to people and society, the pro
relationship of religion to the rest of society,
revivalism, the clergy, and coping with chai

MOROWITZ, Harold J.
COSMIC JOY & LOCAL PAIN: MUSING
distinguished biologist offers a Teilhardian
valuable insights if read carefully. (S-88)

NATIONAL Cou
GENETIC E
of Bioethica

NELSON, J. Rob
HUMAN LIF
ive biblical
spiritual. We

NELSON, Jame
HUMAN ME
Augsburg, 1

✝NEWMAN, Ro
GENESIS C
theologians

NORTH, J.D.
THE MEAS
through the

OWENS, Virgini
AND THE T
Eerdmans,
the world arc
(M-84)

PACKER, J.I., a
CHRISTIAN
man?

PANNENBERG,
THE APOST

PANNENBERG,
FAITH AND
our understa
was influenc
the modern
with human

PAUL, Iain.
SCIENCE A
3). Scot. Ac
demonstrate
that each is
participation
empirical kn

PAUL, Iain.
SCIENCE, T
Culture serie
scientific wo

POLKINGHORN
PARTICLE F

POLLARD, W.G.
CHANCE A

✝PUN, Pattle P.
EVOLUTION
with a progr
bibliography

✝RAMM, Bernar
AN EVANGE
introduction
Christianity.
phy, history,

⊕RITSCH, Dietri
THE LOGIC

BASIC CONCEPTS IN THEOLOGY. Fortress. A study of theology in contemporary society, the search for truth, and how theology is put into practice.

SANTMIRE, H. Paul.
THE TRAVAIL OF NATURE: THE AMBIGUOUS ECOLOGICAL PROMISE OF CHRISTIAN THEOLOGY. Fortress, 1985. An examination of the history of Christian theology as it relates to the goodness and value of the non-human universe, and how the force of religion in America continues to shape public attitudes toward ecology. One of several works on ecological theology by the author. (M-87)

SCHNEIDER, Edward D., ed.
QUESTIONS ABOUT THE BEGINNING OF LIFE. Augsburg, 1985. Covers seven issues: artificial insemination, in vitro fertilization, surrogate motherhood, genetic manipulation, genetic screening and counseling, prenatal diagnosis, and care and treatment of severely handicapped newborns.

SCHWARZ, Hans.
ON THE WAY TO THE FUTURE. rev.ed. Augsburg, 1979. Leading Lutheran evangelical theologian discusses Christian eschatology in light of our current understanding in the sciences, philosophy and theology. Standard work for those interested in future studies, especially from a Lutheran perspective.

SCHWARZ, Hans.
RESPONSIBLE FAITH: CHRISTIAN THEOLOGY IN THE LIGHT OF 20TH CENTURY QUES-TIONS. Augsburg, 1986. A major theological work with helpful discussions of basic science/the-ology issues; i.e., God's creative and sustaining activity and current scientific understanding, the limits of rational inquiry, disclosure of a higher dimension, exclusiveness of the self-disclo-sure in Jesus Christ.

SHANNON, Thomas A.
WHAT ARE THEY SAYING ABOUT GENETIC ENGINEERING? Paulist Press, 1985.

+SHEAFFER, John, and BRAND, Raymond.
WHATEVER HAPPENED TO EDEN? Tyndale, 1980. A book dealing with the energy and environmental crisis, by Brand, a biology professor, and Sheaffer, an engineer. (M-82)

SHETTLES, Landrum, M.D., and RORVIK, David.
RITES OF LIFE—THE EVIDENCE FOR LIFE BEFORE BIRTH. Zondervan, 1983. A detailed examination of life before birth from the time of conception, and the evidence for emotion and feeling in the fetus. Also, the description of medical procedures of abortion. Compelling arguments against abortion by an obstetrician-gynecologist who has specialized in fertility and sterility, sperm biology and human conception. (D-84, M-85)

+SLOCUM, Robert E.
ORDINARY CHRISTIANS IN A HIGH-TECH WORLD. Word, 1986. A useful discussion of the issues associated with its title. (J-87)

STAFLEU, M.D.
THEORIES IN PRACTICE. U.P. of America/Institute for Christian Studies, Toronto, 1987. This book illustrates the nature of theories through the ways they were used during the period of the Copernican Revolution from Copernicus through Newton, with a Christian philosophical under-pinning.

STANLEY, Steven M.
THE NEW EVOLUTIONARY TIMETABLE. Basic Bks., 1984. A lucid presentation of the concept of punctuated equilibrium by a paleontologist. (Not too technical.)

STANNARD, Russell.
SCIENCE AND THE RENEWAL OF BELIEF. SCM Press, Ltd., 1982. (May still be able to order direct: SCM Press, Ltd., 58 Bloomsbury St., London, WC, UK.) An outstanding and very readable book on the relationship between science and relgious belief by a high-energy physicist.

THIELICKE, Helmut.
BEING HUMAN ... BECOMING HUMAN: AN ESSAY IN CHRISTIAN ANTHROPOLOGY. Doubleday, 1984. A masterpiece and very readable.

TOLSTOY, Ivan.
JAMES CLERK MAXWELL. U. of Chicago P., 1983. A very readable account of the life of this great Christian and scientist with an understandable account of the key role that Maxwell played in the revolutionary shift from Newtonian to modern (field) physics. The author is sensitive to Maxwell's personal character and Christian convictions, acknowledging that they may have played a role in his devotion to teach working people about science and possibly as a heuristic,

motivating factor in his development of theoretical physics. A fine book.

✚TORRANCE, Thomas F.
DIVINE AND CONTINGENT ORDER. Oxford U.P., 1981. The importance of the Judeo-Christian view of a contingent universe with respect to the origins of western science.

✚TORRANCE, Thomas F., ed.
THEOLOGICAL DIALOGUE BETWEEN ORTHODOX & REFORMED CHURCHES. Scot. Acad. Press, 1985. This collection is difficult theological reading which contains useful material on possible congruences between basic epistemological structures in theology and natural science. A very valuable section on the Christian Fathers' understanding of God's action in spatial-temporal reality and beyond space and time. Will help a dedicated reader better understand the spiritual-intellectual treasures contained in the Judeo-Christian tradition.

✚TORRANCE, Thomas F.
THEOLOGY IN RECONCILIATION. Eerdmans, 1975.

✚TORRANCE, Thomas F.
THEOLOGY IN RECONSTRUCTION. Eerdmans, 1965.

TRINKLEIN, Fred.
THE GOD OF SCIENCE. Exposition Press, 1982. This book presents answers by 38 leading scientists and technologists to questions such as: Where is the boundary between science and religion? Can the existence of God be scientifically proven? Or disproven? Do scientists believe in miracles? How do scientists view churches and clerics?

✚VAN LEEUWEN, Mary Stewart, et al.
CHRISTIAN VISION: MAN & MIND, Vol. 3. Hillsdale College Press, 1987. Paul Vitz, Thomas Burke and many others contribute to this collection.

✚VAN LEEUWEN, Mary Stewart.
THE SORCERER'S APPRENTICE: A CHRISTIAN LOOKS AT THE CHANGING FACE OF PSYCHOLOGY. InterVarsity Press, 1982. Attacks both the ethics and accuracy of dominant research methods in psychology. An excellent discussion of the scientific methodology of empiricist psychology with a strong argument for a human-science approach to the study of persons as contrasted to a natural-science approach. (D-83)

VON WEISÄCKER, Carl F.
THE WORLDVIEW OF PHYSICS. Chicago, 1952. A look at developments in modern physics which had some influence on Bonhoeffer's thought.

✚WIESTER, John.
THE GENESIS CONNECTION. Thomas Nelson, 1983. Author contends that both "scientistic" and religious fundamentalism "are using science to teach religion." He carefully points out the weak arguments used by both these extremes in the process of relating scriptural accounts to historical geology and evolutionary biology. (S-84)

WILDER-SMITH, A.E.
CREATION OF LIFE: A CYBERNETIC APPROACH TO EVOLUTION. Creation Life Pub., 1970. Primarily a refutation of thesis in *Biochemical Predestination* (Kenyon and Steinman) that matter is governed by predestined properties and is "programmed" to evolve. The author argues from information theory and artificial intelligence for the necessity of a prior intelligence (i.e., God). Good argumentation, but not mathematically or biologically rigorous. (D-73)

WILKINSON, Loren, ed.
EARTHKEEPING: CHRISTIAN STEWARDSHIP OF NATURAL RESOURCES 2nd ed. Eerdmans, 1980. The product of a year of study by seven fellows of the Calvin Center for Christian Scholarship. Using biblical guidelines, authors look at different aspects of stewardship (nature of ecosphere, economics, resource distribution, etc.), and come up with 30 guidelines for Christian stewardship. (J-82)

✚WILLIS, David, ed.
ORIGINS AND CHANGE. ASA Reprint Volume. American Scientific Affiliation, 1978. Excellent classical papers on anthropology and geology covering both general aspects such as the unity of creation, special creation and evolution, and particular aspects such as biogenesis and the various geological evidences. Richard Bube's introduction "We Believe in Creation," is a masterpiece.

WINGREN, Gustaf.
THE FLIGHT FROM CREATION. Augsburg, 1971. An appeal for adequate theological emphasis on First Article concerns.

+YAMAUCHI, Edwin M.
FOES FROM THE NORTHERN FRONTIER: INVADING HORDES FROM THE RUSSIAN STEPPES. Baker, 1982.

+YAMAUCHI, Edwin M.
THE STONES AND THE SCRIPTURES. Baker, 1981. Scholarly text by outstanding biblical archaeologist.

+YOUNG, Davis.
CREATION & THE FLOOD: AN ALTERNATIVE TO FLOOD GEOLOGY & THEISTIC EVOLU-TION. Baker, 1977. This book was written in collaboration with and in commemoration of the author's father, E. J. Young, an Old Testament professor at Westminster Seminary. It details a biblical view of an old earth based on a conservative reformed theology. (J-79, 3 reviews)

YOUNGBLOOD, Ronald, ed.
THE GENESIS DEBATE: PERSISTENT QUESTIONS ABOUT CREATION AND THE FLOOD. Thomas Nelson, 1986. Twenty-two highly regarded theologians alternatively answer pro and con on 11 "persistent questions" surrounding the Genesis debate. (J-89)

(Notes)

CATEGORICAL LISTING OF BOOKS
In & Out Of Print

The following is a somewhat arbitrary division of books into categories, which we hope will nevertheless be helpful. Books are generally listed in only one category, and books for which no category existed were put under the most closely related one. Category heads should be broadly construed. Headings are as follows:

Apologetics
Archaeology & Anthropology
Biblical Interpretation
Biology & Bioethics
Books for Children
Cosmology & Astronomy
Devotional
Education
Engineering
Environment & Resources
General & Fiction
General Science
History of Science

History of Science & Theology
Math Related
Origins: Creation & Evolution
Philosophy of Science
Physics
Politics & Economics
Psychology & Neural Science
Science & Religion
Sociology
Technology & Computers
Theology
Third World

Books that are out of print are marked with an asterisk.

APOLOGETICS

CAMPOLO, Anthony. A REASONABLE FAITH: RESPONDING TO SECULARISM.

CAMPOLO, Anthony. WE HAVE MET THE ENEMY AND THEY ARE PARTLY RIGHT.

GILL, Jerry H. FAITH IN DIALOGUE: A CHRISTIAN APOLOGETIC.

GROOTHUIS, Douglas R. REVEALING THE NEW AGE JESUS: CHALLENGES TO ORTHO-DOX VIEWS OF CHRIST.

*HAYWARD, Alan. GOD IS: A SCIENTIST SHOWS WHY IT MAKES SENSE TO BELIEVE IN GOD.

LEWIS, C.S. MERE CHRISTIANITY.

POLKINGHORNE, John. THE WAY THE WORLD IS: THE CHRISTIAN PERSPECTIVE OF A SCIENTIST.

STANNARD, Russell. GROUNDS FOR REASONABLE BELIEF.

ARCHAEOLOGY & ANTHROPOLOGY

CHENEVIERE, Alain. VANISHING TRIBES: PRIMITIVE MAN ON EARTH.

*DARVILL, Timothy. PREHISTORIC BRITAIN.

EISELEY, Loren. THE UNEXPECTED UNIVERSE.

MORRIS, Walter F. Jr. LIVING MAYA.

MILLARD, Alan. TREASURES FROM BIBLE TIMES.

RUSPOLI, Mario. THE CAVE OF LASCAUX: THE FINAL PHOTOGRAPHS.

SCHOVILLE, Keith N. BIBLICAL ARCHAEOLOGY IN FOCUS.

SMUTS, Barbara, et al., eds. PRIMATE SOCIETIES.

*YAMAUCHI, Edwin M. FOES FROM THE NORTHERN FRONTIER: INVADING HORDES FROM THE RUSSIAN STEPPES.

*YAMAUCHI, Edwin M. THE STONES AND THE SCRIPTURES.

BIBLICAL INTERPRETATION

BILEZIKIAN, Gilbert. BEYOND SEX ROLES: A GUIDE FOR THE STUDY OF FEMALE ROLES IN THE BIBLE.

BONHOEFFER, Dietrich. CREATION & THE FALL AND TEMPTATION.

BRANSON, Mark, and PADILLA, Rene. CONFLICT AND CONTEXT: HERMENEUTICS IN THE AMERICAS.

CASSIRER, Heinz W., trans. GOD'S NEW COVENANT: A NEW TESTAMENT TRANSLATION.

GAVENTA, Beverly R. FROM DARKNESS TO LIGHT: ASPECTS OF CONVERSION IN THE NEW TESTAMENT.

GREIDANUS, Sidney. THE MODERN PREACHER AND THE ANCIENT TEXT: INTERPRETING AND PREACHING BIBLICAL LITERATURE.

HEFLEY, James C. THE TRUTH IN CRISIS: THE CONTROVERSY IN THE SOUTHERN BAPTIST CONVENTION. Vol. 2 & 3.

*JOHNSON, Cedric B. THE PSYCHOLOGY OF BIBLICAL INTERPRETATION.

LEITH, John H. THE REFORMED IMPERATIVE: WHAT THE CHURCH HAS TO SAY THAT NO ONE ELSE CAN SAY.

SANDERS, James A. CANON AND COMMUNITY: A GUIDE TO CANONICAL CRITICISM.

SWARTLEY, Willard M. SLAVERY, SABBATH, WAR AND WOMEN: CASE STUDIES IN BIBLICAL INTERPRETATION.

VON RAD, Gerhard. WISDOM IN ISRAEL. rev. ed.

YAMAUCHI, Edwin M. HARPER'S WORLD OF THE NEW TESTAMENT.

BIOLOGY & BIOETHICS

*ALLEN, David F. and Victoria. ETHICAL ISSUES IN MENTAL RETARDATION: TRAGIC CHOICES/LIVING HOPE.

*ALLEN, David F.; BIRD, Lewis P.; and HERRMANN, Robert L. WHOLE PERSON MEDICINE: AN INTERNATIONAL SYMPOSIUM.

AMBROSE, E.J. THE NATURE & ORIGIN OF THE BIOLOGICAL WORLD.

*ANDERSON, J. Kerby. GENETIC ENGINEERING: THE ETHICAL ISSUES.

*ANDERSON, Norman. ISSUES OF LIFE & DEATH: ABORTION, EUTHANASIA, GENETIC ENGINEERING, BIRTH CONTROL.

BERG, Howard C. RANDOM WALKS IN BIOLOGY.

BIRD, Lewis P., and BARLOW, James. MEDICAL ETHICS: OATHS AND PRAYERS. AN ANTHOLOGY.

BOUMA, Hessel, III, et al. CHRISTIAN FAITH, HEALTH, AND MEDICAL PRACTICE.

*CALLAHAN, D. ABORTION: LAW, CHOICE AND MORALITY.

CANTOR, Norman L. LEGAL FRONTIERS OF DEATH AND DYING.

CAVALIERI, Liebe F. DOUBLE-EDGED HELIX: GENETIC ENGINEERING IN THE REAL WORLD.

*COHEN, B.D. HARD CHOICES: MIXED BLESSINGS OF MODERN TECHNOLOGY.

DESOWITZ, Robert S. THE THORN IN THE STARFISH: HOW THE HUMAN IMMUNE SYSTEM WORKS.

DIXON, Patrick. THE WHOLE TRUTH ABOUT AIDS.

DUNBAR, Robin I.M. PRIMATE SOCIAL SYSTEMS.

*ELLISON, Craig, ed. MODIFYING MAN: IMPLICATIONS AND ETHICS.

FOUNTAIN, Daniel E. HEALTH, THE BIBLE AND THE CHURCH.

GARFIELD, Jay L., and HENNESSEY, P., eds. ABORTION, MORAL AND LEGAL PERSPECTIVES.

GOEL, N.S., and THOMPSON, Richard L. COMPUTER SIMULATIONS OF SELF-ORGANIZATION IN BIOLOGICAL SYSTEMS.

HAUERWAS, Stanley. NAMING THE SILENCES: GOD, MEDICINE, AND THE PROBLEM OF SUFFERING.

HENSHAW, Paul S., and KAPLAN, Sylvan J. INFOPOWER: BIOPHYSICS AND BIOSOCIOLOGY OF MIND.

HERRMANN, Robert L., GENETIC ENGINEERING.

*HERRMANN, Robert L., ed. MAKING WHOLE PERSONS: ETHICAL ISSUES IN BIOLOGY & MEDICINE.

*JONES, D. Gareth. BRAVE NEW PEOPLE: ETHICAL ISSUES AT THE COMMENCEMENT OF LIFE.

JONES, D. Gareth. MANUFACTURING HUMANS.

*JONES, D. Gareth. OUR FRAGILE BRAINS: A CHRISTIAN PERSPECTIVE ON BRAIN RESEARCH.

KELLER, Evelyn F., and FREEMAN, W.H. A FEELING FOR THE ORGANISM: THE LIFE AND WORK OF BARBARA MCCLINTOCK.

LAMMERS, Stephen, and VERHEY, Allen, eds. ON MORAL MEDICINE: THEOLOGICAL PERSPECTIVES IN MEDICAL ETHICS.

MARX, Jean L., ed. A REVOLUTION IN BIOTECHNOLOGY.

*NATIONAL Council of Churches. GENETIC ENGINEERING: SOCIAL AND ETHICAL CONSEQUENCES.

*NELSON, J. Robert. HUMAN LIFE: A BIBLICAL PERSPECTIVE FOR BIOETHICS.

*NELSON, James B., and ROHRICHT, Jo Anne. HUMAN MEDICINE: ETHICAL PERSPECTIVES ON TODAY'S MEDICAL ISSUES.

NOONAN, John T., Jr., ed. THE MORALITY OF ABORTION: LEGAL AND HISTORICAL PERSPECTIVES.

PEACOCKE, Arthur R. GOD AND THE NEW BIOLOGY.

REISSER, Paul C.; REISSER, Teri; and WELDON, John. NEW AGE MEDICINE: A CHRISTIAN PERSPECTIVE ON HOLISTIC HEALTH.

RIFKIN, Jeremy. ALGENY: A NEW WORD—A NEW WORLD.

RUSE, Michael. PHILOSOPHY OF BIOLOGY TODAY.

*SCHNEIDER, Edward D., ed. QUESTIONS ABOUT THE BEGINNING OF LIFE.

SHANNON, Thomas A., ed. BIOETHICS. 3rd ed.

*SHANNON, Thomas A. WHAT ARE THEY SAYING ABOUT GENETIC ENGINEERING?

*SHETTLES, Landrum, M.D. and RORVIK, David. RITES OF LIFE—THE EVIDENCE FOR LIFE BEFORE BIRTH.

SIDER, Ronald J. COMPLETELY PRO-LIFE.

SIEGEL, Bernard S. LOVE, MEDICINE AND MIRACLES.

SMITH, J. Maynard. DID DARWIN GET IT RIGHT? ESSAYS ON GAMES, SEX AND EVOLUTION.

SO, Miriam L. THE BIBLE AND BIOLOGY. 5 vols.

SNYDER, S.H. DRUGS AND THE BRAIN: A SCIENTIFIC AMERICAN BOOK.

VYUYAN, John. IN PITY AND IN ANGER: A STUDY OF THE USE OF ANIMALS IN SCIENCE.

WENNBERG, Robert N. LIFE IN THE BALANCE: EXPLORING THE ABORTION CONTROVERSY.

WRIGHT, Richard T. BIOLOGY THROUGH THE EYES OF FAITH.

YOXEN, Edward. THE GENE BUSINESS: WHO SHOULD CONTROL BIOTECHNOLOGY?

BOOKS FOR CHILDREN

*DUNN, Jean. ASTRONOMY FOR THE YOUNGER SET.

LAWHEAD, Steve. HOWARD HAD A SPACESHIP.

LUCAS, Ernest and Hazel. OUR WORLD: HOW? WHAT? WHEN? WHY?

COSMOLOGY & ASTRONOMY

BARROW, John D., and SILK, Joseph. THE LEFT HAND OF CREATION: THE ORIGIN AND EVOLUTION OF THE EXPANDING UNIVERSE.

BERTOLA, F.; SULENTIC, J.W.; and MADORE, B.F., eds. NEW IDEAS IN ASTRONOMY.

BÖRNER, G. THE EARLY UNIVERSE: FACTS AND FICTION.

BRUNGS, Robert A. YOU SEE LIGHTS BREAKING UPON US: DOCTRINAL PERSPECTIVES ON BIOLOGICAL ADVANCE.

CHAISSON, Eric. UNIVERSE: AN EVOLUTIONARY APPROACH TO ASTRONOMY.

CHAPMAN, Clark R., and MORRISON, David. COSMIC CATASTROPHIES.

*DAVIES, Paul. THE ACCIDENTAL UNIVERSE.

DAVIES, Paul. THE COSMIC BLUEPRINT: NEW DISCOVERIES IN NATURE'S CREATIVE ABILITY TO ORDER THE UNIVERSE.

FERRIS, Timothy. THE RED LIMIT. rev. ed.

HARRISON, Edward. COSMOLOGY: THE SCIENCE OF THE UNIVERSE.

HARRISON, Edward. DARKNESS AT NIGHT: A RIDDLE OF THE UNIVERSE.

HAWKING, Stephen W. A BRIEF HISTORY OF TIME: FROM THE BIG BANG TO BLACK HOLES.

HETHERINGTON, Norriss S. ANCIENT ASTRONOMY AND CIVILIZATION.

JAKI, Stanley L. GOD AND THE COSMOLOGISTS.

KIPPENHAHN, R. LIGHT FROM THE DEPTHS OF TIME.

LESLIE, John. UNIVERSES.

LINDE, A.D. INFLATION AND QUANTUM COSMOLOGY.

MARSCHALL, Laurence A. THE SUPERNOVA STORY.

*NORTH, J.D. THE MEASURE OF THE UNIVERSE.

NOVIKOV, Igor. BLACK HOLES AND THE UNIVERSE.

SILK, Joseph. THE BIG BANG: THE CREATION AND EVOLUTION OF THE UNIVERSE.

STEPHENSON, B. KEPLER'S PHYSICAL ASTRONOMY.

SWERDLOW, N.M., and NEUGEBAUER, O. MATHEMATICAL ASTRONOMY IN COPERNICUS' DE REVOLUTIONIBUS. 2 vols.

UNSOLD, A. and BASCHEK, R.B. THE NEW COSMOS. 3rd ed.

VERSCHUUR, Gerrit L. THE INVISIBLE UNIVERSE REVEALED.

VERSCHUUR, Gerrit L. INTERSTELLAR MATTERS.

WEINBERG, Steven. THE FIRST THREE MINUTES: A MODERN VIEW OF THE ORIGIN OF THE UNIVERSE.

DEVOTIONAL

BLOESCH, Donald G. THE STRUGGLE OF PRAYER.

DEMARAY, Donald E. LAUGHTER, JOY AND HEALING.

HARTZLER, H. Harold. KING FAMILY HISTORY.

*HOUSTON, James M. I BELIEVE IN THE CREATOR.

LINZEY, Andrew, and REGAN, Tom, eds. LOVE THE ANIMALS: MEDITATIONS AND PRAYERS.

MACDONALD, Gordon. ORDERING YOUR PRIVATE WORLD.

SEERVELD, Calvin. ON BEING HUMAN: IMAGING GOD IN THE MODERN WORLD.

EDUCATION

AMERICAN Association for the Advancement of Science. SCIENCE FOR ALL AMERICANS.

BARLOW, Daniel L. EDUCATIONAL PSYCHOLOGY: THE TEACHING-LEARNING PROCESS.

*BERGMAN, Jerry. THE CRITERION: RELIGIOUS DISCRIMINATION IN AMERICA.

COMMITTEE on the Conduct of Science of the National Academy of Science. ON BEING A SCIENTIST.

DE JONG, Arthur J. RECLAIMING A MISSION: NEW DIRECTION FOR THE CHURCH-RELATED COLLEGE.

*DE JONG, Norman, ed. CHRISTIAN APPROACHES TO LEARNING THEORY. Vol. 1 & 2.

DE JONG, Norman, ed. CHRISTIAN APPROACHES TO LEARNING THEORY. Vol. 3.

HEIE, Harold, and WOLFE, David, L., eds. REALITY OF CHRISTIAN LEARNING: STRATEGIES FOR FAITH-DISCIPLINE INTEGRATION.

HERMANN, Kenneth W. EVERY THOUGHT CAPTIVE TO CHRIST.

HOLMES, Arthur F. SHAPING CHARACTER: MORAL EDUCATION IN THE CHRISTIAN COLLEGE.

MORRIS, Henry M., et al, eds. SCIENTIFIC CREATIONISM.

NATIONAL Advisory Group of Sigma Xi. AN EXPLORATION OF THE NATURE AND QUALITY OF UNDERGRADUATE EDUCATION IN SCIENCE, MATHEMATICS AND ENGINEERING.

NELKIN, Dorothy. THE CREATION CONTROVERSY: SCIENCE OR SCRIPTURE IN THE SCHOOLS?

PAZMIÑO, Robert W. FOUNDATIONAL ISSUES IN CHRISTIAN EDUCATION: AN INTRODUCTION IN EVANGELICAL PERSPECTIVE.

PETERSON, Michael L. PHILOSOPHY OF EDUCATION: ISSUES & OPTIONS.

PRICE, David; WIESTER, John L.; and HEARN, Walter R. TEACHING SCIENCE IN A CLIMATE OF CONTROVERSY: A VIEW FROM THE AMERICAN SCIENTIFIC AFFILIATION.

THOMSON, Alexander. TRADITION AND AUTHORITY IN SCIENCE AND THEOLOGY.

VITZ, Paul C. CENSORSHIP: EVIDENCE OF BIAS IN OUR CHILDREN'S TEXTBOOKS.

ENGINEERING

ASA INDUSTRIAL and Engineering Ethics Commission. OVERRULED.

FLORMAN, Samuel C. THE CIVILIZED ENGINEER.

ENVIRONMENT & RESOURCES

ADENEY, Miriam. A TIME FOR RISKING: PRIORITIES FOR WOMEN.

BROWN, Lester R. et al. STATE OF THE WORLD 1988: A WORLDWATCH INSTITUTE RE-PORT ON PROGRESS TOWARDS A SUSTAINABLE SOCIETY.

EHRLICH, Paul R. THE MACHINERY OF NATURE.

GRANBERG-MICHAELSON, Wesley, ed. TENDING THE GARDEN: ESSAYS ON THE GOSPEL AND THE EARTH.

KASUN, Jacqueline. THE WAR AGAINST POPULATION: THE ECONOMICS AND IDEOLOGY OF POPULATION CONTROL.

PETERSON, Dale. THE DELUGE AND THE ARK: A JOURNEY INTO PRIMATE WORLDS.

PRESBYTERIAN Eco-Justice Task Force. KEEPING AND HEALING THE CREATION.

*SHEAFFER, John and BRAND, Raymond. WHATEVER HAPPENED TO EDEN?

VERMEIJ, Geerat J. EVOLUTION AND ESCALATION: AN ECOLOGICAL HISTORY OF LIFE.

WEIR, David. THE BHOPAL SYNDROME: PESTICIDES, ENVIRONMENT AND HEALTH.

*WILKINSON, Loren, ed. EARTHKEEPING: CHRISTIAN STEWARDSHIP OF NATURAL RE-SOURCES. 2nd ed.

GENERAL & FICTION

BARTH, Karl. WOLFGANG AMADEUS MOZART.

BAYLY, Joseph. THE GOSPEL BLIMP AND OTHER STORIES.

BOVA, Ben. WELCOME TO MOONBASE.

NYMAN, Michael. EXPERIMENTAL MUSIC: CAGE AND BEYOND.

OSBORNE, Denis. THE ANDROMEDANS & OTHER PARABLES OF SCIENCE AND FAITH.

PREISS, Byron, ed. THE UNIVERSE.

VITZ, Paul C., and GLIMCHER, Arnold B. MODERN ART AND MODERN SCIENCE: A PARALLEL ANALYSIS OF VISION.

GENERAL SCIENCE

BROAD, William, and WADE, Nicholas. BETRAYERS OF THE TRUTH.

DAVIES, Paul. SUPERFORCE.

DAVIS, Philip J., and PARK, David, eds. NO WAY: THE NATURE OF THE IMPOSSIBLE.

DYSON, Freeman. DISTURBING THE UNIVERSE.

FLOOD, Raymond, and LOCKWOOD, Michael, eds. THE NATURE OF TIME.

FRENCH, A.P., and KENNEDY, P.J., eds. NIELS BOHR: A CENTENARY VOLUME.

GARDNER, Martin. SCIENCE: GOOD, BAD AND BOGUS.

GLEICK, James. CHAOS: MAKING A NEW SCIENCE.

HARDING, Sandra, and O'BARR, Jean F., eds. SEX AND SCIENTIFIC INQUIRY.

HEILBRON, J.L. THE DILEMMAS OF AN UPRIGHT MAN: MAX PLANCK AS SPOKESMAN FOR GERMAN SCIENCE.

JUDSON, Horace F. THE SEARCH FOR SOLUTIONS. abridged ed.

LEITH, T. Harry. BIBLIOGRAPHY For the Preparation of Research Papers in the History & Philosophy & Sociology of Science, Biography of Scientists, Science & Religion, Science & the Humanities, & Education in Science. 7th ed.

MURCHIE, Guy. MUSIC OF THE SPHERES: THE MATERIAL UNIVERSE—FROM ATOM TO QUASAR, SIMPLY EXPLAINED. rev. ed. 2 vols.

NATIONAL Aeronautics and Space Administration. THE SEARCH FOR EXTRATERRESTRIAL INTELLIGENCE.

PAGELS, Heinz R. THE COSMIC CODE: QUANTUM PHYSICS AS THE LAW OF NATURE.

PAGELS, Heinz R. PERFECT SYMMETRY: THE SEARCH FOR THE BEGINNING OF TIME.

PIERCE, John R., and NOLL, A. Michael. SIGNALS—THE SCIENCE OF TELECOMMUNICATIONS.

ROTHMAN, Tony. SCIENCE À LA MODE: PHYSICAL FASHIONS AND FICTIONS.

SPERRY, Roger. SCIENCE AND MORAL PRIORITY: MERGING MIND, BRAIN, AND HUMAN VALUES.

SPIELBERG, Nathan, and ANDERSON, Bryon D. SEVEN IDEAS THAT SHOOK THE UNIVERSE.

TREFIL, James S. A SCIENTIST AT THE SEASHORE.

TREFIL, James S. MEDITATIONS AT SUNSET: A SCIENTIST LOOKS AT THE SKY.

WEINER, J.S. THE PILTDOWN FORGERY.

WHEELER, John A. A JOURNEY INTO GRAVITY AND SPACETIME.

HISTORY OF SCIENCE

BLAEDEL, Niels. HARMONY AND UNITY: THE LIFE OF NIELS BOHR.

BUTTERFIELD, Herbert. ORIGINS OF MODERN SCIENCE. rev. ed.

COHEN, Bernard. REVOLUTION IN SCIENCE.

D'ABRO, A. THE EVOLUTION OF SCIENTIFIC THOUGHT FROM NEWTON TO EINSTEIN.

FUNKENSTEIN, Amos. THEOLOGY AND THE SCIENTIFIC IMAGINATION FROM THE MIDDLE AGES TO THE SEVENTEENTH CENTURY.

GAMOW, George. THE GREAT PHYSICISTS FROM GALILEO TO EINSTEIN.

GINGERICH, Owen, ed. SCIENTIFIC GENIUS AND CREATIVITY.

GOODING, David, and JAMES, Frank A.J.L., eds. FARADAY REDISCOVERED: ESSAYS ON THE LIFE AND WORK OF MICHAEL FARADAY, 1791-1867.

GRIBBIN, John. IN SEARCH OF THE DOUBLE HELIX: QUANTUM PHYSICS AND LIFE.

HARRISON, Edward. MASKS OF THE UNIVERSE.

HENDRY, John. JAMES CLERK MAXWELL AND THE THEORY OF THE ELECTROMAGNETIC FIELD.

HOLTON, Gerald. THEMATIC ORIGINS OF SCIENTIFIC THOUGHT: KEPLER TO EINSTEIN.

JAKI, Stanley L. COSMOS IN TRANSITION: STUDIES IN THE HISTORY OF COSMOLOGY.

JAKI, Stanley L. THE ORIGIN OF SCIENCE AND THE SCIENCE OF ITS ORIGIN.

JAKI, Stanley L. UNEASY GENIUS: THE LIFE AND WORK OF PIERRE DUHEM.

KEVLES, D.J. THE PHYSICISTS: THE HISTORY OF A SCIENTIFIC COMMUNITY IN MODERN AMERICA.

KUHN, Thomas S. THE STRUCTURE OF SCIENTIFIC REVOLUTIONS. 2nd ed.

NUMBERS, Ronald L. CREATION BY NATURAL LAW: LAPLACE'S NEBULAR HYPOTHESIS IN AMERICAN THOUGHT.

OLDROYD, David. THE ARCH OF KNOWLEDGE: AN INTRODUCTORY STUDY OF THE HISTORY OF THE PHILOSOPHY AND METHODOLOGY OF SCIENCE.

PAIS, Abraham. 'SUBTLE IS THE LORD...': THE SCIENCE AND THE LIFE OF ALBERT EINSTEIN.

REBONDI, Pietro. GALILEO: HERETIC.

REICHENBACH, Hans. FROM COPERNICUS TO EINSTEIN.

RICHARDS, Robert J. DARWIN AND THE EMERGENCE OF EVOLUTIONARY THEORIES OF MIND AND BEHAVIOR.

RUSSELL, Colin. SCIENCE & SOCIAL CHANGE IN BRITAIN: 1700-1900.

STAFLEU, Marinus D. THEORIES AT WORK: ON THE STRUCTURE AND FUNCTIONING OF THEORIES IN SCIENCE, IN PARTICULAR DURING THE COPERNICAN REVOLUTION.

STROMBECK, Donald R. THE REASON FOR SCIENCE.

SUGIMOTO, Kenji. ALBERT EINSTEIN: A PHOTOGRAPHIC BIOGRAPHY.

*TOLSTOY, Ivan. JAMES CLERK MAXWELL.

TOOMER, G.J. PTOLEMY'S ALMAGEST.

VICKERS, Brian, ed. ENGLISH SCIENCE: BACON TO NEWTON

WEISSKOPF, Victor F. THE PRIVILEGE OF BEING A PHYSICIST.

WHITROW, G.J., ed. EINSTEIN: THE MAN AND HIS ACHIEVEMENT.

WHITTAKER, Edmund T. A HISTORY OF THE THEORIES OF AETHER AND ELECTRICITY.

ZEE, A. AN OLD MAN'S TOY: GRAVITY AT WORK AND PLAY IN EINSTEIN'S UNIVERSE.

HISTORY OF SCIENCE & THEOLOGY

ALLEN, Diogenes. CHRISTIAN BELIEF IN A POSTMODERN WORLD: THE FULL WEALTH OF CONVICTION.

BARBOUR, Ian G. ISSUES IN SCIENCE AND RELIGION.

*BIRCH, C., and COBB, John. THE LIBERATION OF LIFE.

BROWN, Robert H. THE WISDOM OF SCIENCE: ITS RELEVANCE TO CULTURE & RELI-GION.

*BUBE, Richard H. THE ENCOUNTER BETWEEN CHRISTIANITY & SCIENCE.

ELLUL, Jacques. THE HUMILIATION OF THE WORD.

FIDDES, Victor. SCIENCE AND THE GOSPEL.

HODGSON, Peter E. CHRISTIANITY AND SCIENCE (Christianity and Science Series).

*HOOYKAAS, R. RELIGION AND THE RISE OF MODERN SCIENCE.

HOUGHTON, John. DOES GOD PLAY DICE? A LOOK AT THE STORY OF THE UNIVERSE.

HUMMEL, Charles E. THE GALILEO CONNECTION.

JAKI, Stanley L. THE ROAD OF SCIENCE AND THE WAYS TO GOD.

JAKI, Stanley L. THE SAVIOR OF SCIENCE.

JAKI, Stanley L. SCIENCE AND CREATION: FROM ETERNAL CYCLES TO AN OSCILLATING UNIVERSE.

*JEEVES, Malcolm A. THE SCIENTIFIC ENTERPRISE & CHRISTIAN FAITH.

KLAAREN, Eugene M. RELIGIOUS ORIGINS OF MODERN SCIENCE: BELIEF IN CREATION IN SEVENTEENTH-CENTURY THOUGHT.

LINDBERG, David C., and NUMBERS, Ronald, eds. GOD & NATURE: HISTORICAL ESSAYS ON THE ENCOUNTER BETWEEN CHRISTIANITY AND SCIENCE.

LIVINGSTONE, David N. DARWIN'S FORGOTTEN DEFENDERS: THE ENCOUNTER BE-TWEEN EVANGELICAL THEOLOGY AND EVOLUTIONARY THOUGHT.

LODER, James E. THE TRANSFORMING MOMENT. 2nd ed.

MCINTIRE, C. T., ed. GOD, HISTORY AND THE HISTORIANS: MODERN CHRISTIAN VIEWS OF HISTORY.

MILLER, James B., and MCCALL, Kenneth E., eds. THE CHURCH AND CONTEMPORARY COSMOLOGY.

MITCHELL, Ralph G. EINSTEIN AND CHRIST: A NEW APPROACH TO THE DEFENCE OF THE CHRISTIAN RELIGION.

MORELAND, J.P. CHRISTIANITY AND THE NATURE OF SCIENCE: A PHILOSOPHICAL IN-VESTIGATION.

MURPHY, George L. THE TRADEMARK OF GOD.

MURPHY, Nancey. THEOLOGY IN THE AGE OF SCIENTIFIC REASONING.

NEBELSICK, Harold P. THE CIRCLES OF GOD: THEOLOGY AND SCIENCE FROM THE PRE-SOCRATICS TO COPERNICUS.

NEBELSICK, Harold P. THEOLOGY AND SCIENCE IN MUTUAL MODIFICATION.

PAUL, Iain. KNOWLEDGE OF GOD: CALVIN, EINSTEIN, AND POLANYI.

*PAUL, Iain. SCIENCE AND THEOLOGY IN EINSTEIN'S PERSPECTIVE.

PEACOCKE, Arthur R. CREATION AND THE WORLD OF SCIENCE.

PEACOCKE, Arthur R. INTIMATIONS OF REALITY: CRITICAL REALISM IN SCIENCE AND RE-LIGION.

PETERS, Ted, ed. COSMOS AS CREATION: THEOLOGY AND SCIENCE IN CONSONANCE.

POLKINGHORNE, John. ONE WORLD: THE INTERACTION OF SCIENCE AND THEOLOGY.

*POLLARD, W.G. CHANCE AND PROVIDENCE.

POLLARD, W.G. TRANSCENDENCE AND PROVIDENCE: REFLECTIONS OF A PHYSICIST AND PRIEST.

*SANTMIRE, H. Paul. THE TRAVAIL OF NATURE: THE AMBIGUOUS ECOLOGICAL PROM-ISE OF CHRISTIAN THEOLOGY.

SELL, Alan P.F. DEFENDING & DECLARING THE FAITH: SOME SCOTTISH EXAMPLES, 1860-1920.

*STANNARD, Russell. SCIENCE AND THE RENEWAL OF BELIEF.

TEILHARD DE CHARDIN, Pierre. CHRISTIANITY AND EVOLUTION.

TORRANCE, Thomas F. CHRISTIAN THEOLOGY AND SCIENTIFIC CULTURE.

*TORRANCE, Thomas F. DIVINE AND CONTINGENT ORDER.

TORRANCE, Thomas F. GROUND AND GRAMMAR OF THEOLOGY.

TORRANCE, Thomas F. THE MEDIATION OF CHRIST.

TORRANCE, Thomas F. REALITY AND EVANGELICAL THEOLOGY.

TORRANCE, Thomas F. REALITY AND SCIENTIFIC THEOLOGY.

TORRANCE, Thomas F. SPACE, TIME AND INCARNATION.

TORRANCE, Thomas F. THEOLOGICAL SCIENCE.

*TORRANCE, Thomas F. THEOLOGY IN RECONCILIATION.

*TORRANCE, Thomas F. THEOLOGY IN RECONSTRUCTION.

TORRANCE, Thomas, F. TRANSFORMATION AND CONVERGENCE IN THE FRAME OF KNOWLEDGE: EXPLORATION IN THE INTERRELATIONS OF SCIENTIFIC AND THEOLOGICAL ENTERPRISE.

MATH RELATED

BLOCKSMA, Mary. READING THE NUMBERS: A SURVIVAL GUIDE TO THE MEASURE-MENTS, NUMBERS AND SIZES ENCOUNTERED IN EVERYDAY LIFE.

CHASE, Gene B., and JONGSMA, Calvin. BIBLIOGRAPHY OF CHRISTIANITY AND MATHE-MATICS, 1910-1983.

EKELAND, Ivar. MATHEMATICS AND THE UNEXPECTED.

GHYKA, Matila. THE GEOMETRY OF ART AND LIFE.

*GRANVILLE, H. LOGOS: MATHEMATICS AND CHRISTIAN THEOLOGY.

HUNTLEY, H.E. THE DIVINE PROPORTION: A STUDY IN MATHEMATICAL BEAUTY.

PEDOE, Dan. GEOMETRY AND THE VISUAL ARTS.

ORIGINS: CREATION & EVOLUTION

ACKERMAN, Paul. IT'S A YOUNG WORLD AFTER ALL.

ANDERSON, Bernard W., ed. CREATION IN THE OLD TESTAMENT.

ANDERSON, Bernard W. CREATION VERSUS CHAOS: THE REINTERPRETATION OF MYTHI-CAL SYMBOLISM IN THE BIBLE.

*ANDERSON, J. Kerby, and GUFFIN, Harold G. FOSSILS IN FOCUS.

ANDREWS, Edgar H.; GITT, W.; and OUWENEEL, W.J., eds. CONCEPTS IN CREATIONISM.

ANDREWS, Edgar H. GOD, SCIENCE AND EVOLUTION.

*BENZ, Ernst. EVOLUTION AND CHRISTIAN HOPE.

BIRD, Wendell R. THE ORIGIN OF SPECIES REVISITED. 2 vols.

BLACKMORE, Vernon, and PAGE, Andrew. EVOLUTION: THE GREAT DEBATE.

BLISS, Richard B. ORIGINS: CREATION OR EVOLUTION.

BLOCHER, Henri. IN THE BEGINNING: THE OPENING CHAPTERS OF GENESIS.

BOWLER, Peter J. THE ECLIPSE OF DARWINISM.

BOWLER, Peter J. EVOLUTION: THE HISTORY OF AN IDEA. rev. ed.

BROOKS, Jim. ORIGINS OF LIFE.

BURKE, Derek, ed. CREATION & EVOLUTION: SEVEN VIEWS.

BURRELL, David B., and MCGINN, Bernard, eds. GOD AND CREATION: AN ECUMENICAL SYMPOSIUM.

CAMERON, Nigel. EVOLUTION AND THE AUTHORITY OF THE BIBLE.

CARVIN, Walter P. CREATION & SCIENTIFIC EXPLANATION.

CHAISSON, Eric. COSMIC DAWN: THE ORIGINS OF MATTER AND LIFE.

CHAISSON, Eric. THE LIFE ERA: COSMIC SELECTION AND CONSCIOUS EVOLUTION.

DARWIN, Charles. THE ORIGIN OF SPECIES AND THE DESCENT OF MAN.

DAVIS, Percival, and KENYON, Dean H. OF PANDAS AND PEOPLE: THE CENTRAL QUESTION OF BIOLOGICAL ORIGINS.

DENTON, Michael. EVOLUTION: A THEORY IN CRISIS.

ELDREDGE, Niles. LIFE PULSE: EPISODES FROM THE STORY OF THE FOSSIL RECORD.

ELDREDGE, Niles. TIME FRAMES: THE EVOLUTION OF PUNCTUATED EQUILIBRIUM.

FABIAN, A.C., ed. ORIGINS: THE DARWIN COLLEGE LECTURES.

*FISCHER, Robert B., GOD DID IT, BUT HOW?

FISHER, David E. THE BIRTH OF THE EARTH: A WANDERLIED THROUGH SPACE, TIME, AND THE HUMAN IMAGINATION.

*FRAIR, Wayne, and DAVIS, Percival. A CASE FOR CREATION. 3rd ed.

FRYE, Roland M., ed. IS GOD A CREATIONIST?: THE RELIGIOUS CASE AGAINST CREATION SCIENCE.

GANGE, Robert. ORIGINS AND DESTINY: A SCIENTIST EXAMINES GOD'S HANDIWORK.

GEISLER, Norman L. CREATOR IN THE COURTROOM.

GEISLER, Norman L., and ANDERSON, J. Kerby. ORIGIN SCIENCE: A PROPOSAL FOR THE CREATION-EVOLUTION CONTROVERSY.

GILKEY, Langdon. CREATIONISM ON TRIAL: EVOLUTION AND GOD AT LITTLE ROCK.

GILKEY, Langdon. MAKER OF HEAVEN AND EARTH: THE CHRISTIAN DOCTRINE OF CREATION IN THE LIGHT OF MODERN SCIENCE.

*GILLESPIE, Neal C. CHARLES DARWIN AND THE PROBLEM OF CREATION.

GISH, Duane T. EVOLUTION: THE CHALLENGE OF THE FOSSIL RECORD.

*GISH, Duane T. EVOLUTION: THE FOSSILS SAY NO!

*GODFREY, Laurie R., ed. WHAT DARWIN BEGAN.

GOULD, S. J. THE FLAMINGO'S SMILE: REFLECTIONS IN NATURAL HISTORY.

GOULD, S. J. HENS' TEETH AND HORSES' TOES: FURTHER REFLECTIONS IN NATURAL HISTORY.

*GRAY, Asa. DARWINIANA.

GROVES, Colin P. THEORY OF HUMAN AND PRIMATE EVOLUTION.

HAYES, Zachary. WHAT ARE THEY SAYING ABOUT CREATION?

*HAYWARD, Alan. CREATION & EVOLUTION: THE FACTS & FALLACIES.

HENRY, Carl F.H. GOD, REVELATION & AUTHORITY: GOD WHO SPEAKS & SHOWS, Vol. 6.

HOOVER, A.J. THE CASE FOR TEACHING CREATION.

HORNER, John R., and GORMAN, James. DIGGING DINOSAURS: THE SEARCH THAT UN-RAVELED THE MYSTERY OF BABY DINOSAURS.

HUMMEL, Charles E. CREATION OR EVOLUTION?

HYERS, Conrad. MEANING OF CREATION: GENESIS & MODERN SCIENCE.

JASTROW, Robert. GOD AND THE ASTRONOMERS.

JOHNSON, Phillip E. DARWIN ON TRIAL.

KLOTZ, John W. STUDIES IN CREATION: A GENERAL INTRODUCTION TO THE CREATION-EVOLUTION DEBATE.

KRAMER, William. EVOLUTION AND CREATION: A CATHOLIC UNDERSTANDING.

LAMBERT, David, and Diagram Group Staff. THE FIELD GUIDE TO EARLY MAN.

LARSON, Edward J. TRIAL & ERROR: THE AMERICAN CONTROVERSY OVER CREATION AND EVOLUTION.

*LEITH, T. Harry. THE CONTRASTS AND SIMILARITIES AMONG SCIENCE, PSEUDO-SCIENCE, THE OCCULT AND RELIGION.

LESTER, Lane, and BOHLIN, Raymond G. THE NATURAL LIMITS TO BIOLOGICAL CHANGE.

LEWIN, Roger. BONES OF CONTENTION: CONTROVERSIES IN THE SEARCH FOR HUMAN ORIGINS.

LEWONTIN, R.C. THE GENETIC BASIS OF EVOLUTIONARY CHANGE.

LOVTRUP, Soren. DARWINISM: THE REFUTATIONS OF A MYTH.

MAATMAN, Russell W. THE BIBLE, NATURAL SCIENCE, AND EVOLUTION.

MACBETH, Norman. DARWIN RETRIED: AN APPEAL TO REASON.

MARGULIS L., ed. ORIGINS OF LIFE. 2nd ed.

MARSDEN, George M. FUNDAMENTALISM & AMERICAN CULTURE: THE SHAPING OF TWENTIETH-CENTURY EVANGELICALISM.

MCGOWAN, Chris. IN THE BEGINNING: A SCIENTIST SHOWS WHY THE CREATIONISTS ARE WRONG.

MCIVER, Tom. ANTI-EVOLUTION: AN ANNOTATED BIBLIOGRAPHY.

MCMULLIN, Ernan, ed. EVOLUTION AND CREATION.

*MESSENGER, Ernest C. EVOLUTION AND THEOLOGY.

MOLTMANN, Jürgen. GOD IN CREATION: A NEW THEOLOGY OF CREATION AND THE SPIRIT OF GOD.

MONTAGU, Ashley, ed. SCIENCE AND CREATIONISM.

MONTENAT, Christian; PLATEAUX, Luc; and ROUX, Pascal. HOW TO READ CREATION IN EVOLUTION.

MOORE, James R. POST-DARWINIAN CONTROVERSIES.

MOORE, John N. HOW TO TEACH ORIGINS (WITHOUT ACLU INTERFERENCE).

*MOROWITZ, Harold J. COSMIC JOY & LOCAL PAIN: MUSINGS OF A MYSTIC SCIENTIST.

MORRIS, Henry M. HISTORY OF MODERN CREATIONISM.

MORRIS, Henry M. WHAT IS CREATION SCIENCE?

NEWELL, Norman D. CREATION AND EVOLUTION: MYTH OR REALITY?

*NEWMAN, Robert, and ECKLEMENN, Herman. GENESIS ONE & THE ORIGIN OF THE EARTH.

PARKER, Barry. CREATION: THE STORY OF THE ORIGIN AND EVOLUTION OF THE UNIVERSE.

PITMAN, Michael. ADAM & EVOLUTION: A SCIENTIFIC CRITIQUE OF NEO-DARWINISM.

POLLARD, Jeffrey W., ed. EVOLUTIONARY THEORY: PATHS INTO THE FUTURE.

*PUN, Pattle P. T. EVOLUTION: NATURE & SCRIPTURE IN CONFLICT?

RAMM, Bernard. THE CHRISTIAN VIEW OF SCIENCE AND SCRIPTURE.

ROZENTAL, I.L. BIG BANG BIG BOUNCE: HOW PARTICLES AND FIELDS DRIVE COSMIC EVOLUTION.

SHAPIRO, Robert. ORIGINS: A SKEPTIC'S GUIDE TO THE CREATION OF LIFE ON EARTH.

SKEHAN, James W. MODERN SCIENCE & THE BOOK OF GENESIS.

SMITH, J. Maynard. EVOLUTION NOW.

SPANNER, Douglas C. BIBLICAL CREATION & THE THEORY OF EVOLUTION.

*STANLEY, Steven M. THE NEW EVOLUTIONARY TIMETABLE.

STOKES, William L. THE GENESIS ANSWER: A SCIENTIST'S TESTAMENT FOR DIVINE CREATION.

THAXTON, Charles B.; BRADLEY, Walter L.; and OLSEN, Roger L. MYSTERY OF LIFE'S ORIGIN: REASSESSING CURRENT THEORIES.

THOMPSON, A. BIOLOGY, ZOOLOGY & GENETICS: EVOLUTION MODEL VS. CREATION MODEL.

THURMAN, L. Duane. HOW TO THINK ABOUT EVOLUTION, AND OTHER BIBLE-SCIENCE CONTROVERSIES. 2nd ed.

VAN TILL, Howard J. THE FOURTH DAY: WHAT THE BIBLE AND THE HEAVENS ARE TELLING US ABOUT THE CREATION.

VAN TILL, Howard J.; YOUNG, Davis A.; and MENNINGA, Clarence. SCIENCE HELD HOS-TAGE: WHAT'S WRONG WITH CREATION SCIENCE & EVOLUTIONISM.

WHITCOMB, John C., Jr., and MORRIS, Henry M. THE GENESIS FLOOD.

WICKEN, Jeffrey S. EVOLUTION, THERMODYNAMICS AND INFORMATION: EXTENDING THE DARWINIAN PROGRAM.

*WIESTER, John. THE GENESIS CONNECTION.

*WILDER-SMITH, A. E. CREATION OF LIFE: A CYBERNETIC APPROACH TO EVOLUTION.

*WILLIS, David, ed. ORIGINS AND CHANGE.

WONDERLY, Daniel E. GOD'S TIME-RECORDS IN ANCIENT SEDIMENTS: EVIDENCES OF LONG TIME SPANS IN EARTH'S HISTORY.

WONDERLY, Daniel E. NEGLECT OF GEOLOGIC DATA: SEDIMENTARY STRATA COM-PARED WITH YOUNG-EARTH CREATIONIST WRITINGS.

YOUNG, Davis A., CHRISTIANITY & THE AGE OF THE EARTH.

*YOUNG, Davis A. CREATION & THE FLOOD: AN ALTERNATIVE TO FLOOD GEOLOGY & THEISTIC EVOLUTION.

*YOUNGBLOOD, Ronald, ed. THE GENESIS DEBATE: PERSISTENT QUESTIONS ABOUT CREATION AND THE FLOOD.

PHILOSOPHY OF SCIENCE

AESCHLIMAN, Michael D. THE RESTITUTION OF MAN: C. S. LEWIS AND THE CASE AGAINST SCIENTISM.

*ALEXANDER, Denis. BEYOND SCIENCE.

ALLEN, Diogenes. THREE OUTSIDERS: BLAISE PASCAL, SØREN KIERKEGAARD, SIMONE WEIL.

BARROW, John D., and TIPLER, Frank J. THE ANTHROPIC COSMOLOGICAL PRINCIPLE.

BARROW, John D. THE WORLD WITHIN THE WORLD.

BATESON, Gregory. MIND & NATURE: A NECESSARY UNITY.

BAUER, Henry H. BEYOND VELIKOVSKY: THE HISTORY OF A PUBLIC CONTROVERSY.

BLAKEMORE, Colin, and GREENFIELD, Susan, eds. MINDWAVES: THOUGHTS ON INTELLI-GENCE, IDENTITY AND CONSCIOUSNESS.

BOHM, David. WHOLENESS AND THE IMPLICATE ORDER.

BOHR, Niels. THE PHILOSOPHICAL WRITINGS OF NIELS BOHR.

BRIGGS, John P., and PEAT, F. David. LOOKING GLASS UNIVERSE: THE EMERGING SCI-ENCE OF WHOLENESS.

CANTORE, Enrico. ATOMIC ORDER: AN INTRODUCTION TO THE PHILOSOPHY OF MICRO-PHYSICS.

*CANTORE, Enrico. SCIENTIFIC MAN: THE HUMANIST SIGNIFICANCE OF SCIENCE.

CAPRA, Fritjof. THE TAO OF PHYSICS. 2nd ed.

CASTI, John L. PARADIGMS LOST: IMAGES OF MAN IN THE MIRROR OF SCIENCE.

CHAISSON, Eric. RELATIVELY SPEAKING: RELATIVITY, BLACK HOLES, AND THE FATE OF THE UNIVERSE.

CUSHING, James T. et al, eds. SCIENCE & REALITY: RECENT WORK IN THE PHILOSOPHY OF SCIENCE.

DAVIES, Paul. GOD & THE NEW PHYSICS.

*DAVIES, Paul. OTHER WORLDS.

DYSON, Freeman. INFINITE IN ALL DIRECTIONS: AN EXPLORATION OF SCIENCE AND BE-LIEF.

EINSTEIN, Albert. SIDELIGHTS ON RELATIVITY.

ELLUL, Jacques. THE SUBVERSION OF CHRISTIANITY.

FOLSE, Henry J. THE PHILOSOPHY OF NIELS BOHR: THE FRAMEWORK OF COMPLEMEN-TARITY.

FORD, Norman M. WHEN DID I BEGIN? CONCEPTION OF THE HUMAN INDIVIDUAL IN HIS-TORY, PHILOSOPHY AND SCIENCE.

FRASER, J.T. TIME: THE FAMILIAR STRANGER.

GAMOW, George. ONE TWO THREE...INFINITY: FACTS AND SPECULATIONS OF SCIENCE.

GARDNER, Martin. THE WHYS OF A PHILOSOPHICAL SCRIVENER.

GELWICK, Richard. WAY OF DISCOVERY: AN INTRODUCTION TO THE THOUGHT OF MI-CHAEL POLANYI.

GILSON, Etienne. FROM ARISTOTLE TO DARWIN AND BACK AGAIN: A JOURNEY IN FINAL CAUSALITY.

GLEICK, James. CHAOS: MAKING A NEW SCIENCE.

GOULD, Stephen J. WONDERFUL LIFE: THE BURGESS SHALE AND THE NATURE OF HIS-TORY.

GREENSTEIN, George. THE SYMBIOTIC UNIVERSE: AN UNORTHODOX LOOK AT THE ORI-GIN OF THE COSMOS AND THE DEVELOPMENT OF LIFE.

GREGORY, Richard L., and ZANGWILL, O.L., eds. THE OXFORD COMPANION TO THE MIND.

HENDERSON, Charles P., Jr. GOD & SCIENCE: THE DEATH AND REBIRTH OF THEISM.

HENRY, Carl F.H., ed. HORIZONS OF SCIENCE: CHRISTIAN SCHOLARS SPEAK OUT.

HERSCHEL, John F.W. A PRELIMINARY DISCOURSE ON THE STUDY OF NATURAL PHIL-OSOPHY.

HOFSTADTER, Douglas R. GÖDEL, ESCHER, BACH: AN ETERNAL GOLDEN BRAID.

HOFSTADTER, Douglas R. METAMAGICAL THEMAS: QUESTING FOR THE ESSENCE OF MIND AND PATTERN.

*HOLMES, Arthur F. ALL TRUTH IS GOD'S TRUTH.

HOLMES, Arthur F. CONTOURS OF A WORLD VIEW.

JAKI, Stanley L. ANGELS, APES, & MEN.

JAKI, Stanley L. CHESTERTON, A SEER OF SCIENCE.

*JAKI, Stanley L. COSMOS AND CREATOR.

*JASTROW, Robert. TWO FACES OF REALITY.

LAYZER, D. COSMOGENESIS: THE GROWTH OF ORDER IN THE UNIVERSE.

LONGINO, Helen E. SCIENCE AS SOCIAL KNOWLEDGE: VALUES AND OBJECTIVITY IN SCIENTIFIC INQUIRY.

*MACKAY, Donald M. BRAINS, MACHINES & PERSONS.

*MACKAY, Donald M., ed. CHRISTIANITY IN A MECHANISTIC UNIVERSE.

*MACKAY, Donald M. THE CLOCKWORK IMAGE.

MACKAY, Donald M. HUMAN SCIENCE & HUMAN DIGNITY.

MACKAY, Donald M. SCIENCE AND THE QUEST FOR MEANING.

MURDOCH, D.R. NIELS BOHR'S PHILOSOPHY OF PHYSICS.

NEWBIGIN, Lesslie. FOOLISHNESS TO THE GREEKS: THE GOSPEL AND WESTERN CULTURE.

*PACKER, J.I., and HOWARD, Thomas. CHRISTIANITY: THE TRUE HUMANISM.

*PANNENBERG, Wolfhart. FAITH AND REALITY.

PANNENBERG, Wolfhart. THEOLOGY AND THE PHILOSOPHY OF SCIENCE.

PASCAL, Blaise. PENSÉES.

PATTEE, Howard H., ed. HIERARCHY THEORY: THE CHALLENGE OF COMPLEX SYSTEMS.

*PAUL, Iain. SCIENCE, THEOLOGY AND EINSTEIN.

PEAT, F. David. SUPERSTRINGS AND THE SEARCH FOR THE THEORY OF EVERYTHING.

PEUKERT, Helmut. SCIENCE, ACTION AND FUNDAMENTAL THEOLOGY: TOWARD A THEOLOGY OF COMMUNICATIVE ACTION.

POLANYI, Michael. KNOWING AND BEING.

POLANYI, Michael. PERSONAL KNOWLEDGE: TOWARDS A POST-CRITICAL PHILOSOPHY.

POLKINGHORNE, John. THE QUANTUM WORLD.

PRIGOGENE, Ilya, and STENGERS, Isabelle. ORDER OUT OF CHAOS—MAN'S NEW DIALOGUE WITH NATURE.

PUDDEFOOT, John. LOGIC & AFFIRMATION: PERSPECTIVES IN MATHEMATICS & THEOLOGY.

RATZSCH, Del. PHILOSOPHY OF SCIENCE: THE NATURAL SCIENCES IN CHRISTIAN PERSPECTIVE.

RAVETZ, J.R. SCIENTIFIC KNOWLEDGE & ITS SOCIAL PROBLEMS.

RICHARDS, Stewart. PHILOSOPHY AND SOCIOLOGY OF SCIENCE: AN INTRODUCTION. 2nd ed.

RUCKER, Rudy. INFINITY AND THE MIND: THE SCIENCE AND PHILOSOPHY OF THE INFINITE.

RUSSELL, Colin. CROSS-CURRENTS: INTERACTIONS BETWEEN SCIENCE AND FAITH.

RYAN, Dennis P., ed. EINSTEIN AND THE HUMANTITIES.

*SCHWARZ, Hans. ON THE WAY TO THE FUTURE. rev. ed.

SCOTT, Drusilla. EVERYMAN REVIVED: THE COMMON SENSE OF MICHAEL POLANYI.

SEIELSTAD, George A. AT THE HEART OF THE WEB: THE INEVITABLE GENESIS OF INTELLIGENT LIFE.

SHELDRAKE, Rupert. A NEW SCIENCE OF LIFE: THE HYPOTHESIS OF FORMATIVE CAUSATION. rev. ed.

SHOPE, Robert K. THE ANALYSIS OF KNOWING: A DECADE OF RESEARCH.

SMITH, Wolfgang. COSMOS & TRANSCENDENCE: BREAKING THROUGH THE BARRIERS OF SCIENTIFIC BELIEF.

SMULLYAN, Raymond. FOREVER UNDECIDED: A PUZZLE GUIDE TO GÖDEL.

SNOW, C.P. THE TWO CULTURES: AND A SECOND LOOK. 2nd ed.

SOKOLOWSKI, Robert. THE GOD OF FAITH AND REASON.

SQUIRES, Euan J. THE MYSTERY OF THE QUANTUM WORLD.

*STAFLEU, M.D. THEORIES IN PRACTICE.

STANESBY, Derek. SCIENCE, REASON & RELIGION.

TORRANCE, Thomas F., ed. BELIEF IN SCIENCE AND IN CHRISTIAN LIFE: THE RELEVANCE OF MICHAEL POLANYI'S THOUGHT FOR CHRISTIAN FAITH AND LIFE.

TORRANCE, Thomas F. THE CHRISTIAN FRAME OF MIND: REASON, ORDER, AND OPENNESS IN THEOLOGY AND NATURAL SCIENCE.

TORRANCE, Thomas F. REALITY AND SCIENTIFIC THEOLOGY.

VARGHESE, Roy A., ed. THE INTELLECTUALS SPEAK OUT ABOUT GOD.

VOEGELIN, Eric. SCIENCE, POLITICS AND GNOSTICISM.

WANG, Hao. REFLECTIONS ON KURT GÖDEL.

WHITEHEAD, Alfred N. SCIENCE AND THE MODERN WORLD.

WINFREE, Arthur T. WHEN TIME BREAKS DOWN: THE THREE-DIMENSIONAL DYNAMICS OF ELECTROCHEMICAL WAVES & CARDIAC ARRHYTHMIAS.

YU, Carver. BEING AND RELATION: AN EASTERN CRITIQUE OF WESTERN DUALISM.

ZIMAN, J. AN INTRODUCTION TO SCIENCE STUDIES: THE PHILOSOPHICAL AND SOCIAL ASPECTS OF SCIENCE AND TECHNOLOGY.

PHYSICS

ADAIR, Robert K. THE GREAT DESIGN: PARTICLES, FIELDS, AND CREATION.

BABLOYANTZ, A. MOLECULES, DYNAMICS AND LIFE: AN INTRODUCTION TO SELF-ORGANIZATION OF MATTER.

BELL, John S. SPEAKABLE AND UNSPEAKABLE IN QUANTUM MECHANICS: COLLECTED PAPERS IN QUANTUM PHILOSOPHY.

BLUM, W., et al, eds. HEISENBERG: GESAMMELTE WERKE (COLLECTED WORKS).

CLINE, Barbara L. MEN WHO MADE A NEW PHYSICS: PHYSICISTS AND THE QUANTUM THEORY.

CREASE, Robert F., and MANN, Charles C. THE SECOND CREATION: MAKERS OF THE REVOLUTION IN 20TH CENTURY PHYSICS.

DAVIES, Paul. THE FORCES OF NATURE. 2nd ed.

DAVIES, Paul, and BROWN, J.R., eds. THE GHOST IN THE ATOM: A DISCUSSION OF THE MYSTERIES OF QUANTUM PHYSICS.

DEBRUS, Joachim, and HIRSHFELD, Allen C. eds. THE FUNDAMENTAL INTERACTION: GEOMETRICAL TRENDS.

D'ESPAGNAT, B. IN SEARCH OF REALITY.

DIRAC, Paul A. THE PRINCIPLES OF QUANTUM MECHANICS. 4th ed.

EINSTEIN, Albert, and INFELD, Leopold. THE EVOLUTION OF PHYSICS.

EINSTEIN, Albert. RELATIVITY: THE SPECIAL & GENERAL THEORY.

FEYNMAN, Richard P. and WEINBERG, Steve. ELEMENTARY PARTICLES AND THE LAWS OF PHYSICS.

FEYNMAN, Richard P. THE CHARACTER OF PHYSICAL LAW.

GALLAVOTTI, Giovanni, and ZWEIFEL, Paul F., eds. NONLINEAR EVOLUTION AND CHAOTIC PHENOMENA.

GAL-OR, B. COSMOLOGY, PHYSICS AND PHILOSOPHY. 2nd ed.

GAMOW, George. MR. TOMPKINS IN PAPERBACK.

GAMOW, George. THIRTY YEARS THAT SHOOK PHYSICS: THE STORY OF QUANTUM THEORY.

GEROCH, Robert. GENERAL RELATIVITY FROM A TO B.

GRIBBIN, John. IN SEARCH OF SCHRODINGER'S CAT: QUANTUM PHYSICS AND REALITY.

GRIBBIN, John. THE OMEGA POINT: THE SEARCH FOR THE MISSING MASS AND THE ULTIMATE FATE OF THE UNIVERSE.

HEISENBERG, Werner. PHYSICS AND BEYOND.

HERBERT, Nick. QUANTUM REALITY: BEYOND THE NEW PHYSICS.

HEY, A.J., and Walters, P. THE QUANTUM UNIVERSE.

*HOFFMANN, Banesh. THE STRANGE STORY OF THE QUANTUM. 2nd ed.

JAKI, Stanley L. THE ABSOLUTE BENEATH THE RELATIVE AND OTHER ESSAYS.

JAKI, Stanley L. MIRACLES AND PHYSICS.

JAKI, Stanley L. THE PHYSICIST AS ARTIST: THE LANDSCAPES OF PIERRE DUHEM.

*JAKI, Stanley L. THE RELEVANCE OF PHYSICS.

JAUCH, Josef M. ARE QUANTA REAL?: A GALILEAN DIALOGUE.

KAKU, Michio, and TRAINER, Jennifer. BEYOND EINSTEIN: THE COSMIC QUEST FOR THE THEORY OF THE UNIVERSE.

*LINDSAY, Robert B., and MARGENAU, Henry. FOUNDATIONS OF PHYSICS.

MARCH, Robert H. PHYSICS FOR POETS.

MERMIN, N. David. BOOJUMS ALL THE WAY THROUGH: COMMUNICATING SCIENCE IN A PROSAIC AGE.

MISNER, Charles; THORNE, Kip; and WHEELER, John A. GRAVITATION.

MOTZ, Lloyd, and WEAVER, Jefferson H. THE STORY OF PHYSICS.

*OWENS, Virginia S. AND THE TREES CLAP THEIR HANDS: FAITH, PERCEPTION AND THE NEW PHYSICS.

PAGELS, Heinz R. THE COSMIC CODE: QUANTUM PHYSICS AS THE LAW OF NATURE.

PARK, David. THE HOW & THE WHY: AN ESSAY ON THE ORIGINS & DEVELOPMENT OF PHYSICAL THEORY.

PERKINS, D. INTRODUCTION TO HIGH ENERGY PHYSICS. 3rd ed.

PODOLNY, R. SOMETHING CALLED NOTHING: THE PHYSICAL VACUUM: WHAT IS IT?

POLANYI, Michael. KNOWING AND BEING.

*POLKINGHORNE, John. PARTICLE PLAY.

POLKINGHORNE, John. THE QUANTUM WORLD.

POLKINHORNE, John. ROCHESTER ROUNDABOUT: THE STORY OF HIGH ENERGY PHYSICS.

RIORDAN, Michael. THE HUNTING OF THE QUARK.

ROHRLICH, Fritz. FROM PARADOX TO REALITY: BASIC CONCEPTS OF THE PHYSICAL WORLD.

ROTHMAN, Tony, et al. FRONTIERS OF MODERN PHYSICS: NEW PERSPECTIVES ON COS-MOLOGY, RELATIVITY, BLACK HOLES AND EXTRATERRESTRIAL INTELLIGENCE.

SCHWINGER, Julian. EINSTEIN'S LEGACY: THE UNITY OF SPACE AND TIME.

SQUIRES, Euan J. TO ACKNOWLEDGE THE WONDER: THE STORY OF FUNDAMENTAL PHYSICS.

STEPHENSON, G., and KILMISTER, C.W. SPECIAL RELATIVITY FOR PHYSICISTS.

TREFIL, James S. FROM ATOMS TO QUARKS: THE STRANGE WORLD OF PARTICLE PHYS-ICS.

*VON WEISÄCKER, Carl F. THE WORLDVIEW OF PHYSICS.

YOURGRAU, Wolfgang, and MANDELSTAM, Stanley. VARIATIONAL PRINCIPLES IN DYNAM-ICS AND QUANTUM THEORY.

ZEH, Heinz D. THE PHYSICAL BASIS OF THE DIRECTION OF TIME.

POLITICS & ECONOMICS

ANDERSON, Ray S. MINDING GOD'S BUSINESS.

BERNBAUM, John, ed. ECONOMIC JUSTICE AND THE STATE.

BOCKMUEHL, Klaus E. THE CHALLENGE OF MARXISM.

BUZZARD, Lynn, and COLBY, Kim. PUBLIC SCHOOL POLICY MANUAL.

*CLOUSE, Robert G., ed. WEALTH & POVERTY: FOUR CHRISTIAN VIEWS OF ECONOMICS.

ELLER, Vernard. CHRISTIAN ANARCHY: JESUS' PRIMACY OVER THE POWERS.

ERDAHL, Lowell. PRO-LIFE/PRO-PEACE: LIFE-AFFIRMING ALTERNATIVES TO ABORTION, WAR, MERCY KILLING, AND THE DEATH PENALTY.

GRANBERG-MICHAELSON, Wesley. A WORLDLY SPIRITUALITY: THE CALL TO TAKE CARE OF THE EARTH.

GRANT, George. BRINGING IN THE SHEAVES: TRANSFORMING POVERTY INTO PRODUC-TIVITY.

GRIFFITHS, Brian. THE CREATION OF WEALTH: A CHRISTIAN'S CASE FOR CAPITALISM.

HALL, Douglas J. IMAGING GOD: DOMINION AS STEWARDSHIP.

HUMPHREY, Derek, and WICKETT, Ann. THE RIGHT TO DIE: UNDERSTANDING EUTHANASIA.

KLAY, Robin. COUNTING THE COST: THE ECONOMICS OF CHRISTIAN STEWARDSHIP.

KREEFT, Peter. THE BEST THINGS IN LIFE.

LEAN, Garth. GOD'S POLITICIAN.

LEAN, Garth. ON THE TAIL OF A COMET: THE LIFE OF FRANK BUCHMAN.

LINZEY, Andrew. CHRISTIANITY & THE RIGHTS OF ANIMALS.

MARSHALL, Paul A. THINE IS THE KINGDOM: A BIBLICAL PERSPECTIVE ON THE NATURE OF GOVERNMENT AND POLITICS TODAY.

MONTGOMERY, John W. HUMAN RIGHTS & HUMAN DIGNITY: AN APOLOGETIC FOR THE TRANSCENDENT PERSPECTIVE.

NOLL, Mark A. ONE NATION UNDER GOD?: CHRISTIAN FAITH AND POLITICAL ACTION IN AMERICA.

NOLL, Mark A.; HATCH, Nathan O.; and MARSDEN, George M. THE SEARCH FOR CHRISTIAN AMERICA. exp. ed.

REICHLEY, A. James. RELIGION IN AMERICAN PUBLIC LIFE.

ROTHENBERG, Stuart, and NEWPORT, Frank. THE EVANGELICAL VOTER: RELIGION AND POLITICS IN AMERICA

SCHINDLER, Craig F., and LAPID, Gary G. THE GREAT TURNING: PERSONAL PEACE, GLOBAL VICTORY.

SIDER, Ronald J. RICH CHRISTIANS IN AN AGE OF HUNGER.

SKILLEN, James W. CHRISTIANS ORGANIZING FOR POLITICAL SERVICE: A STUDY GUIDE BASED ON THE WORK OF THE ASSOCIATION FOR PUBLIC JUSTICE.

SMARTO, Donald. JUSTICE AND MERCY.

SMITH, Gary S., ed. GOD AND POLITICS: FOUR VIEWS ON THE REFORMATION OF CIVIL GOVERNMENT.

WADE, Nicholas. A WORLD BEYOND HEALING: THE PROLOGUE AND AFTERMATH OF NUCLEAR WAR.

PSYCHOLOGY & NEURAL SCIENCE

ALLMAN, William F. APPRENTICES OF WONDER: INSIDE THE NEURAL NETWORK REVOLUTION.

ARGYLE, Michael. THE PSYCHOLOGY OF HAPPINESS.

AUGSBURGER, David W. PASTORAL COUNSELING ACROSS CULTURES.

*BARCLAY, Oliver R. THE INTELLECT AND BEYOND: DEVELOPING A CHRISTIAN MIND. rev. ed.

BROWN, L.B. THE PSYCHOLOGY OF RELIGIOUS BELIEF.

BROWNING, Don S. RELIGIOUS THOUGHT AND THE MODERN PSYCHOLOGIES.

*BURKE, Thomas, ed. MAN AND MIND.

CARTER, John, and NARRAMORE, Bruce. THE INTEGRATION OF PSYCHOLOGY AND THEOLOGY: AN INTRODUCTION.

*CLIFT, W.B. JUNG AND CHRISTIANITY.

CLOUSE, Bonnidell. MORAL DEVELOPMENT: PERSPECTIVES IN PSYCHOLOGY AND CHRISTIAN BELIEF.

COLES, Robert. THE MORAL LIFE OF CHILDREN.

COLES, Robert. THE SPIRITUAL LIFE OF CHILDREN.

COLLINS, Gary R. CAN YOU TRUST PSYCHOLOGY?

COLLINS, Gary R. CHRISTIAN COUNSELING: A COMPREHENSIVE GUIDE. rev. ed.

COLLINS, Gary R. THE REBUILDING OF PSYCHOLOGY.

COLLINS, Gary R., ed. RESOURCES FOR CHRISTIAN COUNSELING Series: INNOVATIVE APPROACHES TO COUNSELING (Gary Collins); COUNSELING CHRISTIAN WORKERS (Louis McBurney); SELF-TALK, IMAGERY AND PRAYER IN COUNSELING (H. Norman Wright); and COUNSELING THOSE WITH EATING DISORDERS (Raymond Vath).

COLLINS, Gary R., ed. RESOURCES FOR CHRISTIAN COUNSELING Series: COUNSELING THE DEPRESSED (Archibald Hart); COUNSELING FOR FAMILY VIOLENCE AND ABUSE (Grant Martin); COUNSELING IN TIMES OF CRISIS (Judson Swihart and Gerald Richardson); COUNSELING AND GUILT (Earl Wilson); COUNSELING & THE SEARCH FOR MEANING (Paul Welter); COUNSELING FOR UNPLANNED PREGNANCY AND INFERTILITY (Everett Worthington, Jr.); COUNSELING FOR PROBLEMS OF SELF-CONTROL (Richard Walters); COUNSELING FOR SUBSTANCE ABUSE AND ADDICTION (Stephen Van Cleave, Walter Byrd, Kathy Revell).

COLLINS, Gary R., ed. RESOURCES FOR CHRISTIAN COUNSELING Series: COUNSELING AND SELF-ESTEEM (David Carlson); COUNSELING FAMILIES (George Rekers); COUNSELING AND HOMOSEXUALITY (Earl Wilson); COUNSELING FOR ANGER (Mark Cosgrove); and COUNSELING AND THE DEMONIC (Rodger Bufford).

COLLINS, Gary R., ed. RESOURCES FOR CHRISTIAN COUNSELING Series: COUNSELING AND DIVORCE (David Thompson); COUNSELING AND MARRIAGE (Deloss and Ruby Friesen); COUNSELING THE SICK AND TERMINALLY ILL (Gregg Albers); COUNSELING ADULT CHILDREN OF ALCOHOLICS (Sandra Wilson); and COUNSELING AND CHILDREN (Warren Byrd and Paul Warren).

COLLINS, Gary R., ed. RESOURCES FOR CHRISTIAN COUNSELING Series: COUNSELING BEFORE MARRIAGE (Everett Worthington, Jr.); COUNSELING AND AIDS (Gregg Albers); COUNSELING FAMILIES OF CHILDREN WITH DISABILITIES (Rosemarie Cook); and COUNSELING FOR SEXUAL DISORDERS (Joyce and Clifford Penner).

COLLINS, Gary R. YOUR MAGNIFICENT MIND: THE FASCINATING WAY IT WORKS FOR YOU.

CRABB, Lawrence. INSIDE OUT.

EVANS, C. Stephen. SØREN KIERKEGAARD'S CHRISTIAN PSYCHOLOGY: INSIGHT FOR COUNSELING AND PASTORAL CARE.

FARNSWORTH, Kirk E. WHOLE-HEARTED INTEGRATION: HARMONIZING PSYCHOLOGY & CHRISTIANITY THROUGH WORD & DEED.

FULLER, Andrew R. PSYCHOLOGY AND RELIGION: EIGHT POINTS OF VIEW. 2nd ed.

GAYLIN, Willard. ADAM AND EVE AND PINOCCHIO: ON BEING AND BECOMING HUMAN.

GAZZANIGA, Michael S. MIND MATTERS: HOW MIND AND BRAIN INTERACT TO CREATE OUR CONSCIOUS LIVES.

HARAWAY, Donna. PRIMATE VISIONS: GENDER, RACE AND NATURE IN THE WORLD OF MODERN SCIENCE.

HURDING, Roger F. THE TREE OF HEALING: PSYCHOLOGICAL & BIBLICAL FOUNDATIONS FOR COUNSELING & PASTORAL CARE.

ISBISTER, J.N. FREUD: AN INTRODUCTION TO HIS LIFE AND WORK.

JAKI, Stanley L. BRAIN, MIND AND COMPUTERS, 3rd ed.

JEEVES, Malcolm A., ed. BEHAVIOURAL SCIENCES.

JEEVES, Malcolm A.; BERRY, R.J.; and ATKINSON, David. FREE TO BE DIFFERENT.

JOHNSON-LAIRD, P.N. THE COMPUTER AND THE MIND: AN INTRODUCTION TO COGNI-TIVE SCIENCE.

JONES, Stanton L., ed. PSYCHOLOGY & THE CHRISTIAN FAITH: AN INTRODUCTORY READER.

JOY, Donald M., ed. MORAL DEVELOPMENT FOUNDATIONS: JUDEO-CHRISTIAN ALTERNA-TIVES TO PIAGET-KOHLBERG.

*KIRKPATRICK, William K. PSYCHOLOGICAL SEDUCTION: THE FAILURE OF MODERN PSY-CHOLOGY.

KOHONEN, T. SELF-ORGANIZATION AND ASSOCIATIVE MEMORY. 2nd ed.

*KOTESKEY, Ronald L. PSYCHOLOGY FROM A CHRISTIAN PERSPECTIVE.

LANGER, Ellen J. MINDFULNESS.

*LINDQUIST, Stanley E. REACH OUT: BECOME AN ENCOURAGER.

LINN, Matthew.; FABRICANT, Sheila.; and LINN, Dennis. HEALING THE EIGHT STAGES OF LIFE.

LUCKY, Robert W. SILICON DREAMS: INFORMATION, MAN AND MACHINE.

MALONY, H. Newton, ed. WHOLENESS AND HOLINESS: READINGS IN THE PSYCHOL-OGY/THEOLOGY OF MENTAL HEALTH.

MCGINNIS, Alan Loy. BRINGING OUT THE BEST IN PEOPLE: HOW TO ENJOY HELPING OTHERS EXCEL.

MOBERLY, Elizabeth R. PSYCHOGENESIS: THE EARLY DEVELOPMENT OF GENDER IDEN-TITY.

MYERS, David G. and JEEVES, Malcolm A. PSYCHOLOGY THROUGH THE EYES OF FAITH.

MYERS, David G. PSYCHOLOGY. 2nd ed.

MYERS, David G. SOCIAL PSYCHOLOGY. 2nd ed.

NEHER, Andrew. THE PSYCHOLOGY OF TRANSCENDENCE.

PECK, M. Scott. PEOPLE OF THE LIE: THE HOPE FOR HEALING HUMAN EVIL.

PECK, M. Scott. THE ROAD LESS TRAVELED.

PENROSE, Roger. THE EMPEROR'S NEW MIND: CONCERNING COMPUTERS, MINDS, AND THE LAWS OF PHYSICS.

PHILIPCHALK, Ronald P. PSYCHOLOGY AND CHRISTIANITY: AN INTRODUCTION TO THE CONTROVERSIAL ISSUES IN PSYCHOLOGY.

PROPST, L. Rebecca. PSYCHOTHERAPY IN A RELIGIOUS FRAMEWORK.

ROBINSON, Daniel N. AN INTELLECTUAL HISTORY OF PSYCHOLOGY.

SCHULTZ, Duane P., and SCHULTZ, Sydney E. A HISTORY OF MODERN PSYCHOLOGY. 4th ed.

SHELLY, Judith A., and JOHN, Sandra D., eds. SPIRITUAL DIMENSIONS OF MENTAL HEALTH.

SHUSTER, Marguerite. POWER, PATHOLOGY, PARADOX: THE DYNAMICS OF GOOD & EVIL.

SMEDES, Lewis B. CHOICES: MAKING RIGHT DECISIONS IN A COMPLEX WORLD.

SMEDES, Lewis B. MERE MORALITY: WHAT GOD EXPECTS FROM ORDINARY PEOPLE.

TOURNIER, Paul. A LISTENING EAR: REFLECTIONS ON CHRISTIAN CARING.

VAN DEN AARDWEG, Gerard J. ON THE ORIGINS AND TREATMENT OF HOMOSEXUALITY: A PSYCHOANALYTIC REINTERPRETATION.

*VAN LEEUWEN, Mary Stewart et al. CHRISTIAN VISION: MAN & MIND, Vol. 3.

VAN LEEUWEN, Mary Stewart. GENDER & GRACE: LOVE, WORK & PARENTING IN A CHANGING WORLD.

*VAN LEEUWEN, Mary Stewart. THE SORCERER'S APPRENTICE: A CHRISTIAN LOOKS AT THE CHANGING FACE OF PSYCHOLOGY.

VAN LEEUWEN, Mary Stewart. THE PERSON IN PSYCHOLOGY: A CONTEMPORARY APPRAISAL.

VITZ, Paul C. PSYCHOLOGY AS RELIGION: THE CULT OF SELF-WORSHIP.

VITZ, Paul C. SIGMUND FREUD'S CHRISTIAN UNCONSCIOUS.

WALLACH, Michael A., and WALLACH, Lise. PSYCHOLOGY'S SANCTION FOR SELFISH-NESS: THE ERROR OF EGOISM IN THEORY & THERAPY.

WHITE, John. PUTTING THE SOUL BACK IN PSYCHOLOGY.

WILLIAMS, Redford. THE TRUSTING HEART: GREAT NEWS ABOUT TYPE A BEHAVIOR.

WORTHINGTON, Everett L., Jr. MARRIAGE COUNSELING: A CHRISTIAN APPROACH TO COUNSELING COUPLES.

SCIENCE & RELIGION

AMBROSE, E.J. THE MIRROR OF CREATION.

ANDREWS, Edgar H. CHRIST & THE COSMOS.

BARBOUR, Ian G. MYTHS, MODELS AND PARADIGMS: A COMPARATIVE STUDY IN SCIENCE AND RELIGION.

BARBOUR, Ian G. RELIGION IN AN AGE OF SCIENCE (The Gifford Lectures Ser.: Vol 1)

BARRETT, Eric C., and FISHER, David. SCIENTISTS WHO BELIEVE: 21 TELL THEIR OWN STORIES.

BIRTEL, Frank T., ed. RELIGION, SCIENCE, & PUBLIC POLICY.

BLACKWELL, Richard J. GALILEO, BELLARMINE, AND THE BIBLE.

BRAND, Paul, and YANCEY, Philip. FEARFULLY AND WONDERFULLY MADE.

BRAND, Paul, and YANCEY, Philip. IN HIS IMAGE.

BROWN, Colin. MIRACLES AND THE CRITICAL MIND.

*BUBE, Richard H. THE HUMAN QUEST: A NEW LOOK AT SCIENCE & CHRISTIAN FAITH.

*BUBE, Richard. SCIENCE AND THE WHOLE PERSON: A PERSONAL INTEGRATION OF SCIENTIFIC AND BIBLICAL PERSPECTIVES.

*DYE, David. FAITH AND THE PHYSICAL WORLD.

ELLUL, Jacques. WHAT I BELIEVE.

FOX, Matthew and SWIMME, Brian. MANIFESTO FOR A GLOBAL CIVILIZATION.

GOLDSTEIN, B.R. THE ASTRONOMY OF LEVI BEN GERSON (1288-1344).

GREENE, John C. DARWIN AND THE MODERN WORLD VIEW.

HAWTHORNE, Tim. WINDOWS ON SCIENCE AND FAITH.

JAKI, Stanley L. CHANCE OR REALITY AND OTHER ESSAYS.

JAKI, Stanley L. THE ONLY CHAOS AND OTHER ESSAYS.

KAISER, Christopher B. CREATION AND THE HISTORY OF SCIENCE.

MAATMAN, Russell. UNITY IN CREATION.

MACKAY, Donald M. THE OPEN MIND AND OTHER ESSAYS: A SCIENTIST IN GOD'S WORLD.

MACKAY, Donald M. SCIENCE AND THE QUEST FOR MEANING.

MANGUM, John M., ed. THE NEW FAITH-SCIENCE DEBATE: PROBING COSMOLOGY, TECHNOLOGY, AND THEOLOGY.

MIDGLEY, Mary. EVOLUTION AS A RELIGION: STRANGE HOPES & STRANGER FEARS.

MITCHELL, Ralph G. EINSTEIN AND CHRIST: A NEW APPROACH TO THE DEFENSE OF THE CHRISTIAN RELIGION.

MORRIS, Henry M., and PARKER, G.E. THE BIBLICAL BASIS FOR MODERN SCIENCE.

MORRIS, Henry M. MEN OF SCIENCE, MEN OF GOD.

NOVAK, David, and SAMUELSON, Norbert. CREATION AND THE END OF DAYS.

PANNENBERG, Wolfhart. METAPHYSICS AND THE IDEA OF GOD.

*PAUL, Iain. SCIENCE AND THEOLOGY IN EINSTEIN'S PERSPECTIVE.

POLKINGHORNE, John. SCIENCE AND CREATION: THE SEARCH FOR UNDERSTANDING.

POLKINGHORNE, John. SCIENCE AND PROVIDENCE: GOD'S INTERACTION WITH THE WORLD.

POLLARD, W.G. TRANSCENDENCE AND PROVIDENCE: REFLECTIONS OF A PHYSICIST AND PRIEST.

ROLSTON, Holmes, III. SCIENCE AND RELIGION: A CRITICAL SURVEY.

ROSS, Hugh. THE FINGERPRINT OF GOD.

RUSSELL, Robert J.; STOEGER, William R.; and COYNE, George V., eds. PHYSICS, PHILOSOPHY, AND THEOLOGY: A COSMIC QUEST FOR UNDERSTANDING.

SCHROEDER, Gerald L. GENESIS AND THE BIG BANG: THE DISCOVERY OF HARMONY BETWEEN MODERN SCIENCE AND THE BIBLE.

SOSKICE, Janet M. METAPHOR AND RELIGIOUS LANGUAGE.

STANNARD, Russell. SCIENCE AND THE RENEWAL OF BELIEF.

TEMPLETON, John M., and HERRMANN, Robert L. THE GOD WHO WOULD BE KNOWN: REVELATIONS OF THE DIVINE IN CONTEMPORARY SCIENCE.

THOMSON, Alexander. TRADITION AND AUTHORITY IN SCIENCE AND THEOLOGY.

*TRINKLEIN, Fred. THE GOD OF SCIENCE.

UHLIG, Herbert H. LIFE, SCIENCE AND RELIGIOUS CONCERNS: THEIR INTERRELATIONS AND LIFE'S MEANING.

VAN TILL, Howard J., et al. PORTRAITS OF CREATION: BIBLICAL AND SCIENTIFIC PERPSECTIVES ON THE WORLD'S FORMATION.

SOCIOLOGY

ANKER, Roy M., et al. YOUTH, POPULAR CULTURE, AND THE ELECTRONIC MEDIA.

BALSWICK, Jack O., and BALSWICK, Judith K. THE FAMILY: A CHRISTIAN PERSPECTIVE ON THE CONTEMPORARY HOME.

BELLAH, Robert N., et al. HABITS OF THE HEART: INDIVIDUALISM AND COMMITMENT IN AMERICAN LIFE.

BILEZIKIAN, Gilbert. BEYOND SEX ROLES: A GUIDE FOR THE STUDY OF FEMALE ROLES IN THE BIBLE.

CAMPOLO, Anthony. WHO SWITCHED THE PRICE TAGS?

CAPON, Robert F. HEALTH, MONEY, AND LOVE ... AND WHY WE DON'T ENJOY THEM.

*COLLINS, Gary, R., ed. OUR SOCIETY IN TURMOIL.

COMISKEY, Andrew. PURSUING SEXUAL WHOLENESS: HOW JESUS HEALS THE HOMOSEXUAL.

DESANTO, Charles P., and POLOMA, Margaret M. SOCIAL PROBLEMS: CHRISTIAN PERSPECTIVES.

ELLUL, Jacques. THE SUBVERSION OF CHRISTIANITY.

FORE, William. TELEVISION & RELIGION: THE SHAPING OF FAITH & VALUE.

FOSTER, Richard J. MONEY, SEX AND POWER.

GAEDE, Stan D. BELONGING: OUR NEED FOR COMMUNITY IN CHURCH AND FAMILY.

GAEDE, Stan D. WHERE GODS MAY DWELL: ON UNDERSTANDING THE HUMAN CONDITION.

GARRISON, Charles E. TWO DIFFERENT WORLDS: CHRISTIAN ABSOLUTES AND THE RELATIVISM OF SOCIAL SCIENCE.

*GOUDZWAARD, Bob. IDOLS OF OUR TIME.

GROOTHUIS, Douglas R. UNMASKING THE NEW AGE.

*GRUNLAN, Stephen, and REINER, Milton, eds. CHRISTIAN PERSPECTIVES ON SOCIOL-OGY.

*GUINNESS, Os. THE GRAVEDIGGER FILE: PAPERS ON THE SUBVERSION OF THE MOD-ERN CHURCH.

HAMMOND, Phillip E., ed. THE SACRED IN A SECULAR AGE: TOWARD REVISION IN THE SCIENTIFIC STUDY OF RELIGION.

HEDDENDORF, Russell. HIDDEN THREADS: SOCIAL THOUGHT FOR CHRISTIANS.

JOHNSTON, Jon. CHRISTIAN EXCELLENCE: ALTERNATIVE TO SUCCESS.

KETTLER, Christian D., and SPEIDELL, Todd H., eds. INCARNATIONAL MINISTRY: THE PRESENCE OF CHRIST IN CHURCH, SOCIETY, AND FAMILY.

KIMMEL, Allan J. ETHICS AND VALUES IN APPLIED SOCIAL RESEARCH.

KOENIG, Harold G.; SMILEY, Mona; and GONZALES, JoAnn P. RELIGION, HEALTH, AND AGING: A REVIEW AND THEORETICAL INTEGRATION.

KUHN, Thomas S. THE STRUCTURE OF SCIENTIFIC REVOLUTIONS. 2nd ed.

LEMING, Michael R.; DEVRIES, Raymond G.; and FURNISH, Brendon F.J., eds. THE SOCIO-LOGICAL PERSPECTIVE: A VALUE-COMMITTED INTRODUCTION.

LINGENFELTER, Sherwood G. and MAYERS, Marvin K. MINISTERING CROSS-CULTURALLY: AN INCARNATIONAL MODEL FOR PERSONAL RELATIONSHIPS.

LYON, David. SOCIOLOGY AND THE HUMAN IMAGE.

LYON, David. THE STEEPLE'S SHADOW: ON THE MYTHS & REALITIES OF SECULARIZA-TION.

MARSHALL, Paul A.; GRIFFIOEN, Sander; and MOUW, Richard J., eds. STAINED GLASS: WORLD VIEWS AND SOCIAL SCIENCE.

MARSHALL, Paul A., and VANDERVENNEN, Robert E., eds. SOCIAL SCIENCE IN CHRISTIAN PERSPECTIVE.

MARSDEN, George, ed. EVANGELICALISM AND MODERN AMERICA.

MOBERG, David O. WHOLISTIC CHRISTIANITY: AN APPEAL FOR A DYNAMIC, BALANCED FAITH.

*MOBERG, David O. THE CHURCH AS A SOCIAL INSTITUTION: THE SOCIOLOGY OF AMER-ICAN RELIGION. 2nd ed.

NEWBIGIN, Lesslie. THE GOSPEL IN A PLURALIST SOCIETY.

PERKINS, Richard. LOOKING BOTH WAYS: EXPLORING THE INTERFACE BETWEEN CHRIS-TIANITY & SOCIOLOGY.

POLOMA, Margaret M. THE ASSEMBLIES OF GOD AT THE CROSSROADS: CHARISMA AND INSTITUTIONAL DILEMMAS.

POSTMAN, Neil. CONSCIENTIOUS OBJECTIONS: STIRRING UP TROUBLE ABOUT LAN-GUAGE, TECHNOLOGY, AND EDUCATION.

REDEKOP, Calvin, and BENDER, Urie A. WHO AM I? WHAT AM I?: SEARCHING FOR MEAN-ING IN YOUR WORK.

RUPPRECHT, David and Ruth. RADICAL HOSPITALITY.

SINE, Tom. MUSTARD SEED CONSPIRACY.

STAFFORD, Tim. THE SEXUAL CHRISTIAN.

WALTER, J.A. NEED: THE NEW RELIGION.

WARNER, R. Stephen. NEW WINE IN OLD WINESKINS: EVANGELICALS AND LIBERALS IN A SMALL-TOWN CHURCH.

WUTHNOW, Robert. MEANING AND MORAL ORDER: EXPLORATIONS IN CULTURAL ANAL-YSIS.

TECHNOLOGY & COMPUTERS

ALEKSANDER, Igor, and BURNETT, Piers. THINKING MACHINES: THE SEARCH FOR ARTIFI-CIAL INTELLIGENCE.

AUGSBURGER, Myron, and CURRY, Dean C. NUCLEAR ARMS: TWO VIEWS ON WORLD PEACE.

BRANDIN, David H., and HARRISON, M.A. THE TECHNOLOGY WAR: A CASE FOR COMPETI-TIVENESS.

BURGESS, Jeremy; MURTEN, Michael; and TAYLOR, R. MICROCOSMOS.

BYRNE, Kevin, ed. RESPONSIBLE SCIENCE: THE IMPACT OF TECHNOLOGY ON SOCIETY.

DYSON, Freeman. WEAPONS AND HOPE.

EMERSON, Allen, and FORBES, Cheryl. THE INVASION OF THE COMPUTER CULTURE: WHAT YOU NEED TO KNOW ABOUT THE NEW WORLD WE LIVE IN.

FORESTER, Tom. THE HIGH-TECH SOCIETY: THE STORY OF THE INFORMATION TECH-NOLOGY REVOLUTION.

GRANT, George. TECHNOLOGY AND JUSTICE.

HARDISON, O.B., Jr. DISAPPEARING THROUGH THE SKYLIGHT: CULTURE AND TECHNOL-OGY IN THE TWENTIETH CENTURY.

HODGSON, Peter E. OUR NUCLEAR FUTURE?

HOLTON, Gerald. THE ADVANCEMENT OF SCIENCE, AND ITS BURDENS: THE JEFFERSON LECTURE AND OTHER ESSAYS.

JOHNSON, Douglas W. COMPUTER ETHICS: A GUIDE FOR THE NEW AGE.

LEFEVER, Ernest W., and HUNT, E. Stephen, eds. THE APOCALYPTIC PREMISE: NUCLEAR ARMS DEBATED.

LOEB, Paul. NUCLEAR CULTURE: LIVING & WORKING IN THE WORLD'S LARGEST ATOMIC COMPLEX.

LYON, David. THE SILICON SOCIETY.

MACAULAY, David. THE WAY THINGS WORK: FROM LEVERS TO LASERS, CARS TO COM-PUTERS—A VISUAL GUIDE TO THE WORLD OF MACHINES.

MITCHAM, Carl, and GROTE, Jim, eds. THEOLOGY AND TECHNOLOGY: ESSAYS IN CHRIS-TIAN ANALYSIS AND EXEGESIS.

MITCHAM, Carl, and MACKEY, Robert, eds. PHILOSOPHY AND TECHNOLOGY: READINGS IN THE PHILOSOPHICAL PROBLEMS OF TECHNOLOGY.

MONSMA, Stephen, et al. RESPONSIBLE TECHNOLOGY: A CHRISTIAN PERSPECTIVE.

ROSZAK, Theodore. THE CULT OF INFORMATION: THE FOLKLORE OF COMPUTERS AND THE TRUE ART OF THINKING.

SCHUURMAN, Egbert. TECHNOLOGY AND THE FUTURE: A PHILOSOPHICAL CHALLENGE.

*SLOCUM, Robert E. ORDINARY CHRISTIANS IN A HIGH-TECH WORLD.

WALDROP, M. Mitchell. MAN-MADE MINDS: THE PROMISE OF ARTIFICIAL INTELLIGENCE.

THEOLOGY

ALLEN, Diogenes. PHILOSOPHY FOR UNDERSTANDING THEOLOGY.

ALLEN, Diogenes. QUEST: THE SEARCH FOR MEANING THROUGH CHRIST.

ANDERSON, Bernard W., ed. CREATION IN THE OLD TESTAMENT.

ANDERSON, Ray S., and FUERNSEY, Dennis B. ON BEING FAMILY: A SOCIAL THEOLOGY OF THE FAMILY.

ANDERSON, RAY S. THEOLOGY, DEATH AND DYING.

AULÉN, Gustav. CHRISTUS VICTOR.

BARTH, Karl. DOGMATICS IN OUTLINE.

BEATY, Michael D., ed. CHRISTIAN THEISM AND THE PROBLEMS OF PHILOSOPHY (Library of Religious Philosophy, Vol. 5).

BLOESCH, Donald G. THE FUTURE OF EVANGELICAL CHRISTIANITY: A CALL FOR UNITY AMID DIVERSITY.

BLOESCH, Donald G. THEOLOGICAL NOTEBOOK Vol. 1: 1960-1964.

BOCKMUEHL, Klaus E. BOOKS: GOD'S TOOLS IN THE HISTORY OF SALVATION.

BOCKMUEHL, Klaus E. LISTENING TO THE GOD WHO SPEAKS: REFLECTIONS ON GOD'S GUIDANCE FROM SCRIPTURE & THE LIVES OF GOD'S PEOPLE.

BOCKMUEHL, Klaus E. LIVING BY THE GOSPEL: CHRISTIAN ROOTS OF CONFIDENCE AND PURPOSE.

BOCKMUEHL, Klaus E. THE UNREAL GOD OF MODERN THEOLOGY: BULTMANN, BARTH, AND THE THEOLOGY OF ATHEISM: A CALL TO RECOVERING THE TRUTH OF GOD'S RE-ALITY.

BONHOEFFER, Dietrich. ETHICS.

BONHOEFFER, Dietrich. LETTERS AND PAPERS FROM PRISON. enl. ed.

CHESTNUT, Glen F. IMAGES OF CHRIST.

COBB, John B., Jr. GOD AND THE WORLD.

CRAIG, W.L. THE ONLY WISE GOD.

ELLUL, Jacques. THE PRESENCE OF THE KINGDOM. 2nd ed.

ERLER, Rolf J., and MARQUARD, Reiner, eds. A KARL BARTH READER.

FORD, David F., ed. THE MODERN THEOLOGIANS: AN INTRODUCTION TO CHRISTIAN THE-
OLOGY IN THE TWENTIETH CENTURY. 2 vols.

GILL, Jerry H. MEDIATED TRANSCENDENCE: A POSTMODERN REFLECTION.

GREEN, Garrett. IMAGINING GOD: THEOLOGY AND THE RELIGIOUS IMAGINATION.

*GRUENLER, Royce G. THE INEXHAUSTIBLE GOD.

GRUENLER, Royce G. THE TRINITY IN THE GOSPEL OF JOHN.

*GUTHRIE, Shirley C., Jr. DIVERSITY IN FAITH, UNITY IN CHRIST.

HALL, Douglas J. IMAGING GOD: DOMINION AS STEWARDSHIP.

HARDY, Edward R., ed. CHRISTOLOGY OF THE LATER FATHERS.

*HENRY, Carl F.H. QUEST FOR REALITY: CHRISTIANITY & THE COUNTER CULTURE.

JAKI, Stanley L., ed. LORD GIFFORD & HIS LECTURES: A CENTENARY RETROSPECT.

JAKI, Stanley L. THE PURPOSE OF IT ALL.

JENSON, Robert W. THE TRIUNE IDENTITY: GOD ACCORDING TO THE BIBLE.

*JUNGEL, Eberhard. GOD AS THE MYSTERY OF THE WORLD.

KAISER, Christopher B. THE DOCTRINE OF GOD.

KAUFMAN, Gordon D. THEOLOGY FOR A NUCLEAR AGE.

KRAFT, Charles. CHRISTIANITY WITH POWER: EXPERIENCING THE SUPERNATURAL.

LINDBECK, George A. THE NATURE OF DOCTRINE: RELIGION AND THEOLOGY IN A
POSTLIBERAL AGE.

MACDONALD, George. PROVING THE UNSEEN.

MATHENY, Paul D. DOGMATICS AND ETHICS: THE THEOLOGICAL REALISM AND ETHICS
OF KARL BARTH'S CHURCH DOGMATICS.

MAVRODES, George I. BELIEF IN GOD: A STUDY IN THE EPISTEMOLOGY OF RELIGION.

MOLTMANN, Jürgen. GOD IN CREATION: A NEW THEOLOGY OF CREATION AND THE
SPIRIT OF GOD.

ODEN, Thomas C. THE LIVING GOD.

PANNENBERG, Wolfhart. ANTHROPOLOGY IN THEOLOGICAL PERSPECTIVE.

*PANNENBERG, Wolfhart. THE APOSTLE'S CREED IN THE LIGHT OF TODAY'S QUES-
TIONS.

PANNENBERG, Wolfhart. CHRISTIANITY IN A SECULARIZED WORLD.

PANNENBERG, Wolfhart. JESUS: GOD AND MAN. 2nd ed.

PLACHER, William C. UNAPOLOGETIC THEOLOGY: A CHRISTIAN VOICE IN A PLURALISTIC CONVERSATION.

POYTHRESS, Vernon S. SYMPHONIC THEOLOGY: THE VALIDITY OF MULTIPLE PERSPEC-TIVES.

*RAMM, Bernard. AN EVANGELICAL CHRISTOLOGY: ECUMENIC & HISTORIC.

*RITSCH, Dietrich. THE LOGIC OF THEOLOGY: A BRIEF ACCOUNT OF THE RELATIONSHIP BETWEEN BASIC CONCEPTS IN THEOLOGY.

SCHAEFFER, Francis A. ESCAPE FROM REASON.

SCHAEFFER, Francis A. THE CHURCH AT THE END OF THE 20TH CENTURY: THE CHURCH BEFORE THE WATCHING WORLD. 2nd ed.

SCHAEFFER, Francis A. THE GOD WHO IS THERE.

*SCHWARZ, Hans. RESPONSIBLE FAITH: CHRISTIAN THEOLOGY IN THE LIGHT OF 20TH CENTURY QUESTIONS.

SIRE, James W. THE UNIVERSE NEXT DOOR: A BASIC WORLD VIEW CATALOG. 2nd ed..

TEILHARD DE CHARDIN, Pierre. THE PHENOMENON OF MAN.

*THIELICKE, Helmut. BEING HUMAN ... BECOMING HUMAN: AN ESSAY IN CHRISTIAN ANTHROPOLOGY.

THOMPSON, John, ed. THEOLOGY BEYOND CHRISTENDOM: ESSAYS ON THE CENTE-NARY OF THE BIRTH OF KARL BARTH.

TILLICH, Paul. DYNAMICS OF FAITH.

TORRANCE, Thomas F. KARL BARTH: BIBLICAL AND EVANGELICAL THEOLOGIAN.

*TORRANCE, Thomas F., ed. THEOLOGICAL DIALOGUE BETWEEN ORTHODOX & RE-FORMED CHURCHES.

TORRANCE, Thomas F. SPACE, TIME AND INCARNATION.

TREFIL, James S. READING THE MIND OF GOD: IN SEARCH OF THE PRINCIPLE OF UNI-VERSALITY.

VAN HUYSSTEEN, Wentzel. THEOLOGY AND THE JUSTIFICATION OF FAITH: CONSTRUCT-ING THEORIES IN SYSTEMATIC THEOLOGY.

*WINGREN, Gustaf. THE FLIGHT FROM CREATION.

THIRD WORLD

ADENEY, Miriam. GOD'S FOREIGN POLICY.

BATCHELOR, Peter. PEOPLE IN RURAL DEVELOPMENT.

*BROWNE, S. G.; DAVEY, F.; and THOMSON, W. A. R., eds. HERALDS OF HEALTH: THE SAGA OF CHRISTIAN MEDICAL INITIATIVES.

*FREUDENBERGER, C. Dean. FOOD FOR TOMORROW?

JENNINGS, George J. ALL THINGS, ALL MEN, ALL MEANS—TO SAVE SOME.

JENNINGS, George J. HADITH: A COMPOSITE MIDDLE EASTERN VILLAGE UNDER A MISSIONS CONSULTANT'S GAZE.

JENNINGS, George J. A MISSION CONSULTANT VIEWS MIDDLE EASTERN CULTURE AND PERSONALITY.

JENNINGS, George J. WITHOUT A PEER: WELCOME INTO THE MIDDLE EAST.

LIU, Zongren. TWO YEARS IN THE MELTING POT.

SIDER, Ronald J., ed. EVANGELICALS & DEVELOPMENT: TOWARD A THEOLOGY OF SOCIAL CHANGE.

SINCLAIR, Maurice. GREEN FINGER OF GOD.

ASA BOOK SERVICE

Arrangements have been made for Logos Bookstore of Bloomington, Indiana to carry and/or order books from the Annotated Book List. STOP (Single Title Order Plan) orders from small presses may take 1-3 months for processing by the publishers. (Small presses include such publishers as Helmers & Howard, Radix, Belknap Press, etc., and some college and university presses.)

Some titles included in the Book List are available only through direct ordering from the publisher/supplier. In these cases, the addresses are noted within the listings.

ORDER PLACEMENT:

Send or call in your orders to:

ASA Book Service c/o Logos Bookstore
314 E. Kirkwood
Bloomington, IN 47401
Tel. (812) 334-2304
Attn: Jeff Crosby

BILLING FOR ASA/CSCA MEMBERS:

Members will be billed with shipment of books. Payment is expected within 10 days of billing. Please do not send check or prepayment: prices and availability are subject to change without notice. Please provide your name, address, telephone number, and ASA/CSCA membership number. (ASA/CSCA membership number appears above the address on any mailing list or billing form from ASA.)

BILLING FOR NON-MEMBERS:

Non-members must inquire as to the total cost and send payment before books are shipped. Please write to or call Logos Bookstore.

METHOD OF PAYMENT:

Credit card billing is available (Visa, Mastercard, Discover, and American Express). Shipping and handling costs for domestic orders: $3.00 for first book, $1.00 for each additional book. Shipping and handling costs for foreign orders will be determined for each individual order. Back orders will be charged actual shipping cost. Sales tax will be charged where applicable.

(Notes)

ASA BOOK SERVICE ORDER FORM

(Cut out and use this form, or a photocopy)

SEND OR CALL IN YOUR ORDERS TO:

ASA Book Service, c/o Logos Bookstore
314 E. Kirkwood
Bloomington, IN 47401
(812) 334-2304
Attn: Jeff Crosby

Please refer to book service information on page 97.

AUTHOR	TITLE

For ASA members, the Book Service will ship and bill with payment due 10 days after the books arrive. Non-members are requested to pre-pay. VISA, Mastercard, Discover, or American Express accepted. All domestic orders will be billed $3.00 for the first book and $1.00 for each additional book for shipping and handling. Foreign orders will be billed individually for shipping and handling. Sales tax will be charged where applicable.

BILL TO:

Name _____

Address _____

City _____ State _____ Zip _____

Telephone _____ ASA/CSCA membership # _____

SHIP TO (if different from above):

Name _____

Address _____

City _____ State _____ Zip _____

METHOD OF PAYMENT:

Check enclosed____

VISA _____   Mastercard_____   Discover_____   American Express____

Account #_____ Exp. date_____

(Notes)

ASA BOOK SERVICE ORDER FORM
(Cut out and use this form, or a photocopy)

SEND OR CALL IN YOUR ORDERS TO:

ASA Book Service, c/o Logos Bookstore
314 E. Kirkwood
Bloomington, IN 47401
(812) 334-2304
Attn: Jeff Crosby

Please refer to book service information on page 97.

AUTHOR	TITLE

For ASA members, the Book Service will ship and bill with payment due 10 days after the books arrive. Non-members are requested to pre-pay. VISA, Mastercard, Discover, or American Express accepted. All domestic orders will be billed $3.00 for the first book and $1.00 for each additional book for shipping and handling. Foreign orders will be billed individually for shipping and handling. Sales tax will be charged where applicable.

BILL TO:

Name _____

Address _____

City _____ State _____ Zip_____

Telephone _____ ASA/CSCA membership #_____

SHIP TO (if different from above):

Name _____

Address _____

City _____ State _____ Zip_____

METHOD OF PAYMENT:

Check enclosed____

VISA _____   Mastercard_____   Discover____   American Express____

Account #_____ Exp. date_____

101

(Notes)

ASA AUDIO TAPE LIST

The following audio tapes are available for purchase, at $5/tape plus postage, from The Sanders Christian Foundation. Postage amounts and other ordering information can be found on the order forms on pages 107 and 109. Tapes available from other sources are listed beginning on page 127.

🐚　　🐚　　🐚　　🐚　　🐚

ASA ANNUAL MEETINGS & SPECIAL FORUMS AND COURSES

ASA ANNUAL MEETINGS

August, 1990 - Messiah College, Grantham, PA

Tape #	Author and Title
ASA90-1	Hostetter, D. Ray, Welcome
	Hess, Gerald, Announcements
ASA90-2	Livingstone, David, Lecture
ASA90-3	Livingstone, David, Lecture
ASA90-4	Priebe, Duane, Address
ASA90-5	Priebe, Duane, Address
	Livingstone, David and Priebe, Duane, Panel Discussion
ASA90-6	Livingstone, David and Priebe, Duane, Panel Discussion
ASA90-7	Wiester, John, "Is Evolution Evolving into a Religion?"
	Price, J. David, "The California Science Framework & Its Implications for Science Education"
	Wonderly, Daniel, "Why Was the Anti-Creationism Movement Able to Arise So Rapidly Following the Arkansas Creation Trial?"
ASA90-8	Bagby, Roland, "Does God Approve of Teaching Evolution?"
	Kanagy, Sherman, "Is the Use of Science in Religious Apologetics Merely a Form of Scientism?"
	Stahl, John, "The Bible's Use of Object Lessons From the Natural World"
	Moore, Eric, "Imagination in the Teaching of Science"
ASA90-9	Murphy, George, "The Origin of Matter and Pattern in Modern Cosmology"
	Bergman, Jerry, "High Energy Physics at the Crossroads"
	Faries, Dillard, "Objectivity & Objective Reality in Darwin, Evolution, Modern Physics & an Understanding of God"
ASA90-10	Shank, Norman, "Implications of a Creative Cosmos: Modeling Causes"
	Adams, Paul "Chance Within Design"
	Drozdek, Adam, "Awe & Arrogance in Science"
	Chase, Gene, "Mathematics as Created: Four Theses"
ASA90-11	Annual Business Meeting
ASA90-12	Johnson, Phillip, Banquet
ASA90-13	Wilcox, D.; Johnson, P.; Van Till, H., Symposium, "Teaching Evolution in the Science Classroom: Education or Indoctrination?"
ASA90-14	Symposium (continued)
ASA90-15	Symposium (continued)
ASA90-16	Olson, Edwin, "A Case for Dualism as the Correct Way to Understand Human Nature"
	Fischer, Dick, "Finding Adam's Historical Niche: Clues from Scripture
ASA90-17	Siemens, David, "The Uncreative Creator of the Creationists"
ASA90-18	Beverly, Ted, "Viewing the Natural World as Creation: A View From Early Judaism (400BC-200AD)"
	Yamauchi, Edwin "Gnostic Views of Creation"
ASA90-19	Wood, Kurt, "The Scientific Exegesis of the Qur'an: A Case Study in Relating Science and Scripture"

	Davis, Edward B., "A Whale of a Tale: Fundamentalist Fish Stories"
ASA90-20	Wise, Kurt, "Lost Foundations: Scripture and the Assumptions of Science"
	Mullins, Jeff, "Creation Science: Science, Pseudoscience, or Disguised Religion?"
ASA90-21	Neidhardt, W. Jim, "One Scientist's Reflections on the Contribution of Harold P. Nebelsick to the Science/Theology Dialogue"
ASA90-22	Frair, Wayne, "Homology: Where is it Going?"
	Mills, Gordon, "Protein Similarities & Ancestral Relationships"
ASA90-23	Rüst, Peter, "How Has Life & Its Diversity Been Produced?"
	Thaxton, Charles, "Intelligent Design"
ASA90-24	Bullock, Wilbur, "The Origin of Species & the Cause of Disease"
	Rice, Stanley, "Shared Themes in Biology & Christian Theology"
ASA90-25	Lindquist, Stanley, "Counseling Techniques for Third World Cultures: Limitations of Psychological & Linguistic Applications"
	Swearengen, Jack, "Arms Control & the Kingdom of God"
ASA90-26	Hoshiko, Tomuo, "Transgenic Animals: Medical Marvel or Slippery Slope?"
	Hollman, Jay, "The Teleology of Lipidology"
	Eichheofer, Gerald, "PEAR: Neither Fruit, Nor Religion, Nor Normal Science"
ASA90-27	Miller, Keith, "Theological Reflections on a Continuous Creation View"
	Studenroth, John, "The Glory of God as Revealed in the Microscope"

August, 1989 - Indiana Wesleyan University, Marion, IN

ASA89-1	Jones, Howard W., Jr., Keynote Lecture, "Assisted Reproduction: Factors Influencing a Clinician's Ethical Decision"
ASA89-2	Swanson, James, Keynote Response, "One Scientist's Ethical Dilemma"
ASA89-3	Munro, Donald W., "Human Genetic Engineering"
ASA89-4	Herrmann, Robert L., Ph.D., "Gene Therapy"
ASA89-5	Vibert, Peter J., "Genetic Screening"
ASA89-6A&B	Jones, Howard W., Jr., and Swanson, James, Discussion Panel, "Biomedical Ethics"
ASA89-7	Rice, Stanley, "Limitations of Human Genetic Engineering"
	Bouma, Hessell, III, "Breakthroughs & Ethical Issues in Human Gene Engineering"
	Monsma, William B., "The Abolition of Humanity"
ASA89-8	Hoshiko, Tomuo, " Forbidden Knowledge"
	Mills, Mary Jane, "Medicines in the Ancient World"
	Yamauchi, Edwin, "Aphrodisiacs, Contraception, Abortion, & Infanticide in Antiquity"
ASA89-9	Murphy, George L., "Chiasmic Cosmology as the Context for Bioethics"
	Ducharme, Howard M., "The Immorality of IVF & the Incarnation"
ASA89-10	Hummel, Charles, "Hermeneutics & Science" paper read by Jim Neidhardt
	Wilcox, David L., "On Putting the Axe to the Roots"
	Mills, Gordon C., "Presuppositions of Science as Related to Origins"
ASA89-11	Cain, Dallas E., "Genesis 1 Paraphrase in Reality"
	Haas, John W., Jr., "Science & Faith in Western Europe"
	Kanagy, Sherman P., II, "The Appropriateness of Discussion of Alleged Miraculous Events in Institutions of Public Science Education"
ASA89-12	Hoshiko, Barbara R., "Course on the Spiritual Dimension of Nursing at a Secular University"
	Jennings, George J., "Ecological Imperatives for Development of Programs in the Middle East"
ASA89-13	Nelson, James E., "Seeking the Human Face of Medicine"
	Ross, H. Miriam, "The World's Children"
ASA89-14	Hoshiko, Barbara R., "How Patients & Families Can Potentiate Excellence in Nursing Care"
	Wagner, William E., "Institutional Review Boards"
ASA89-15	Richardson, J.E., "Now It's YOUR Business—The New Age"
	Lechner, Joseph H., "Radiohaloes: The Creator's Fingerprints?"
	Bergman, Gerald, "Physics of Time"

SPECIAL ASA FORUMS AND COURSES

Gene-Splicing Conference, Eastern College, St. Davids, PA - June 27-30, 1987
National conference organized by ASA

ASA87-1	Anderson, V.E., "Public Perception of Recombinant DNA Technology"
ASA87-2	Bird, L., "Universal Principles of Biomedical Ethics & Their Applications to Gene-splicing"
ASA87-3	Friedmann, Theodore, "Human Gene Therapy"
ASA87-4	Jones, W., "Use of DNA Technology to Study Molecular Mechanisms of Steroid Hormone Action"
ASA87-5	Kimbrell, A., "Environmental Concerns in Recombinant DNA Technology"
ASA87-6	Kingsbury, D., "Regulatory Concerns in Recombinant DNA Technology"
ASA87-7	Nelson, J.R., "Theological Issues in Recombinant DNA Technology"
ASA87-8	Olsen, K., "Development of Therapeutic Proteins by Recombinant DNA Technology"
ASA87-9	Robertson, D., "Gene-Splicing Research & Applications in Plant Systems"
ASA87-10	Walters, L., "The Ethics of Human Gene Therapy"

Talks by Donald MacKay

ASADM-1	MacKay, D., "Biblical Perspectives on Human Engineering" (Wheaton College, 1976)
ASADM-2	MacKay, D., "Brain Science & Christian Realism" (Gordon College, 1986)

(Notes)

AUDIO TAPE ORDER FORM
(Cut out and use this form, or a photocopy)

Order from:
ASA Tape Service
c/o The Sanders Christian Foundation
P.O. Box 2094
South Hamilton, MA 01982-0094

QTY.	TAPE #	SPEAKER & TITLE	COST (@ $5/tape)

Total Cost $_____

Mass. Residents Add 5% Sales Tax $_____

Postage & Handling $_____

Amount Enclosed $_____

Make Checks Payable to: Sanders Christian Foundation

POSTAGE CHARGES:

Special 4th Class (USA only)		First Class (USA only)	
1-4 Tapes:	$2.00	Single Tape:	$1.50
5-7 Tapes:	$3.00	2-4 Tapes:	$3.00
8+ Tapes:	$4.00	5-7 Tapes:	$4.00

Foreign Orders will be billed for postage.

Canadian Orders — First Class Only.

MAIL TAPES TO:

Name_____

Address_____

City_____ State_____ Zip_____

(Notes)

AUDIO TAPE ORDER FORM
(Cut out and use this form, or a photocopy)

Order from:
ASA Tape Service
c/o The Sanders Christian Foundation
P.O. Box 2094
South Hamilton, MA 01982-0094

QTY.	TAPE #	SPEAKER & TITLE	COST (@ $5/tape)

Total Cost$ _____

Mass. Residents Add 5% Sales Tax $_____

Postage & Handling $_____

Amount Enclosed $_____

Make Checks Payable to: Sanders Christian Foundation

POSTAGE CHARGES:

Special 4th Class (USA only)

1-4 Tapes:	$2.00
5-7 Tapes:	$3.00
8+ Tapes:	$4.00

First Class (USA only)

Single Tape:	$1.50
2-4 Tapes:	$3.00
5-7 Tapes:	$4.00

Foreign Orders will be billed for postage.

Canadian Orders — First Class Only.

MAIL TAPES TO:

Name_____

Address_____

City_____ State_____ Zip_____

(Notes)

ASA VIDEO TAPE LIST

Your Local Section or other group may borrow or purchase the following VHS video tapes from ASA. Video tapes for loan can be obtained for the cost of shipping. Video tapes for sale can be purchased for the cost of the tape(s) plus shipping. All video tapes are sent by first class insured mail. PLEASE NOTE: A borrowed video tape must be returned to ASA within 6 weeks by insured mail.

❦   ❦   ❦   ❦   ❦

VIDEO TAPES FOR LOAN

ASA Promotional Video

Filmed in Ipswich, Massachusetts and at Eastern College (during the 1987 Gene-Splicing Conference), this promotional video captures the essence of ASA's mission to integrate science and Christian faith. Perfect format for local promotion of ASA. (9 minutes)
$5 postage charge

VIDEO TAPES FOR SALE

1986 ASA Annual Meeting - Houghton College, Houghton, NY

Myers, Dr. David G., Series of three lectures: "Current Trends in Psychology—Myths & Realities"; "Yin & Yang in Psychological Research & Christian Belief"; "Practical Implications of Psycho-Social Research for the Church"
Set of 3 tapes @ $15/tape plus $4 postage charge

Technology & Humanity—Plenary Session by ASA's Social Ethics Commission: Lars Granberg, "Thielicke on Humanity & Personality—An Overview"; Thomas Burke, "Historical Perspectives on Technology—A Theological Appraisal"; Robert VanderVennen, "World Views for Technology"; Duane Kauffmann, "Is Technology Master or Servant? Perspectives on Science, Community & Self"
Set of 2 tapes @ $15/tape plus $4 postage charge

Creation, Evolution & Education—Plenary Session by ASA's Creation Commission and ad hoc Committee for Integrity in Science Education: David Wilcox, "Three Models of Making: Prime Mover, Craftsman, & King"; J. David Price, "Teaching Science in a Climate of Controversy: ASA's Outreach to Science Teachers"; Walter Hearn, "ASA's Responsibility & Opportunity" Discussion
Set of 2 tapes @ $15/tape plus $4 postage charge

Gene-Splicing Conference, Eastern College, St. Davids, PA - June, 1987

Session I	Elving Anderson, "Public Perception of Recombinant DNA Technology"
Session II	Leroy Walters, "Ethics of Human Gene Therapy"; Theodore Friedman, "Human Gene Therapy"
Session III	Weldon Jones, "Use of Recombinant DNA Technology to Study the Molecular Mechanisms of Steroid Hormone Action"; Kenneth Olson, "Development of Therapeutic Proteins by Recombinant DNA Technology"
Session IV	J. Robert Nelson, "Theological Issues in Recombinant DNA Technology"; Lewis P. Bird, "Universal Principles of Biomedical Ethics & Their Applications to Gene-Splicing" (Robert Herrmann, moderator; Panel Response (Robert Herrmann, moderator; James Swanson; Donald Munro; William Durbin; Richard Morgan; Jay W. MacMoran)
Session V	Donald Robertson, "Gene-Splicing Research & Applications in Plant Systems";

Session VI

Andrew Kimbrell, "Environmental Concerns in Recombinant DNA Technology"
David Kingsbury, "Regulatory Concerns in Recombinant DNA Technology"

1 tape each @ $15/tape plus $4 postage charge

Annual Meeting 1987 - Colorado Springs, CO - August 1987

Ehlers, Dr. Vernon, Series of three lectures: "Applied Earthkeeping I: Purpose & Principles," "Applied Earthkeeping II: Problems & Politics," "Applied Earthkeeping III: Problems & Promise"
Set of 2 tapes @ $15/tape plus $4 postage charge

Other Videotapes Available

Gingerich, Owen, "Let There Be Light: Scientific Cosmogony & Biblical Creation." This lecture has been presented throughout the US and Canada on behalf of the ASA, featuring our proposed PBS TV series.
$15/tape plus $4 postage charge

Herrmann, Robert L., "Ethical Problems in Biotechnology," presented in 1984 at Messiah College.
$15/tape plus $4 postage charge

Biotechnology & the Human Condition, Forum at Park Street Church in 1984: V. Elving Anderson, "Guidelines for Genetic Engineering"; J. Robert Nelson, "Genetics & Zoethics—The Chance to Enhance Human Life"; Ruth Hubbard, "Women's Options & the New Prenatal Technologies"; Lewis P. Bird, "Biblical Perspectives on Genetic Engineering."
Set of 2 tapes @ $15/tape plus $4 postage charge

OTHER ASA MATERIALS

Teaching Science in A Climate of Controversy A 48 page booklet addressing issues science teachers must face when teaching creation/evolution. Available from the ASA for $6.00/single copy; $5.00/2-9 copies (same address); $4.00/10 or more copies (same address). If orders are prepaid, prices include postage in North America.

SEARCH: Scientists Who Serve God An occasional publication of the ASA exploring current science trends and the men and women involved in science/faith issues. A four page insert from *Perspectives on Science and Christian Faith,* the ASA Journal, *SEARCH* is available separately at 15¢ per copy + $1.50 postage & handling for multiple copies (pre-paid orders only, please). Perfect for educational supplements, teaching aids and handouts. Contact the ASA office for a list of available editions. Indicate featured scientist when ordering.

Subscription to *Perspectives on Science & Christian Faith,* the Journal of the American Scientific Affiliation. Reserve your year of challenging reading for $25 (individuals) or $35 (institutions). Take advantage of our special rate for gift subscriptions: only $20/year (individuals).

Contemporary Issues in Science & Christian Faith: An Annotated Bibliography: A Resource Book An annotated listing of books on science and religion plus many other resources dealing with science and Christian faith issues. Available from ASA for $10.50 plus $1.50 postage and handling (in North America), prepaid. Discounted price for ASA members (with membership number): $8.50 plus $1.50 postage and handling in North America. Volume discounts available.

Prospective Member's Packet If you or others would be interested in learning more about ASA, send us names and addresses at the address below. We will be glad to mail each person an ASA information packet, which includes a sample copy of *Perspectives on Science and Christian Faith.* Your name will be mentioned to anyone you suggest unless we are otherwise instructed.

American Scientific Affiliation
P.O. Box 668
Ipswich, MA 01938

All prices and terms are subject to change.

113

(Notes)

ASA ORDER FORM
(Cut out and use this form, or a photocopy)

Order from:
American Scientific Affiliation
P.O. Box 668
Ipswich, MA 01938

ORDERED BY:_____

Address_____

City_____ State_____ Zip_____

PLEASE SEND THE FOLLOWING VIDEO TAPES:

Name & Description of Program_____

_____

Cost of Tape(s) plus Postage Charge $_____

PLEASE SEND THE FOLLOWING MATERIALS:

Qty.	Description	Price	Postage	Total
____	*Teaching Science*	____		_____
____	*SEARCH*	15¢/ea.	$1.50	_____
____	*Contemporary Issues Resource Book*	$10.50	$1.50	_____
____	*Prospective Member's Packet*	FREE		_____

PLEASE ENTER GIFT SUBSCRIPTIONS TO *PERSPECTIVES ON SCIENCE AND CHRISTIAN FAITH:*

Name_____

Address_____

City_____ State_____ Zip_____

Sign gift card:_____

Name_____

Address_____

City_____ State_____ Zip_____

Sign gift card:_____

Number of gift subscriptions_____ @ $20/year (individuals)   Total $_____

TOTAL ENCLOSED $_____

115

ASA ORDER FORM

(Cut out and use this form, or a photocopy)

Order from:
American Scientific Affiliation
P.O. Box 668
Ipswich, MA 01938

ORDERED BY:_____

Address_____

City_____ State_____ Zip_____

PLEASE SEND THE FOLLOWING VIDEO TAPES:

Name & Description of Program_____

_____

Cost of Tape(s) plus Postage Charge $_____

PLEASE SEND THE FOLLOWING MATERIALS:

Qty.	Description	Price	Postage	Total
____	*Teaching Science*	____		_____
____	*SEARCH*	15¢/ea.	$1.50	_____
____	*Contemporary Issues Resource Book*	$10.50	$1.50	_____
____	*Prospective Member's Packet*	FREE		_____

PLEASE ENTER GIFT SUBSCRIPTIONS TO *PERSPECTIVES ON SCIENCE AND CHRISTIAN FAITH:*

Name_____

Address_____

City_____ State_____ Zip_____

Sign gift card:_____

Name_____

Address_____

City_____ State_____ Zip_____

Sign gift card:_____

Number of gift subscriptions_____ @ $20/year (individuals)   Total $_____

TOTAL ENCLOSED $_____

(Notes)

PROGRAM & MEETING SUGGESTIONS

PROMOTIONAL INFORMATION

The ASA national office offers on loan a 9-minute promotional video tape capturing the essence of ASA's mission to integrate science and Christian faith. Filmed in Ipswich, Massachusetts and at Eastern College, this is a perfect format for local promotion of ASA. This video tape is available for order in the section of this book titled ASA Video Tapes.

ASA LOCAL SECTIONS

ASA members meet together in local sections with varying degrees of frequency and formality. Large sections in the New York City area and in the San Franscisco Bay area meet frequently, elect a slate of officers, and collect section dues. Smaller sections meet just twice a year, perhaps spring or fall or on some special occasion. The Rocky Mountain Section, for example, has an all-day program once or twice a year, and the Cleveland Section schedules a major lecture in conjunction with the University Christian Forum at Case-Western Reserve University.

A list of ASA Local Sections and their contact persons follows. Addresses can be found in the ASA-CSCA Directory or gotten from the ASA national office in Ipswich, MA.

Central California	Stanley Lindquist
Cleveland-Case Western	Tom Hoshiko
Chicago-Wheaton	Marilyne Flora-Raymond Brand
Delaware Valley	Frank Roberts-Dave Wilcox
Eastern Tennessee	Evans Roth
Indiana	Ann Hunt
Los Angeles	Stan Moore-George Bate
New England	Jack Haas
New York-New Jersey	W. James Neidhardt
North Central	V. Elving Anderson-Bill Monsma
Oklahoma	Ken Dormer
Oregon-Washington	Dave Willis-Dennis Feucht
Rocky Mountain	ELdon Hitchcock-John Vayhinger
St. Louis	James Armbrecht
San Diego	Jerry Albert-Fred Jappe
San Francisco Bay	Richard Bube-Ken Lincoln
Southwest	Fred Hickernell
Texas	Gordon Mills
Washington-Baltimore	Paul Arveson-David Swift
Western Michigan	Roger Griffioen
Western New York	Don Munro

A list of CSCA Local Sections and contact persons follows.

Guelph-Ontario	Steven Scadding
Hamilton	Donald McNally
Ottawa	Richard Herd
Toronto	Daniel Osmond
Vancouver	Lawrence Walker

119

ORGANIZING YOUR OWN ASA SECTION OR STUDY GROUP

Should you live in an area not served by a local section, and wish to meet others interested in Science-Christian Faith issues, we suggest that you locate others through the ASA membership directory. Information on the procedure to be followed in obtaining a charter as a local section can be obtained from the ASA national office.

Other Christian professional organizations may also be able to supply information on interested persons in your area. Refer to the section in this book titled Christian Professional Societies. In addition, you may find that pastors of local churches have knowledge of church members who are scientists.

The choice of program activities is dependent upon the group, but most sections seek out local or visiting speakers. The following section in this book titled ASA Speakers Bureau provides a list of speakers who may be available. Larger groups, or groups located in a college or university community, often find it desirable to plan one or two public meetings each year, bringing a well-known speaker to the campus as a way to attract others to the group. It is generally necessary to provide an honorarium, so campus support may be necessary. The departments of the school which are most familiar with the visitor will often be willing to provide for some or all of the expense.

Local sections may also use video tapes as part of program activities. Refer to the section in this book titled ASA Video Tape List for a selection from the national office.

Some groups represent a large geographical area and so find it useful to arrange an annual day-long conference with overnight accommodations for those travelling some distance.

The ASA national office welcomes inquiries from members and friends concerning opportunities to meet for fellowship and study in your home area or when traveling. Local sections are responsible for collecting section dues and other monies and receipting members. However, any transactions involving ASA's Federal (or Massachusetts state) tax exempt number in conducting local section business must be carefully recorded and a summary of income and disbursements and copies of any tax notices (i.e. statement of earned interest, 1099's, etc.) must be submitted to our office before Feb. 1 of each year for auditing purposes.

ASA SPEAKERS BUREAU

The following persons have indicated their willingness to speak to ASA/CSCA groups. Their names, addresses, phone numbers, and principal topics are listed. We have more information on file on each of them, and we'll be happy to send this information out to members on request. Alternatively, the speakers may be contacted directly. Most speakers will require reimbursement if traveling a distance, unless they happen to be traveling in your area. We hope to continue to expand this list—please send names and complete addresses of your suggestions for additional speakers.

ARNDT, J. Richard, Ph.D.; Director, Advising and Testing;
California State University, Fresno; Fresno, CA 93470-0066, (209) 278-2924 (work) or (209)432-3212 (home).

"Myth: Science is in Conflict with the Christian Faith"—or variations on this theme.

"Are Creation and Evolution Really Contradictory?"—Presentation on misunderstandings surrounding the scientific enterprise and Christian faith, including clarification of the Creation-Evolution controversy.

BENSON, Purnell, 21 Maple Avenue, Madison, NJ 07940, (201) 377-8050.

"Jesus as a Psychologist"

"The Writer of John's Gospel and Letters as Psychologist and Philosopher"

"What We Know About God as the Mind Controlling the Universe"

BERGMAN, Jerry, Ph.D., 321 Iuka, Montpelier, OH 43543, (419) 485-3602.

"The Wonder of the Human Body"—A study of the incredible machine and its incredible details and feats.

"Was Man First?"—A discussion of the many human mechanical innovations which had their origin in the natural world.

"Who Were the Neanderthals?"—Discusses our understanding of this ancient race, and our growth from early interpretations of them as brutish, and our modern understanding of them as members of the human race, fully equal and fully human.

"The UFO Mystery"—Where do UFOs come from, and what is a reasonable conclusion relative to their existence or nonexistence?

"The New Palley's Argument From High Energy Physics"—shows how the research of physics is reintroducing Palley's watch argument to cosmology.

Eight additional topics available; complete listing available from Dr. Bergman at above address, or the ASA office.

BUBE, Richard H., Ph.D., 753 Mayfield Avenue, Stanford, CA 94305, (415) 723-2535.

"The Relationship between Scientific and Theological Descriptions"

"The Significance of Being Human: Genes and Souls"

"Ethical Guidelines in Critical Issues of Life and Death"

"A Christian Perspective on Ecology"

"Is the Bible Scientifically Credible?"

"The Scientific Structure of the World: Parts and Wholes"

BULLOCK, Wilbur L., Ph.D., 13 Thompson Lane, Durham, NH 03824, (603) 868-2725.

"Biblical Perspectives on Environmental Problems"—an overview of biblical attitudes toward God's creation and human stewardship.

"Creation and Evolution: What are the REAL Issues?—The infallible Scriptures tell us God *did* it (not *how*); fallible science investigates *how* (not *why*).

"God, Germs, and Genes"—A comparison of Christian reaction to the theory of natural selection and the Christian reaction to the germ theory of disease.

"The 'Black Death' and AIDS"—Christians and pestilence.

BUSWELL, James O., III, Ph.D., Wm. Carey Intl. University, 1539 E. Howard Street, Pasadena, CA 91104, (818) 797-1200.

"Evangelical Perspectives on Creation and Evolution (Especially Human Evolution)" —1 to 4 lectures.

"Missionary Anthropology and its Application to Fulfilling the Great Commission"

"The American Indian as Representative of Tribal Peoples in Every Continent" (illustrated).

DAVIS, Edward B., Ph.D., Dept. of Mathematical Sciences, Messiah College, Grantham, PA 17027, (717) 766-2511 ext. 6840.

"Rationalism and Voluntarism in 17th Century Science"—explores the relationship between divine freedom and empirical science.

"Isaac Newton, Divine Sovereignty, and the Rejection of Rationalistic Natural Philosophy"— Newton's notion of an active deity who undermines an attempt at *a priori* science.

"Understanding Creationism: A Brief Historical Survey, with suggestions about the Current Debate"

"A Whale of a Tale: Fundamentalist Fish Stories"—The story of the story about a modern Jonah.

Can lead a discussion on almost any historical science/Christianity issue.

DYE, David L., 12825 SE 45th Pl., Bellevue, WA 98006, (206) 746-0498.

"The Bible as Data: A way of looking at inspiration"—A consistent Christian world view that accounts for the data.

FEUCHT, Dennis L., 5275 Crown Street, West Linn, OR 97068, (503) 656-1400.

"The Mind/Brain Problem and Artificial Intelligence"

"Knowledge Representation and Theology"

(Currently developing a series of talks on basic science/Christianity issues, primarily for radio.)

FISCHER, Dick, 6623 Williamsburg Blvd., Arlington, VA 22213.

"Adam's Historical Niche: Clues From Scripture"

HAAS, John W., Jr., Ph.D., Gordon College, Wenham, MA 01984, (508) 927-2300 or (508) 468-1295 (home).

"Christianity and the Scientific Revolution: A Look at the Influence of Christian Faith on the Development of Modern Science"

HARTZLER, H. Harold, Ph.D., 901 College Ave, Goshen, IN 46526, (219) 534-3700.

"Faith and the Scientific Method"—Faith is a necessity in the work of the scientist.

"Prophetic Accuracy of the Bible"—The principle of probability is used to show that the Bible is inspired.

"Design in Astronomy"—The study of astronomy is an aid in showing the need for a designer of the physical universe.

HEDDENDORF, Russell, Ph.D., 1501 Aladdin Rd., Lookout Mountain, TN 37350, (404) 820-1529.

"The 'Call' to Science"—argues for the Christian concept of "Calling" as a basis for doing scientific work instead of the "Career."

"Being 'In the World'"—attempts to explain the meaning of the phrase "in the world and not of it," especially as it applies to the role of the scientist.

"The Sociology of Science"—argues for recognition of the sociological bases of science, especially as influenced by the work of Thomas Kuhn.

HEFLEY, James C., Ph.D., 31 Holiday Drive, Hannibal, MO 63401, (314) 221-2462.

"Media & Morality: How the Mass Media Impact Our Lives and What We Can Do About It"

"Communicating Christian Values in an Information Society"

"Textbooks, Education, & Propaganda: What the Great Textbook War Is All About"

"Good News, Bad News, Mixed News: What's the Best News for Christian Communicators?"

"Writing for Publication"

"Crisis in the Southern Baptist Convention: Case History of a Denomination in Conflict"

HERRMANN, Robert L., Ph.D., American Scientific Affiliation, PO Box 668, Ipswich, MA 01938, (508) 356-5656.

"Biblical Perspectives on Human Engineering"—A look at genetic engineering, *in vitro* fertilization, and other reproductive technologies.

"Prospects for Gene Therapy—Ethical & Theological Implications"—An examination of the new treatment of genetic disease.

"God & the New Science"—A discussion of signals of transcendence in the new physics and the new biology.

HUMMEL, Charles E., Ph.D., 17 Worcester Street, Grafton, MA 01519, (508) 839-5495.

"The Galileo Connection"—biblical and scientific views of nature.

KANAGY, Sherman P., II, Ph.D., 1213 Ohio Street, Valparaiso, IN 46383, (219) 464-3247 (home) or (219) 785-5200 (work).

"What Was the Star of the Magi?"—various astronomical and other explanations which have been suggested for the star.

"Issues in the Creationism/Evolution Controversy"—Deals with the issue of the origin of man, the earth, and the universe—scientific, philosophical, and religious aspects along with discussion related to educational implications.

"An Astronomer Examines Astrology"—A critique of astrology from scientific, philosophical, and religious perspectives.

"Distinguishing Legitimate Science From its Counterfeits (The Pseudosciences)—Examples of topics commonly considered pseudoscientific are: astrology, para-psychology (ESP), UFOlogy (flying saucers), the colliding planet theories of I. Velikovsky, scientific and biblical creationism, Big Foot and the Loch Ness Monster, pyramidology (alleged occult mysteries of the Great Pyramids), the legend of Atlantis, mysteries of the Bermuda Triangle, and so on. Topics may also be done separately.

25 additional topics available; complete listing available from Dr. Kanagy at above address, or the ASA office.

KEY, Thomas, c/o Kyview C.M. Church, Rt. 6 Box 290A, Laurel, MS 39440.

"Theories of Creationism: Description and Evaluation"
"A Biologist Examines the Book of Mormon"
"How Did the Races Originate?"
"When Does the Soul Enter the Body?"
"Scientific Concepts in the Bible"
"How Evolutionism Stands Today"
"Canopy Theory"

KOBE, Donald H., Ph.D., 1704 Highland Park Road, Denton, TX 76205, (817) 387-7803 (home) or (817) 565-3272 (office).

"Luther & Science"—Martin Luther's attitudes toward science.
"Christianity & Science"—Relation of the Bible to modern science.
"Anthropic or Theistic Principle in Cosmology?"

LEWTHWAITE, Gordon R., Ph.D., 18908 Liggett Street, Northridge, CA 91324-2844, (818) 349-5308.

A variety of topics in the following areas:
"Christianity, Science, and their Relationship"
"Biblical Geography"—touching on either the geography behind the Bible, or the geographical context of biblical Israel.
"Christianity and Ecology"
"Christianity and Marxism"

MIXTER, Russell, Ph.D., 120 Windsor Park Dr. A206, Carol Stream, IL 60188, (708) 668-2032.

"Creation & Evolution"—specific creation followed by limited evolution.
"Aging"—attitudes and activities.

MUNRO, Donald W., Ph.D., Dept. of Biology, Houghton College, Houghton, NY 14744, (716) 567-2211 ext. 299 or (716) 567-8811 (home).

"Christian Tensions in the Field of Bioethics"—basically philosophical with illustrations from the various areas.
"Christian Tensions in Genetic Engineering"—historical, ethical, and the promises and perils. Also interested in preparing a similar talk on euthanasia.

NEIDHARDT, W. Jim, Ph.D., Physics Dept., New Jersey Institute of Technology, Newark, NJ 07102, (201) 596-3555 (work) or (201) 584-0436 (home).

"Science as Personal Knowledge: An Open-Ended Form of Truth"—Science is a form of personal knowledge in that it is communal, motivated by faith, and similar to other forms of human creativity; i.e., artistic creativity. Since science originates as a direct response to human experience of the Universe's inexhaustible structure, it is an open-ended form of truth.
"Personal Knowledge and Human Creativity—Some Reflections from Judeo-Christian Theology & Michael Polanyi's Conception of Science"—Discussed are the personal character of all knowledge, the stages of the knowing process, the objectivity of personal knowledge, and a Biblical model of human creativity.
Six additional topics available from the ASA office, or from Dr. Neidhardt.

NEWMAN, Robert C., Ph.D., 115 S. Main Street (or Biblical Theol. Sem., 200 N. Main Street), Hatfield, PA 19440, (215) 368-5000 (work) or (215) 855-4046 (home).

"Relating the Bible & Science"
"Origin of the Universe"
"Genesis One & the Origin of the Earth"
"Scientific Problems of Evolution"
"Self-Reproducing Automata and the Origin of Life"

OSMOND, Daniel H., Ph.D., 301 Rushton Road, Toronto, Ontario M6C 2X8, CANADA, (416) 653-5746.

"Creation/Evolution"—You can have a Creator who operates through His own evolution mechanisms.
"Science and Ethics"—Ethics do not arise out of science, but from the scientist.
"Christianity and Vocation"—Being Christian in the workplace.
"Science and Faith"

PRICE, J. David, Ph.D., P. O. Box 157, Springville, CA 93265, (209) 539-3880.

"Creation vs. Philosophical Naturalism"
"The Argument is not Creation vs. Evolution, But Creator vs. No-Creator"

PRICE, Martin L.., Ph.D., Executive Director, Educational Concerns for Hunger Organization (ECHO), 17430 Durrance Road, N. Ft. Myers, FL 33917, (813) 543-3246.

"God's Abundant Resources for the Fight Against Wold Hunger"—Lecture with slides, preferably to a general student audience, concerning ECHO's approach, motivation for this kind of scientific research, and the needs and opportunities for this research on the mission field.

PUN, Pattle, Ph.D., Biology Department, Wheaton College, Wheaton, IL 60187, (708) 260-3725.

"Evolution, Nature and Scripture in Conflict?"—The issue is presented from scientific, philosphical and theological perspectives. A progressive creationist position will be presented.

RICE, Stanley, Dept. of Biology, Huntington College, Huntington, IN 45750, (219) 356-6000 x 2001 (work).

"The General Revelation: Interpreting the Natural World as God's Communication to Us"—explores fundamental concepts that are found in the Bible, human history and experience, and biology; expands on themes expressed in *Perspectives* 39(3) and 41(1).
"Science Calls Us to Worship"—Biblical lessons from the natural world, with demonstrations, suitable for church use.

SCHAEFER, Henry F., III, Ph.D., Center for Computational Quantum Chemistry, University of Georgia, Athens, GA 30602, (404) 542-2067.

"Modern Science and the Christian Faith"—history of science material and some creation vs. evolution. Two fifty-minute lectures.
"The Way of Discovery"—personal testimony from scientific perspective. Thirty minutes.

SHANK, Norman E., Ph.D., Messiah College, Grantham, PA 17027, (717) 766-2511 (work) or (717) 766-7059 (home).

"Christianity, Materialism, and Science"—Science does not require, or support, a materialistic world view.

SHELDON, Joseph K., Ph.D., Eastern College, St. Davids, PA 19087, (215) 341-5860.

"Environmental Stewardship and the Emergence of a Theology of Creation"
"Antipredation Strategies in Animals and Plants"

SIEMENS, David F., Jr., Ph.D., 2703 E. Kenwood Street, Mesa, AZ 85213-2340, (602) 834-9188.

"The Christian Origins of Science"—Why did science begin only in Christendom with committed Christians?
"The Nature of Scientific Theories and their Limitations"—What a scientific theory is—its strengths and limitations.
"Creation Revealed"—What exactly does the Bible say?

VAN TILL, Howard J., Ph.D., Calvin College Physics Department, Grand Rapids, MI 49546, (616) 957-6341.

"The Cosmos: Nature or Creation?"—A popular-level talk dealing with 3 questions: (1) What is the cosmos like? (slide-illustrated; an astronomer's perspective) (2) What is the "status" of the cosmos? (3) Where do we see the Creator at work in the cosmos?
"The Legend of the Shrinking Sun"—A case study comparing professional science and "creation-science" in action.

WALKER, Laurence C., Ph.D., 514 Millard Dr., Nachogdoches, TX 75961, (409) 569-9754.

"The Nature of Man in Resource Use and Abuse"
"Silviculture of Longleaf Pine"
"Development of U. S. Forestry Policies"
"Ecology in the Woods"
"How Regulation Affects the Price of a House"

WILCOX, David L., Ph.D., Biology Department, St. Davids, PA 19087, (215) 341-5864.

"Adam, Where Are You? A Paradigm Shift in Paleoanthropology"—A summary of current new findings, especially mitochondrial DNA & the biblical record.
"How Blind the Watchmaker? The Adequacy of NeoDarwinism as Creator"—Will cumulative selection serve?
"A Two Hierarchy Model for Living Things: Blueprints & Bodies"—Implications for biological change.

YAMAUCHI, Edwin, Ph.D., History Department, Miami University, Oxford, OH 45056, (513) 529-5141 (work) or (513) 523-2819 (home).

"Old Testament Archaeology"
"Ancient Persian Capitals"
"The Dead Sea Scrolls"
"The Life of Jesus & Archaeology"
"Herodian Archaeology"
"Persia and the Bible"—capital cities of ancient Iran, and their relevance to such books as Esther and Nehemiah.
The above are all slide lectures. Additional topics are available from the ASA office, or from Dr. Yamauchi.

MISCELLANEOUS RESOURCES

VIDEO TAPES

"The Creation of the Universe." Outstanding 90-minute PBS documentary hosted by science journalist Timothy Ferris. $19.95 plus $4 shipping & handling. Order direct: Barnes & Noble, 126 Fifth Ave., New York, NY 10011-5666.

"The Rotten Truth." 30 minute video from CTV. Order direct: *Science News,* 1719 North Street, NW, Washington, DC 20036. $14.95 plus $2.00 shipping & handling.

SLIDE/TAPE PRESENTATION

"God's Abundant Resources." 28 minute program from ASA member Martin Price at ECHO (Educational Concerns for Hunger Organization), RR # 2 Box 852, N. Ft. Myers, FL 33903. (No charge for loan.) Features many of the underexploited food crops, rooftop gardens, no-till gardening, as well as an introduction to the kinds of agricultural and gardening problems faced by missionaries, and how ECHO is able to strengthen their work with new ideas, techniques and seeds.

STUDY GUIDE

The Galileo Connection: Resolving Conflicts Between Science & the Bible, Study Guide, available from author Charles E. Hummel, 17 Worcester St., Grafton, MA 01519.

CSCA MATERIALS

CSCA (contact Norman MacLeod, 41 Gwendolen Ave., Willowdale, Ont. M2N 1A1, CANADA) offers the following resources:

"Creation & Evolution." 30 minute tape/slide program usually presented with discussion led by a CSCA member.
"Here's Life." 60 minute videotape featuring debate between Dr. Daniel Osmond (U. of Toronto) and Dr. Kelly Seagraves on Christian approaches to creation and evolution.
"Puzzle of the Ancient Wing." 30 minute videotape from the CBC show "Man Alive" dealing with the issue of origins.
"Platform Series." 60 minute videotaped discussion on creation and evolution filmed live before a student group at St. Pius High School in Ottawa.
"This is My Story." 30 minute audio cassette tape for Salvation Army radio program on issues of science & faith.

AUDIO TAPES AVAILABLE FROM OTHER SOURCES

Christians in an Age of Science

A taped series of classes offered at the Wheaton Bible Church. Order direct: Dr. Raymond H. Brand, Department of Biology, Wheaton College, Wheaton, IL 60187. Speakers & subjects:

Spradley, Dr. Joseph, "The Universe Displayed"
Wolf, Dr. Herb, "The Science of Scripture Interpretation"

Parmerter, Dr. Stan, "Timeless Question of Age"
Parmerter, Dr. Stan, "Man-Made Life Forms"
Chappell, Dr. Dorothy, "Functional Design in Plants"
Hoerth, Prof. Al, "Ancient Civilizations"
Mixter, Dr. Russell, "Adam & Fossil Man"
Sheaffer, Dr. Jack, "Eden Regained"
Funck, Dr. Larry, "Stewards of Energy"
Holmes, Dr. Arthur, "Scientists & the Bomb"
Brand, Dr. Ray, "Continents Adrift?"
Pun, Dr. Pattle, "Progressive Creation"

Ethical Issues in Human Experimentation & Medical Decision Making

Tapes of a March 1986 Science Symposium. Order direct: Science Division, Wheaton College, Wheaton, IL 60187. Speakers & subjects:

Swift, David L., "Ethics of Human Experimentation in Public Health"
Macpherson, Trevor A., "Fetal Development, In-Vitro Fertilization, & Fetal Research"
Knighton, David R., "Difficult Decisions in the Surgical Care Unit" and "Lessons Learned from the
　　　　Healing Wound"
Myers, Terry L., "The Ethical Dilemma of Human Birth Defects"
Gorsuch, Richard L., "Ethical Issues in Psychological Research"
Panel Discussion, "How do we deal with a human being as an experimental object?"

"Science & Christianity"

Tape of an ASA panel and the Rev. Craig Barnes at the First Presbyterian Church of Colorado Springs, CO during the 1987 ASA Annual Meeting (August 2, 1987), centering on relationships between science and Christianity. Order direct: First Presbyterian Church, 219 East Bijou Street, Colorado Springs, CO 80903, (303) 471-3763.

AUDIO TAPE CATALOGS

Fuller Theological Seminary Media Services Tape Catalog

Catalog of tapes containing chapel sermons and special lectures held at FTS since 1973. Collection includes tapes which relate to issues of science. Order direct: Fuller Theological Seminary Media Services; FTS, Box 115; Pasadena, CA 91182-3110. In California: (818) 584-5227. Out of state: 1(800) 235-2222.

The Listening Library Catalog of Recordings of Princeton Theological Seminary

Catalog of tapes of lectures, sermons and campus events from Princeton Theological Seminary. Tapes are organized by speaker and date and are coded by subject. Collection includes tapes which relate to issues of science. Order direct: Department of Instructional Media, Princeton Theological Seminary, CN821, Princeton, NJ 08542.

Regent College Audio Cassette Catalogue

Catalog of tapes on graduate theological and biblical studies from Regent College, Canada's largest graduate school of theology. Tapes are organized by speaker/title and by subject. Contributors include several ASA members. Order direct: Regent College, 2130 Wesbrook Mall, Vancouver, B.C., Canada V6T 1W6. In Canada: (604) 224-3245. In the U.S.: 1(800) 663-8664.

Westminster Media 1990/91 Audio Catalog

Revised, updated, and expanded catalog of 2000+ tapes from Westminster Theological Seminary organized by speaker and by subject. Limited quantity of catalogs. Order direct: Westminster Media, P.O. Box 27009, Philadelphia, PA 19118.

CHRISTIAN PROFESSIONAL SOCIETIES

American Scientific Affiliation, P.O. Box 668, Ipswich, MA 01938.

American Society of Missiology, 616 Walnut Avenue, Scottsdale, PA 15683.

Association of Christian Economists, c/o Dr. John Mason, Gordon College, 255 Grapevine Road, Wenham, MA 01984.

Association of Christian Engineers and Scientists, Mr. Orvin Olson, P.O. Box 244, Vernonia, OR 97064.

Association of Christian Librarians, P.O. Box 4, Cedarville, OH 45314.

Association of Christians in Mathematical Sciences, Dr. Robert L. Brabenec, Dept. of Mathematics, Wheaton College, Wheaton, IL 60187.

Christian Association for Psychological Studies, Inc., Dr. Robert R. King, Jr., Executive Secretary, P.O. Box 890279, Temecula, CA 92589-0279.

Christian Career Women, Ms. Sandy Hovatter, 4235 Coe Avenue, North, Olmstead, OH 44070.

Christian Educators Association, P.O. Box 50025., Pasadena, CA 91115.

Christian Foresters' Fellowship, Prof. Dennis Lynch, School of Natural Resources, Colorado State University, Ft. Collins, CO 80521.

Christian Legal Society, 4208 Evergreen, Suite 222, Annandale, VA 22003.

Christian Medical & Dental Society, Dr. Hal Habecker, 1616 Gateway Blvd. P.O. Box 830689, Richardson, TX 75083.

Christian Political Science Organization, Prof. Corwin Schmidt, Department of Political Science, Calvin College, Grand Rapids, MI 49546 **or** Prof. Stephen Monsma, Department of Political Science, Pepperdine University, Malibu, CA 90265.

Christian Sociological Society, Prof. Larry Ingram., Dept. of Sociology, University of Tennessee at Martin, TN 38238.

Christian Veterinary Mission, 19303 Fremont Avenue N., Seattle, WA 98133.

Conference on Christianity and Literature, Dr. Jewel Spears Brooker, Collegium of Letters, Eckerd College, St. Petersburg, FL 33711.

Conference on Faith and History, Prof. Richard Pierard, Secretary-Treasurer, Dept. of History, Indiana State University, Terre Haute, IN 47809.

Evangelical Philosophical Society, Dr. David Clark, Secretary-Treasurer, c/o Bethel Theological Seminary, 3949 Bethel Drive, St. Paul, MN 55112.

Evangelical Theological Society, Dr. Simon J. Kistemaker, 5422 Clinton Boulevard, Jackson, MS 39209.

Fellowship of Artists for Cultural Evangelism, 1605 E. Elizabeth Street, Pasadena, CA 91104.

Fellowship of Christian Librarians and Information Services, Dr. Eva Kiewitt, The Christain Broadcasting Network, Inc., CBN Center, Virginia Beach, VA 23463.

Fellowship of Christian Musicians, Bill Anderson, Director, Instrumental Music Dept., Ponca City H.S., Fifth & Overbrook, Ponca City, OK 74601.

Institute for Christian Studies, 229 College Street, Toronto, Ontario, M5T 1R4.

North American Association of Christians in Social Work, P.O. Box 7090, St. Davids, PA 19087-7090.

Nurses Christian Fellowship, 6400 Schroeder Road, P.O. Box 7895, Madison, WI, 53707.

Society of Christian Philosophers, Prof. Kenneth J. Konyndyk, Secretary-Treasurer, Dept. of Philosophy, Calvin College, 3201 Barton Street, S.E., Grand Rapids, MI 49546-4388.

(Notes)

(Notes)